Tolkie

The Lord of the Rings

Sources of Inspiration

edited by
Stratford Caldecott & Thomas Honegger

WALKING TREE PUBLISHERS

2008

Cormarë Series

No 18

Series Editors

Peter Buchs • Thomas Honegger • Andrew Moglestue • Johanna Schön

Library of Congress Cataloging-in-Publication Data

Caldecott, Stratford and Thomas Honegger (eds.)

Tolkien's The Lord of the Rings. Sources of Inspiration

ISBN 978-3-905703-12-2

Subject headings:

Tolkien, J. R. R. (John Ronald Reuel), 1892-1973 – Criticism and interpretation
Tolkien, J. R. R. (John Ronald Reuel), 1892-1973 – Language
Fantasy fiction, English - History and criticism
Middle-earth (Imaginary place)
Literature, Comparative

Cover artwork by Anke Eissmann (www.anke.edoras-art.de)

With many thanks to Doreen Triebel MA for proofreading the entire manuscript.

© Walking Tree Publishers, Zurich and Jena 2008.

Printed by Lightning Source in the United Kingdom and the United States.

TO MY MOTHER,

MOYRA,

WHO KNOWS

THE WISDOM IN STORIES.

(S.C.)

TO DTG

GROW AND PROSPER

(T.H.)

Table of Contents

Part Three—Mythos and Logos

A group-picture of some of the conference participants outside the Rector's Lodgings showing, among others, Philip Munday, Verlyn Flieger, Alison Milbank, Frances Cairncross, Alison Fincher, Catherine Simon, Bonnie Marques, Penelope Cote, Rachel Cote, Mgr Tom Sullivan, Sue Bridgewater, Stratford Caldecott, Edmund Weiner, Patrick Curry, Marek Oziewicz, Jeremy Marshall, Peter Gilliver, Martin Sternberg, Father Guglielmo Spirito, Marcel Buelles and Thomas Honegger.
(Picture courtesy of Father Guglielmo Spirito)

Foreword

FRANCES CAIRNCROSS

Among all the colleges of Oxford University, Exeter has surely one of the richest recent literary traditions. In the past century, it educated several authors of note: Alan Bennett, Philip Pullman and Martin Amis among them. But before them all comes JRR Tolkien, who came to Exeter as an undergraduate in 1911 and stumbled there on his abiding interest in Old and Middle English.

Tolkien arrived with a scholarship to read not English, but Greats—the name given to *Literae Humaniores*, a degree that Oxford still offers today in classical literature, history and philosophy. Halfway through, having taken a passable but not distinguished degree, he decided to switch to English. This momentous decision was, I'm happy to say, taken on the advice of Dr Farnell, my predecessor as Rector of Exeter.

The account of his time in the College by Humphrey Carpenter, in his 1977 biography, makes clear that Tolkien hugely enjoyed his undergraduate days, and made the most of his time there. So where better to hold a conference on the author? Carpenter (*Biography* 60) is unkind about our college's appearance, writing of its "insipid frontage by George Gilbert Scott and its chapel, a tasteless copy of the Sainte Chapelle." But he also waxes lyrical about the Fellows' Garden, describing the tall silver birch (actually, planted in 1908 and probably just a sprig in Tolkien's day) and the soaring horse-chestnut and plane that until recently graced the view down into Radcliffe Square. The conference delegates spent long evenings before and after dinner strolling on the lawns and informally continuing the day's formal discussions.

In those early and formative years at Exeter College, many of the underpinnings of Tolkien's adult life were laid. He courted Edith Bratt, whom he was to marry a year after he graduated. He increasingly experimented with language, including the Earendel verses that were his 'mad hobby', as he called it. And he played a part in College life, founding the Apolausticks, an undergraduate club ('devoted to self-indulgence') as well as attending the College Essay Club and Dialectical Club. None of those societies survives, but one that does is the Stapeldon Society, still the main undergraduate body. Tolkien was Secretary of the Stapeldon Society from October 1913 and President from January 1914, for a full term in each case. We hold in our archives some of the minutes that Tolkien wrote, proclaiming his early literary promise. Take, for instance, this passage from the minutes of a meeting in 1913:

> At the 791st meeting of the Stapeldon Society held on Dec 1st 1913 one of the world's great battles between democracy and autocracy was fought and won, and as is usual in such conflicts the weapons of the democracy were hooliganism and uproar [...] It is for the society to see that the events of that meeting do not, with their precedent, forbode a graver disformation of the society's whole character, a transfer of authority from the chair to the floor.
>
> Long before the officers had even passed the curtain the ominous sounds of a gigantic house athirst for their blood could be heard. Even in the Porch a dull booming murmur like the bay of the Bloodhounds in 'Red Axe' reached the ears of loafers; who promptly swelled the throng, entering, when the door jammed, by way of the windows, so that when on the stroke of 8 the President's face appeared beyond the curtain a record House was assembled upon all the chairs seats tables floor-space and laps available. From the moment the President took the chair until 2 hours later the House seethed with riot and noise, so that no minutes of the conventional sort are to be looked for.
>
> [...] Man after man arose to speak flushed with the wine of wrath, and man after man was quashed, crushed, and squashed into oblivion with the magic of Rule 9 Section (b) [...]

Alas, none of our undergraduates writes like that today. But the influence of Tolkien remains. This third week of January 08, the author's daughter, Priscilla, is talking to a gathering of students about her father's life and work. So the memory of someone born at the start of 1892 will be carried forward, in the minds of today's 18-year-olds, perhaps to the 2060s. It is a wonderful manifestation of the continuity that an Oxford college provides.

Frances Cairncross
The Rector's Lodgings
January 2008

Walter Hooper, Priscilla Tolkien, and Robert Murray SJ during the reception at the Rector's Lodgings. (Picture courtesy of Stratford Caldecott)

Sources of Inspiration

INTRODUCTION[*] BY
STRATFORD CALDECOTT

Many of the various chapters of this volume started life as papers delivered at an important international Tolkien Studies conference in Oxford in the summer of 2006. The initiative for the conference came from Exeter College, where it was held, and specifically from the Rector, Frances Cairncross, to whom we are all tremendously indebted. Exeter was the college where the young Tolkien spent several formative years studying as an undergraduate (1911-15), at first in Classics then switching to English Language and Literature. Later, of course, he had a distinguished academic career in other universities and colleges, and became famous for *The Hobbit* and *The Lord of the Rings*. The College has been understandably proud to have been so closely associated with this great writer, but up until 2006 had never organized a conference to draw attention to its connection with him. The growth of Tolkien Studies as an academic specialty, especially in America, made this a particularly good time for an international conference in Oxford. In some ways it could be said to have marked the 'coming of age' of Tolkien Studies.

Many of Tolkien's fellow-academics in the 1950s and 60s regarded his mythological and children's writing as a foolish hobby that was consuming his energies and time, and preventing him from devoting himself to the writing of lectures and important academic works. He was, after all, employed as a tutor and lecturer at Oxford, and it is true that this fantasy writing did take up a lot of time and formidable amounts of mental energy. We can appreciate this more now that the twelve volumes of posthumous writings (*The History of Middle-earth*) have been edited and published by his son Christopher. As far as the literary establishment goes, many distinguished writers during Tolkien's lifetime regarded *The Lord of the Rings* simply as 'bad literature'. Very few of

---

[*] This Introduction is partly based on Robert Lazu's interview with Stratford Caldecott for the Romanian journal *Adevarul Literar si Artistic* ('Literary and Artistic Truth').

them (W.H. Auden and C.S. Lewis are notable exceptions) understood that he was single-handedly reviving an ancient and important genre of storytelling.

In the last decade or so things began to change. A new generation of literary critics emerged, many of whom had read Tolkien's stories with enthusiasm as children. The continuing popular success of the books became a phenomenon that itself required explanation. As the breadth of learning and scholarship underlying the stories became more apparent, so too did their relevance to a range of academic disciplines from philology and anthropology to religious studies and theology. Hence the emergence of Tolkien Studies as a scholarly discipline in its own right, especially with the establishment of a journal by that name by West Virginia University Press in the United States, edited by Douglas Anderson, Michael Drout, and Verlyn Flieger in 2004.

The aim of the Exeter College conference was specifically to consolidate the emergence of this new field of studies by acknowledging its existence and importance from within the University of Oxford, and at the same time to bring North American scholars in touch with Europeans who shared this interest—in other words, to encourage the development of the discipline and to help internationalize it. I should add, however, that the fascination of this discipline lies precisely in its open-endedness, and no one is in favour of creating a new academic clique. By its nature, Tolkien Studies is interdisciplinary, and if it is to continue to grow it will do so by engaging the broadest possible range of academics and writers. Tolkien's writing simply opens doors, makes connections, and raises questions. We must always remember that Tolkien's fantasy writing was a 'work in progress', unfinished during his lifetime and subject to continual revision by the author right up to his death.

Tolkien's fantasy writing was immensely influential. As we know, it spawned a host of imitators—many of whom even insisted on publishing their works in the form of a trilogy, though this structure was quite accidental as far as Tolkien was concerned—creating a new genre-category for many booksellers. It is not quite accurate to say that Tolkien originated this genre, however. Literature of the same approximate type was being written in the late nineteenth and early twentieth centuries by William Morris, George MacDonald, E.R. Eddison, Robert E. Howard, T.H. White and many others. And, of course, Tolkien was himself deliberately drawing upon old traditions of storytelling and legend-making, especially the tradition of the heroic saga, dating back to the Greeks, the Vikings and *Beowulf*. Nevertheless his work does stand out as unique in many respects, not least because of the way he purified and to some extent Christianized the traditions he incorporated. He drew threads and colours from many places and times, but the tapestry is his own. He was partly writing an original work of fiction, and partly reconstructing (or pretending to reconstruct) a missing tradition of Anglo-Saxon folklore: this was a considerable creative task in its own right, even if it had to disguise itself as the mere copying or transmission of ancient texts.

As for the term 'fantasy', Tolkien tended to use it for the art of 'sub-creation' in its highest form. Man, he believed, was created in the image and likeness of his Creator, and therefore must be creative in an analogous way. The closest we come to imaging the divine act of creation is in the construction of a whole invented world. The difference is that we can only construct it from materials that already lie to hand in our memory and imagination, whereas God creates *ex nihilo* (from nothing). To the extent it is our own work, a sub-creation will naturally reflect our own imperfection, and the limitations of our imagination. Tolkien's limitations were less than some of his imitators. Many writings in the genre of 'fantasy literature' fall far short of the consistency and richness of detail that we find in Tolkien—and some may strike the reader as far less 'wholesome' in a psychological or spiritual sense. One of the characteristics that attracts readers to Tolkien is a sense of radiance, of grace, immanent in his writing, which he on occasion was not unwilling to attribute to a Higher Power working through him. Perhaps this is partly due to the fact that he was driven to write as a way of making sense of the world, and of making known the qualities of truth, goodness, and beauty that he had found in Catholicism. He certainly believed that this world—even death and suffering—ultimately made sense in a religious perspective, and this sense of certainty, or this hope, communicates itself to his readers, whatever their own beliefs may be.

England seems to breed fantasists. Three living examples, whose popularity rivals that of Tolkien, are Terry Pratchett, Philip Pullman, and J.K. Rowling. In each case, however, the genre is slightly different. None of the three is trying to do exactly what Tolkien does, even when they are to some extent influenced by it. Tolkien's Middle-earth presents itself as a (mythological) past stage of our world, whereas Rowling's story is set in an alternative version of our present, in which the wizarding world exists somehow in parallel with ours but is kept hidden. Pullman, too, employs the device of alternative worlds. Rowling's style is partly satiric (this is the case with Pratchett, too, where the charm lies in the jokes more than in the constructed world *per se*). Her magic is largely a device for making us look at our world with fresh eyes (what Tolkien, following Chesterton, might call 'Mooreeffoc fantasy')—for example, the potions class resembles a chemistry lesson, and the Quidditch tournaments are like our school sports but conducted on broomsticks. Apart from the unusual levels of satire, the genre is a mix of sword and sorcery, detective stories, and English boarding-school adventure, with a dash of romance (Jane Austen is a big influence on Rowling, she has admitted). Her love of word-play and etymology does slightly echo Tolkien's fascination with language, but the real resemblance between them, I think, lies elsewhere.

At the heart of both Rowling's as of Tolkien's stories is a concern with loving heroism and self-sacrifice. For all his faults, Harry Potter is attractive to us because he is not only brave but also loving. The mystery of the love that saved his life when he was a baby, when his mother died to save him, is in his blood and runs throughout the books of the series. And Harry is never alone—he is always with his close friends, Ron and Hermione, who form with him a kind of 'fellowship' a bit like that of the Hobbits. The centrality of this friendship, and the mysterious importance of love, is a very important link between the two authors. (Pullman, of course, also presents us with versions of loving heroism, complicated by the fact that he is reacting against aspects of Christianity that Tolkien and Rowling—certainly Tolkien—accept. Some would say that these complications enrich his work, others that they render it ultimately incoherent.)

Morally speaking, to the extent that fantasy movies and stories of these types function as pure entertainment or even escapism, they are pretty neutral—and no doubt they are better for us, more healthy and constructive, than other types of fantasy in which people like to indulge. But to the extent that they keep alive a sense of mystery, of life itself as a quest, of heroism and virtue, they can have a tremendous influence for good. I know someone who uses clips from these movies (and others, such as *Spider-Man* and *Star Wars*) to help young people in prison rediscover their sense of dignity and purpose. Sometimes they learn to understand themselves better by comparing themselves with the different members of the Fellowship of the Ring. In all sorts of ways, and on many different levels, we can learn from such stories. Whether we can then make the leap and apply what we have learned within our everyday lives is maybe another question. And from a Christian point of view, as C.S. Lewis said with reference to George MacDonald, these stories can also help to 'baptize our imaginations', preparing us to understand better the meaning of the Christian revelation, the figure of Jesus Christ, who is prefigured and reflected in many of Tolkien's characters. If in this way the ground is prepared for a spiritual and intellectual recovery of Christian faith and culture in Europe I myself would see that as a great thing. The stories certainly do not *force* Christianity on anyone, and a purely 'pagan' reading of *The Lord of the Rings* remains perfectly possible. (I would add only that, if so, it is a paganism that is not incompatible with Catholic Christianity, but that is a point that would take much more space to develop. I will expand upon this in my own contribution to this volume.)

So there are many reasons for reading Tolkien, many possible interpretations, and much benefit to be derived. Tolkien's work remains unfinished, and in a sense open-ended. He himself hoped it would inspire others to acts of creativity. Above all, one reads for *enjoyment.* It would be a sad thing if the rise of Tolkien Studies turned him into one more worthy author of a Great Book to be studied for examinations. Perhaps some of that is inevitable, because that is the way the world works. Of course, to accept Tolkien's work into the canon of modern English literature would be to erase boundaries between disciplines and entrenched positions that many generations have spent time and energy consolidating. The popular cult of Tolkien and the proliferation of inferior imitations have made it more difficult to take him seriously. But I am convinced that the academic world will come to terms with Tolkien's achievement in its own way eventually, even if it is more difficult to predict how it ends up categorizing him. He will never be in the category of a Dante or a Shakespeare. Maybe he will be closer to *War and Peace,* or his beloved *Beowulf.* Perhaps they will accept into their canon not just Tolkien's *Lord of the Rings* but a whole category of 'mythopoeic' literature that up to now has been excluded. The positive benefits of that would surely outweigh the negative. I hope that the Oxford Tolkien conference, and other conferences now being planned, will contribute to this process.

PART ONE

BIOGRAPHICAL

The Apolausticks, Exeter College, May 1912 (for further information, see page 22).

Tolkien, Exeter College and the Great War[1]

JOHN GARTH

Summary

This paper examines J.R.R. Tolkien's life as an undergraduate from 1911 to 1915, focusing on his friendships and extra-curricular activities, and assessing the impact of the First World War on his Oxford college.

J.R.R. Tolkien arrived at Exeter College in 1911 at the age of 19 as an Exhibitioner—the holder of a scholarship worth £60 a year—after a summer spent partly in the Swiss Alps on the walking holiday that ultimately gave him inspiration for Rivendell and the Misty Mountains. But *The Hobbit* and *The Lord of the Rings* lay far out of sight, and at this stage he had barely tapped into his creative potential: we have only seen evidence of a handful of poems written before this point—the only published example, 'The Battle of the Eastern Field', being a mock-heroic parody quite alien in spirit to the writings that were to make him famous.[2] There was scant sign that Tolkien was anything more than a gifted young man in pursuit of a degree in Classics (also known as

---

[1] The paper may be regarded as a supplement to my book, *Tolkien and the Great War: The Threshold of Middle-earth* (Garth 2003), which contains much further information about this period in Tolkien's life, particularly pertaining to his friendships from King Edward's School, Birmingham; his military career; and his academic and creative development. The text of this paper is an expanded version of the talk originally delivered on 21 August 2006 at the Oxford Tolkien Conference. Quotations from Exeter College archives are reproduced with thanks to the Rector and Fellows of Exeter College; the photograph of the Apolausticks and quotations from the papers of J.R.R. Tolkien are reproduced by kind permission of the Tolkien Estate; quotations from the papers of T.W. Earp are reproduced with thanks to the Tate Gallery. Thanks are also due to Christopher and Priscilla Tolkien for their comments.

[2] Tolkien later assigned dates of composition between March 1910 and September 1911 to his earliest eight extant poems (*Chronology* 19, 23, 25, 28). The parodic 'The Battle of the Eastern Field' appeared pseudonymously in the March 1911 issue of the *King Edward's School Chronicle* (22-27).

Literae Humaniores or 'Greats') amid a host of sociable distractions. By the time he left Exeter in the summer of 1915, the world had gone to war; while Tolkien had outgrown his minority, become engaged, and abandoned Classics for English. He had also begun a sequence of visionary artworks, produced a spate of poetry, and—leaving now the creative pursuits of other students far behind—he had begun inventing both a language and a world for it to describe. His association with Exeter was long-lasting: his eldest son John in turn took his Bachelor of Arts in English Language and Literature here in 1939; he himself became honorary fellow at the start of 1958, when he was Merton Professor of English Language and Literature, and he left £300 to the college in his will.[3] But during the years surrounding the First World War, this college witnessed the transformation of an undergraduate into the creator of Middle-earth.

I Antecedents

An antecedent may be observed in another schoolboy who had arrived at Exeter College from King Edward's School, Birmingham, six decades earlier, and in the friend he made here. Edward Burne-Jones had matriculated alongside William Morris in 1852 and vowed with him to forge an artistic brotherhood for a "crusade and Holy Warfare against the age, 'the heartless coldness of the times.'"[4] Morris and Burne-Jones had been disappointed by the standard of Oxford teaching at that time and had headed off to greater things, but not before the university had quickened their interest in medievalism, and not before they had left their own medievalist mark, notably in the Arthurian fresco at the Oxford Union and the tapestry in Exeter College Chapel—visions that seemed to reunite the seat of learning with a gilded romantic past. Tolkien once compared his informal King Edward's School club, the T.C.B.S., to the Pre-Raphaelite brotherhood which Burne-Jones joined; and when he arrived at Exeter he was probably already interested in the precedent set by him and Morris.

---

[3] *The Times*, 27 July 1939, 16; *The Times*, 2 January 1958, 8; Tolkien also left £500 to Trinity College and £200 to Pembroke College; *The Times*, 11 January 1974, 16.

[4] Edward Burne-Jones, *Memorials*, vol. 1, 84, quoted in Thompson (1991:5).

II Extra-curricular activities

By 1911 Britain was engaged in an arms race with Germany, but international tensions were only a dim backdrop to a slightly feverish gaiety in the population at large, and young Oxbridge undergraduates were no exception. In the words of a close contemporary of Tolkien's, this was Oxford "in the last years of the Affluent Age—absurd, delightful, totally irresponsible, and totally self-assured—moulded on a way of life that appeared unshakeably pre-ordained yet was about to vanish like the fabric of a dream" (Dodds 1977:33).[5] A similar impression of a now-bygone idyll, in which any hint of change is a cause for alarm, is conveyed in an unpublished letter from Tolkien more than half a century later recalling his arrival, soon after his Swiss walking trip, in the "excellent motor-car" of his erstwhile English teacher, R. W. Reynolds:[6]

> In it I was by him transported to Oxford when I came 'up' in 1911 and lunched at 'The Mitre'. A great privilege. I remember in particular his disapproval of the then new buildings of Brasenose. And also that at that beginning of 'winter term', everyone was in flannels and boating. It was the end of the legendary summer of 1911.

Despite the halcyon weather, it was already the end of the second week in October. Michaelmas Term began the following Sunday, and two days later Tolkien matriculated as a member of the university.

Having left King Edward's School in Birmingham feeling like a "young sparrow kicked out of a high nest," Tolkien seems to have been determined now to make up for his loss by boisterousness that descended occasionally into bumptiousness.[7] The signed programme that he kept as a memento of the initiatory Freshman's Annual Wine event, held at the end of October with songs and a dance in Exeter College's hall, gives no hint of the atmosphere of

---

[5] Dodds matriculated at University College in October 1912.

[6] Unpublished letter from Tolkien to Hermione Jolles, R.W. Reynolds's daughter, 6 March 1964. The author would like to thank Arnold Jolles for his kindness in supplying a copy of this letter. Brasenose's New Quad, designed by T.G. Jackson (a friend of William Morris's and an Arts & Crafts pioneer), was completed the year of Tolkien's arrival at Oxford.

[7] *Biography* 49.

the occasion, but it was a lively affair, and probably from some perspectives boorish. An indication of this appears in the papers of one of Tolkien's fellow freshmen, T.W. Earp, who mentions the "brutality of 'Freshers' Port' and rags"—rags being riotous or mischievous student high jinx.[8] It is unclear whether the unconventional and insecure Earp suffered some unwanted horse-play or simply looked down on his peers as brutes. But we need not think that Tolkien, already clubbable and outwardly more conventional than Tommy Earp, saw the gathering as anything other than convivial, and he was certainly not deterred from attending again the following year.[9]

As a whole, Tolkien's first two years at Exeter College were far from industrious. He and other Old Edwardians at Oxford were an inactive bunch, as one (possibly Tolkien himself) confided anonymously in their former school magazine: "In fact we have done nothing; we have been content with being."[10] Exeter was as good a place as any to do nothing. His food was provided in hall or brought by a college servant or 'scout' to his rooms, a bedroom and sitting-room on Staircase 8 in the first year and Staircase 7 in the second year; these were in the Tudor-style 'Swiss Cottage' (since demolished) that stood at the Broad Street end of Turl Street.[11] His college library borrowings for Classics are almost non-existent: only one in his entire first year, Grote's *History of*

---

[8]   T.W. Earp, unpublished synopsis of a planned autobiography that would have covered the period to armistice 1918 and its immediate aftermath. Earp papers, Tate Gallery Archives TGA 9124/1 (in a 16 December 1949 letter from publishers Eyre and Spottiswoode).

[9]   Tolkien preserved his signed programme for the 1912 event, too. Other souvenirs show Tolkien attended college 'Smoking Concerts' (including two in the space of four days that November) comprising light orchestral music, songs, comic recitations and even banjo; and (the following May) a performance of Samuel Coleridge-Taylor's *The Death of Minnehaha* by the college music society (*Chronology* 29).

[10] Unsigned report, 'Oxford Letter', *King Edward's School Chronicle*, December 1911, 100.

[11] Tolkien sketched Turl Street in about 1913 (*Artist and Illustrator* 23, 24). For the Swiss Cottage, see *Family Album* 31.

Greece, signed out for less than two weeks.[12] The Oxford 'sleepies' stopped him from working—a by-product of what the Exeter College fellow Lewis Farnell (1934:268) called "the inertia of the Thames valley which is against all re-forming disturbance."[13] Yet the 'sleepies' do not seem to have stopped him from enjoying himself. He might entertain friends for breakfast, or chat late into the night over a pipe. His longest account of undergraduate life describes how he and a friend 'captured' a bus during an evening of riotous 'ragging' by students.[14] He sketched shady Turl Street from his window and, for the cover of a smoking concert invitation, he added a foursome of undergraduates staggering along tipsily under the Nazgûl-like gaze of proctors in the form of owls.[15] Tolkien played tennis; he also continued playing rugby, though standards were higher than at school and he did not excel.[16]

III Religion

Earp, perhaps rather jaundiced, found the college filled with "young sportsmen and future parsons," and indeed a career in the Church was followed by nearly one in ten Old Exonians.[17] But in recent years Exeter had actually been more popular among Catholic students than any other college; they attended St Aloysius's in the Woodstock Road, the church that gave its name to Sebastian

---

[12] Tolkien checked out Vol. 5 of Grote's history on November 25 to December 6, at the same time as Eliot's *Finnish Grammar* and Joseph Wright's *English Dialect Grammar*; Exeter College library register, Exeter College Archives.

[13] *Biography* 73.

[14] *Biography* 54. Ragging as Tolkien uses it here implies riotous behaviour but not victimisation, the sense in which T.W. Earp uses the word.

[15] The 'smoker' invitation was for an event held on 9 November 1913 (see Priestman 1992:26).

[16] Indeed, Tolkien had "done well to get an occasional place in an exceptionally strong College 'pack'"; 'Oxford Letter', signed Oxoniensis, *King Edward's School Chronicle*, December 1912, 85.

[17] Earp papers. Maddicott (1998:46) gives the leading graduate careers as the Church (8%), the law (5%) and schoolteaching (4%).

Flyte's Catholic teddy bear in *Brideshead Revisited*.[18] At the outset, Tolkien was taken under the wing of a couple of Catholics in the year above him, one of them probably Tony Shakespeare, a law student who had been born in Harborne outside Birmingham and had attended the Oratory School—home of Tolkien's guardian, Father Francis Morgan.[19] In a letter of October 1914 Tolkien tells his wife-to-be Edith Bratt, facetiously or otherwise, that Shakespeare and fellow classicist Lionel Thompson (an Anglican) had "prevented me doing work on the sabbath, as I had proposed to do" (*Letters* 7).[20]

Despite the support of friends who shared his faith, the first few terms passed, Tolkien later confessed, "with practically none or very little practice of religion." He later came to feel that his failings and misdemeanours, recorded at the time in a diary, were a reaction to the fact that he was forbidden by his Catholic guardian from seeing the Anglican Edith until 1913, when he reached the age of 21.[21] He recalled, "It was extremely hard, painful and bitter, especially at first. The effects were not wholly good: I fell back into folly and slackness and misspent a good deal of my first year at College" (*Letters* 53). Such comments should be taken with a grain of salt: as Priscilla Tolkien has pointed out to me, her father was intensely scrupulous in matters of religion, and was prone to discomfort and self-recrimination over the slightest lapse; he certainly never strayed from the Roman Catholic faith into which he had followed his mother at the age of eight. In fact, his crimes as a student were

---

[18]   *The Catholic Encyclopaedia* 1913, www.newadvent.org/cathen/11365c.htm.

[19]   Exeter College had been strongly Catholic in sympathies during the religious upheavals of the Tudor period, owing to its connections with the conservative West Country, but had become Puritan after intervention by Queen Elizabeth's commissioners in 1578 (see Hibbert 1988:133). Carpenter (*Biography* 53) does not name the Catholics who befriended Tolkien at Exeter.

[20]   Correspondence with Jenny Thompson, Lionel Thompson's granddaughter. Evidently Edith had at least heard of these two fellow undergraduates before; Tolkien makes no attempt at introduction. Thompson, from Nottinghamshire, was three years younger than Tolkien but matriculated in his year; judging by his borrowing record in the Exeter College library register, he shared an interest in William Morris.

[21]   *Biography* 58.

probably no more unusual than the regret he felt looking back from a more mature perspective.

IV Social life

The diary of an American friend at Exeter, Allen Barnett, gives a glimpse of the grim reality of one typical day in 1913: "Went back to the jolly inn in the morning with Tolkien and we both got quite merry and made awful fools of ourselves when we got back to college. He put white shoe polish in my four-in-nines [apparently a kind of traditional American braided rug]..."[22] By chance a national daily newspaper, *The Daily Graphic*, affords a glimpse of another day in the lives of Tolkien and Barnett when they went to look at the charred remains of a boathouse destroyed the night before by militant suffragettes; a photograph shows the two undergraduates at the forefront of the onlookers, small and indistinct but perfectly recognisable.[23] (Barnett, who was a farmer's son and Rhodes Scholar, has since acquired some fame in relation to the dubious idea that hobbits were inspired by his tales of simple Kentucky tobacco-growers.)[24]

Exeter's Sub-Rector, responsible for discipline, noted that Tolkien was "v. lazy" and had been warned in summer 1912 that he might lose his annual scholarship money, but that his behaviour since had "much improved"—hardly surprising, given that £60 then was the equivalent of roughly £4,000 now. Perhaps a couple of incidents of 1913 escaped the Sub-Rector's attention, however. The first was a trivial prank played on a fellow student, Milton Hoffman, a Rhodes Scholar from Michigan. In February one of Tolkien's friends at Exeter, R.H. Gordon, was loudly censured by the Stapeldon Society—the closest thing the college had to a student union—for apparently

---

[22] Grotta (1978:42). While Grotta's book is far from reliable, his quotations from Barnett's papers provide a glimpse of Tolkien's Exeter College experiences and friendships that is absent from Carpenter's *Biography*.

[23] 'Boats and boathouse destroyed by fire at Oxford', *The Daily Graphic*, 4 June 1913, 3. Tolkien noted: "Barnett and I walked down to see the ruins and have come out large in photograph" (Douglas A. Anderson to the author).

[24] Grotta (1978:106).

appearing on the nearby towpath beside the Isis "in a large overcoat and carrying a stick or cane ... and tripping Mr. Hoffman up and almost causing him to fall into the River"; yet is seems it was not Gordon's doing at all, for, as the minutes of the meeting record, "Mr. Tolkien rose and said it was he who tripped Mr. Hoffman." The minutes are sadly opaque: was Tolkien on the towpath with Gordon, slyly sticking a foot out to land his friend in trouble, or was he alone, so muffled by the overcoat that he could pass for Gordon?

The second 1913 incident (though clearly an even greater source of amusement to the assembled students) was sufficiently serious to warrant intervention by the civil authorities: a town-versus-gown dust-up that also involved fellow Exonian Austin Blomfield. On 12 May the Stapeldon Society called upon Tolkien, who at the time held the elected post of Deputy Jester, for an account of his 'adventures' on the previous night.

> With the modesty of the true hero, he attempted to minimise his share in the proceedings and introduced Mr Blomfield in the new role of dauntless champion of the 'Varsity's honour. Mr Blomfield thereupon proudly exhibited an abrasion on his comely countenance, caused it would appear by the stupid mistake of a townee who thought his face to be another portion of the anatomy and kicked it accordingly.

Tolkien "then went on to describe his arrest and subsequent release and told how on returning to the College he had delighted the spectators by a magnificent, if unavailing, attempt to scale the Swiss Cottage and had spent the rest of the evening in climbing in and out of Mr Barnet's [sic] window." Despite some ambiguity in these society minutes, it was indeed Tolkien, not Blomfield, who was arrested and later tried to scale the Swiss Cottage. In a letter the following month, his schoolfriend Rob Gilson, now at Cambridge, commented: "Rumours of your adventures and encounters with the arms of the law have reached me in vague form and I await expectantly the promised explanation to the TCBS assembled."[25] Christopher Tolkien has told me that when his father recounted the incident many years later, he added that he had heard one of the police officers say to another, "Let's take this little one," before grabbing him from behind.

---

[25]   Letter from R.Q. Gilson to Tolkien, 10 June 1913; Tolkien family papers, Bodleian Library, Oxford.

V The Apolausticks and the Chequers Club

Not all of Tolkien's extra-curricular activities were so disreputable. *The King Edward's School Chronicle* noted: "Tolkien, if we are to be guided by the countless notices on his mantlepiece, has joined all the Exeter Societies which are in existence."[26] With a fellow classicist, Colin Cullis, he attended the Essay Club, which was then newly revitalised, and was elected Critic and later President in 1914. Tolkien was also an active member of the Stapeldon Society (on which more later). Beyond the college, he attended meetings and dinners held by the Old Edwardians in Birmingham and London, and he read papers to bodies including Corpus Christi's Sundial Society and the Psittakoi ('Parrots'), devoted to the discussion of literature.[27] However, these official societies and gatherings were not enough to satisfy Tolkien's social needs. At Exeter he also wanted a *comitatus* like the T.C.B.S.—a like-minded band of brothers with whom he could conspire—so he founded one.[28]

Undergraduate societies were by no means unusual: the 22 clubs whose records are held in Exeter's archive must be a fraction of the many that have come and gone at the college.[29] The Greek-derived name of the society that Tolkien set up with Colin Cullis in late 1911 or early 1912, 'the Apolausticks', may have been chosen because the co-founders, and several other members, were classicists; indeed, the group contained five of the seven classicists at Exeter from the 1911 intake. Tolkien himself was the first President. A group photograph, taken in May 1912, has long been familiar to readers of Humphrey Carpenter's 1977 *J.R.R. Tolkien: A Biography*. Carpenter identified only Tolkien and Cullis, but in the final stages of revision of this paper, another copy of the photograph has come to light, complete with a key identifying all

---

[26] 'Oxford Letter', signed Oxoniensis, *King Edward's School Chronicle*, December 1912, 85.

[27] Postcard from Tolkien to Edith Bratt, 2 February 1913, in *Family Album* 35; *Chronology* 65. Sundial Society minutes, Corpus Christi College Archives, Oxford. Dodds (1977:31).

[28] The Apolausticks was in existence by 1 June 1912, when Tolkien proposed the toast, "The Club", at an Apolausticks dinner (Priestman 1992:25).

[29] Hibbert (1988:96).

the other faces. The print belonged to *Lionel Thompson*, who appears sitting cross-legged on a mat directly in front of Tolkien.[30]

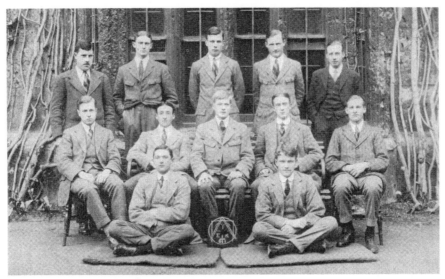

The Apolausticks, Exeter College, May 1912

Standing, from left to right: Allen Barnett, M.W.M. Windle (France 1915), G.S. Field, O.O. Staples (France 1915), R.H. Gordon (France 1916).
Seated: W.R. Brown (Belgium 1917), W.W.T. Massiah-Palmer (Secretary, Macedonia, 1919 L/Co), C. Cullis (President, unfit for service), J.R.R. Tolkien, J. Mackreth (France 1916).
On the floor: H.G.L. Trimingham, L.L.H. Thompson [survived the war]

Names, together with places and dates of death, are from Thompson's annotations, courtesy of Jenny Thompson and Andrew Thompson. Picture reproduced from Humphrey Carpenter, *J.R.R. Tolkien: A Biography* (1st edition 1977), courtesy of the Tolkien Estate.

The seating arrangement for the 12 men partly reflects the pecking order within the Apolausticks. Seated at the centre above the club monogram is an imposing *Colin Cullis*, who had succeeded Tolkien as club President in April.

---

[30]   I am most grateful to Jenny Thompson and Andrew Thompson, grandchildren of L.L.H. Thompson, for providing me with his notes from the back of his copy of the Apolausticks photograph. The information he provides about particular members has been supplemented here (as for other Exeter College students) by How (1928) and, frequently, the 'Debt of Honour Register' of the Commonwealth War Graves Commission as well as other sources.

Cullis is flanked by *J.R.R. Tolkien* on one side and on the other by Secretary *Werner William Thomas Massiah-Palmer*, the son of a Cornish butler and his German wife.[31] The monogram simply combines the Greek letters in the name APOLAUSTIKOI.[32]

Along with Thompson, other classicists pictured are *Robert Hope Gordon*, he of the towpath tripping incident (and, like Tolkien and Cullis, holder of a scholarship); and *Michael William Maxwell Windle*, a budding anthropologist and a particularly close friend to Tolkien, according to Barnett's reminiscences.[33] Windle, though related to the leading Catholic scientist Sir Bertram Windle, was an Anglican, the son of the vicar of Odiham in Hampshire: the Apolausticks, like the T.C.B.S., were non-denominational. At least one member looks to have figured among the 'future parsons' that Earp noticed in high numbers at the college: *John Mackreth*, pictured sitting to Tolkien's right, who was a Theology student and son of the vicar of All Souls, Brighton. Of greater interest to Tolkien, perhaps, would have been the fact that Mackreth was a relative of Robert Baden-Powell, hero of Mafeking and founder in 1907 of the Scout Movement.[34]

Unlike the T.C.B.S., but true to the composition of Exeter College, the Apolausticks were also international. *Allen Barnett* (his heavy-set, glowering, moustachioed face easily recognisable next to Windle's at top left in the photograph) was not the only Rhodes Scholar: another was *Osric Ormond Staples*, from Philippolis in the Orange Free State, less than 100 miles from Bloemfontein, where Tolkien (seated directly in front of him in the photograph) was

---

[31] Listed on the Exeter College chapel war memorial simply as William Thomas Massiah-Palmer.

[32] Arden R. Smith to the author. The triangular shape in the middle is both alpha and lambda, the incomplete square is pi, the circle encompassing all is omicron; ypsilon is inside the upper portion of the alpha, and the rest of the letters are scrambled up below it.

[33] Windle was also known, at least to his family, as Max.

[34] John Mackreth was Robert Stephenson Smyth Baden-Powell's first cousin, twice removed: his mother Madeline was a great-granddaughter of the latter's grandfather (see Baden Clay 2001). Tolkien had devised a 'Scout code' in a 1909 notebook, 'The Book of the Foxrook' (see Wynne and Smith 2000).

born.[35] A third Rhodes Scholar, *Harold Gilbert Lutyens Trimingham* (cross-legged in front of Massiah-Palmer), was a member of one of Bermuda's leading mercantile families but had been schooled at Dulwich College, where he had presumably known Cullis, an exact contemporary.

Not surprisingly in a college that drew nearly a third of its students from just eight schools, the great majority of the Apolausticks were the products of grammar schools or of the great public schools.[36] The former constituency included Tolkien, Lionel Thompson, and *William Ernest Hall* (not in the Apolausticks photograph), a publisher's son born in Darjeeling, India. The latter group included R.H. Gordon, educated at Fettes near Edinburgh; *Geoffrey Simpson Field*, a solicitor's son from Reading in Berkshire but educated at Marlborough; and *Christian Albert Hastings Fairbank* (not in the Apolausticks picture), who was the son of the surgeon to King George V's household at Windsor, not to mention a descendant of Plantagenets, and had gone to Eton. Two of the Apolausticks, however, had been privately tutored: Massiah-Palmer and the man seated at left of him, *Walter Rolfe Brown*, son of a chartered accountant from Wimbledon. Massiah-Palmer, born in 1885 and almost 28 years old when the group was photographed, was by some years the eldest Apolaustick, followed by Allen Barnett (born in 1888). The rest were born in 1892, like Tolkien, or 1893, like R.H. Gordon, the youngest member, and so were between 18 and 20 years old when they stood for the portrait in May 1912. All the identifiable members, however, matriculated at Oxford in October 1911.

The scrawny Tolkien and the stocky Barnett also feature in a joint 1914 photograph of the Rugby and Boat clubs, while Fairbank was a member of the college rowing Eight in 1912.[37] The fact that the quotient of Earp's "young sportsmen" seems so low among the Apolausticks is hardly surprising, perhaps,

---

[35]   William Jervois, resident genealogist at the Albany Museum, Grahamstown, South Africa.

[36]   Marlborough had the most students at Exeter, with Eton and Exeter School also in the top eight (Maddicott 1998:46).

[37]   The joint Rugby and Boat Club photograph is reproduced in Priestman (1992:25) and also in Topliffe (1992:33). Allen Barnett also appears next to Tolkien in a 1913 group portrait of the college.

given the *raison d'être* of the group. *Apolaustic* means 'concerned with or wholly devoted to seeking enjoyment; self-indulgent', according to the *Oxford English Dictionary*. A supporting quotation refers to "The lordly, apolaustic, and haughty undergraduate"—so the club's name neatly combines arrogance and self-mockery.[38] Among its self-indulgences were "large and extravagant dinners" that left a hole in Tolkien's pocket, according to Humphrey Carpenter. These seem to have been annual affairs: on 1 June 1912 the Apolausticks dined at the Randolph Hotel and on 31 May 1913 they sat down at an unrecorded venue for a six-course dinner. While most other meetings were held more modestly in members' college rooms—once a week during term, initially on Saturdays and later on Wednesdays—the conversation was helped along at least once by Swedish punch.[39]

Culture was not entirely eschewed, although as may be expected in the rather giddy pre-war atmosphere the undergraduates seem not to have developed the kind of cultural idealism seen during the war in the T.C.B.S. The patchy evidence suggests that on the whole the Apolausticks discussed decidedly light literary subjects including Lewis Carroll, the nineteenth-century versifiers C.S. Calverley and J.K. Stephen, and the current era's arch-wits G.K. Chesterton and George Bernard Shaw. A weightier topic was the Belgian symbolist writer Maurice Maeterlinck, who was discussed in Tolkien's rooms on 9 March 1912: Maeterlinck had won the Nobel Prize for Literature the previous year, and as the author of the celebrated fairy play, *L'Oiseau Bleu* (1908), may have held more than a passing interest for Tolkien. Tolkien himself presented a paper (subject unknown) on 11 May 1912, and on Saturday 15 June he proposed the motion "That a belief in ghosts is essential to the welfare of a people", scraping victory in the debate by a single vote.[40] While this motion seems at first glance rather eccentric, it constitutes an early example of

---

[38]   *The Oxford English Dictionary*, 1st edition, Vol. 1, 388. Tolkien was already an inveterate dictionary-monger; his sole contribution to Exeter's undergraduate suggestions book was for the purchase of "a good English dictionary" (Hibbert 1988:135). A programme of Apolausticks meetings for Hilary Term 1912 exists in Tolkien's papers (*Chronology* 30).

[39]   *Biography* 53; *Chronology* 31-35, 42, and *Guide* 956.

[40]   *Chronology* 33.

Tolkien's interest in myth and the fantastical as cornerstones of a nation's self-hood—an interest which would lead him to develop 'The Book of Lost Tales' as a mythology for England.

The Apolausticks presumably continued to meet regularly at least until the summer of 1913, by which time Allen Barnett was club President. However, in January 1914 Tolkien and Cullis obtained the Sub-Rector's leave to hold suppers for nine in undergraduate rooms on Saturday nights that term: this permission, as Tolkien later noted, was the 'germ' of the Chequers Club, a successor to the Apolausticks which seems likely to have included many of the same members.[41] In the absence of a complete programme of the activities of the Apolausticks and the Chequers, it is impossible to say whether their membership included other undergraduates than those named in the surviving records, but Tolkien's circle clearly included others at Exeter. One such friend, not among the Apolausticks we can identify, was probably Henry Allpass, with whom Tolkien apparently corresponded during the war; at Exeter to read German, he was a member of the socialist Fabian Society and was once called "the best topical poet in Oxford," publishing his technically sophisticated light verse in the university's *Isis* newspaper.[42] When Tolkien recalls his own abortive attempt to write "a diary with portraits (some scathing some comic some commendatory) of persons or events seen" before he turned to 'The Book of Lost Tales', he seems to be describing the kind of writing in which Allpass specialised.[43]

---

[41] Christina Scull and Wayne G. Hammond (*Chronology* 50) note that many of the signatures on Tolkien's Chequers Club menu from 18 June 1914 belong to former members of the Apolausticks; it seems that both clubs generally numbered about 12 members.

[42] 'A.B.A.', prefatory note to Allpass (1920); Henry [or Harry] Blythe King Allpass is given the nickname 'Rex' on the title page.

[43] *Letters* 85. Tolkien seems to imply that he made this experiment in prose during his military service, and prior to writing 'The Book of Lost Tales' (though not, perhaps, prior to his mythological verse of early 1915).

VI The Stapeldon Society

Given that the Apolausticks at one time or another included at least 14 of the 59 Exeter undergraduates who matriculated in 1911, it is unsurprising to see many of its members—and Tolkien perhaps most prominently—taking active roles in the Stapeldon Society. Tolkien himself began his dizzy climb to power at the bottom, in the College Charges Investigation Committee in 1912, but in late 1913 he rose to Secretary, with R.H. Gordon as President. The minutes, in Tolkien's flowing hand, brim with humour and delight in language:[44]

> Mr Massiah-Palmer made a lewd remark, which it is sad to note was received with thunderous mirth. A maggot, moldiewarp, or mealie-worm saved from drowning in coffee was rescued from Mr Staples' clutches and attended to by Mr Kindersley the noted insect-fancier.

Finally Tolkien was elected Stapeldon President for the Hilary Term of 1914, with Colin Cullis as Secretary and W.E. Hall as Treasurer—a triumphant hat-trick for the Apolausticks. Tolkien's report of that meeting is a mock epic:

> At the 791st meeting of the Stapeldon Society held on December 1st 1913 one of the world's great battles between democracy and autocracy was fought and won, and as is usual in such conflicts the weapons of the democracy were hooliganism and uproar [...].
>
> Long before the officers had even passed the curtain the ominous sounds of a gigantic house athirst for their blood could be heard. Even in the Porch a dull booming murmur like the bay of the Bloodhounds in 'Red Axe' reached the ears of loafers; who promptly swelled the throng, entering when the door jammed, by way of the windows [...].

Tolkien goes on to explain that Gordon, as outgoing President, had foolishly brought a bottle of port in to drink, a bad example promptly followed by the rabble. A misplaced presidential ruling added to the combustible atmosphere:

---

[44] Report of 27 October 1913 meeting, Stapeldon Society minutes, Exeter College Archives. Not all of these words appear to refer to insects. The *Oxford English Dictionary* has no entry for either *mealie-worm* or *moldiewarp*, but defines *mealworm* as a kind of beetle larva, *mealy-bug* as one of a variety of sap-sucking insects, and *mouldwarp* as a mole (literally 'earth thrower'). *The English Dialect Dictionary* casts no further light on these words.

The House—especially typified by Mr H.S. Price—flushed in his
face and with the veins of anger bulging in his forehead [—] pro-
tested against this ruling with an extraordinary uproar the like of
which has never been heard in this room before. Man after man
arose to speak flushed with the wine of wrath, and man after man
was quashed, crushed, and squashed into oblivion with the magic
of Rule 9 section (b); until the House began to resent Rule 9(b) as a
personal foe, and to heave with an uncontrollable antagonism on
each mention of it.

The only way in which members in the further corners could tell
of the progress of business was by the changes of colour in the
presidential countenance, which ranged from a rich violet to a dull
cream. [...]

When Mr Trevor Oliphant arose with the white face of bitter
determination, and demanded that the House go back to Private
Business for the discussion of the shelved constitutional question,
all bounds, all order, and all else was forgotten; and in one long riot
of raucous hubbub; of hoarse cries, brandished bottles, flying
match-stands, gowns wildly flourished, cups smashed, and lights
extinguished, the House declared its determination to have its will
and override the constitution. From the midst of this uproar a Red
Devil of Fu-ji-ya leapt from Mr Palmer's bosom and hit the secretary [Tolkien himself] square on the nose.

For precisely one calendar hour did the House battle with noise
and indignation for its desire. It was at one time on the point of
dissolving and becoming another society; at another it was vocifer-
ating for Rule 40; at another for Rule 10; at another for no Rules at
all, or for the President's head, or his nether-garments.

The meeting ended, Tolkien notes, with "a vote of admiration for the rock-
like obstinacy with which the President had withstood this unparalleled storm
of rebellion and insubordinate riot."[45]

The entry, for all that it matches the parodic thrust of 'The Battle of the
Eastern Field', is notable for being the earliest known prose narrative by
Tolkien, and for demonstrating his already fluent grasp of vivid detail, his
ability to crank up dramatic tension, and his interest in the clash of order and
chaos. Of course, Tolkien did not write all this merely for his own entertainment, and certainly not for the benefit of posterity: according to protocol, the

---

[45]   J.R.R. Tolkien, report of 1 December 1913 meeting, Stapeldon Society minutes.

minutes of the previous meeting would have been read back to the house when it next met, so here was an opportunity to amuse the assembled members of the Stapeldon. Cullis, taking over secretarial duties for the first meeting of Tolkien's own presidency the following term, noted how "the memory and imagination of the House had been stirred by the cinematographically vivid minutes of the last meeting."[46]

VII Extra-curricular work

Amid all this clubbability, Tolkien had not been entirely lazy. In his first term, he had been inspired by his new environment to write poetry, one fragment of which, 'From the many-willow'd margin of the immemorial Thames', was eventually published in the college's *Stapeldon Magazine* beneath another by his contemporary, Hugh Reginald Freston (known as Rex).[47] Tolkien also worked on a series of strange, symbolist sketches in a volume he titled 'The Book of Ishness'—an outlet for his private broodings and his more inchoate creative urges. More important than poetry or drawings, though, had been his discovery in the college library during his first term back in 1911 of Sir Charles Eliot's *Finnish Grammar*. In due course, it led Tolkien eventually, as we shall see, to spend long hours on his old hobby, the invention of languages, with a lexicon of what he came to call Qenya, the language of the Elves. He later compared the discovery of this ostensibly dry little book to Keats's first glimpse inside Chapman's Homer—a fairly bald statement of his growing preference for non-classical learning.

VIII Failure at Classics

Tolkien was not uninterested in work *per se*, but only in his chosen degree course. His real passion for story had once been awakened by Homer, and his first encounters with poetry had been when he was asked to translate it into Latin at school, but he later said that his "love for the classics took ten years to

---

[46]   Colin Cullis, report of 26 January 1914 meeting, Stapeldon Society minutes.

[47]   *The Stapeldon Magazine* (journal of Exeter College, Oxford) December 1913, 11.

recover from lectures on Cicero and Demosthenes."[48] According to his *Times* obituary, the problem was that there was no resident classical tutor at Exeter when Tolkien arrived, but this does not appear to have been the case: the subject was taught there by the college's respected classicist fellow Lewis Farnell, assisted from Hilary Term (January to March) 1912 by the young, brilliant Eric Arthur Barber.[49] It seems that Tolkien simply let himself down. He later blamed a fruitless attempt at learning the Finnish of the mythological poem, the *Kalevala*, saying that "when [Honour Moderations] should have been oc-

---

[48] *Letters* 172, 213. Anonymous obituary, 'Professor J. R. R. Tolkien Creator of Hobbits and inventor of a new mythology', *The Times*, Monday, Sep 3, 1973, 15. The obituary does not state who delivered these lectures. Memoirs by classicists in Tolkien's immediate generation give a very different impression. Dodds (1977:28-29) enthuses about A.B. Poynton's lectures on Cicero's *Orations* and especially about Gilbert Murray's on the *Bacchae* of Euripides: "To hear Murray read aloud and interpret a passage of Greek poetry brought successive generations of his students the intoxicating illusion of direct contact with the past, and to many of them a permanent enlargement of their sensibility [...]. When after Moderations I had occasional serious thoughts of abandoning Classics and switching to some other field, perhaps the still fairly recent English School, it was the memory of Murray's lectures more than anything else which deterred me from making the change." Strong (1961:166) concurs that Murray's "quality shone in everything he did" and adds, "I never met anyone who was unaware of this radiance or was unaffected by it."

[49] Lewis Farnell (who had a special interest in mythology that ought to have appealed to Tolkien) was also senior tutor responsible for the general educational administration of the college (Farnell 1934:266), and perhaps was unable to give his undivided attention to direct tutoring in classics. In Hilary Term 1912 Barber, who was resident at Merton College and held a Prize Fellowship there, was invited to assist Farnell in the classical teaching at Exeter. He took up residence at Exeter in Trinity Term 1912 as a 'Lecturer' (in this context, a college tutor) but was only elected to a Fellowship there in October 1913. (E.A. Barber, 'Vita' (MS autobiography), Exeter College Archives, Box R.I.i., with thanks to John Maddicott.) Cf. *Biography* 54. With Carpenter's unsourced statement that Barber was "a dry teacher", contrast Barber's obituary (*The Times*, Wednesday, May 26, 1965, 14): "As a tutor Barber was first rate, and it was rarely that Exeter could not boast a number of First Classes in 'Mods' out of all proportion to the size of the College. His lectures he generally dictated, or at least delivered at little more than dictation speed. This made them somewhat 'dry', but those of his listmen who had the nous to recognize their excellence formed a faithful and appreciative audience." Tolkien attended Barber's memorial service in the college chapel on Saturday 5 June 1965. *The Times*, 7 June 1965, 10.

cupying all my forces I once made a wild assault on the stronghold of the original language and was repulsed with heavy losses."[50]

On reaching the age of 21 and becoming engaged to Edith Bratt at the start of 1913, he promised her he would work harder and began a tally of hours spent at the grindstone.[51] There was a flurry of library borrowings: Sophocles's *Oedipus Tyrannus* and *Electra* and Aeschylus's *Eumenides*, *Agamemnon* and *Choephoroe*, though not the hated Cicero and Demosthenes, whom candidates were expected to translate. However, it was too late: he achieved a mediocre Class II in his mid-course Honour Moderations. He was not alone: of the seven candidates fielded by Exeter, Colin Cullis, Michael Windle and R.H. Gordon fared just as badly, two did even worse, and only the diligent Lionel Thompson achieved a First.[52]

IX Switch to English

Perhaps it was fortunate for Tolkien that Lewis Farnell, Exeter's new Rector or principal, was one of those who had helped agitate for the establishment, in 1894, of Oxford's Honours School (or faculty) of English Language and Literature. The study of English literature was generally sneered at as somehow essentially feminine until the mid-years of the 20th century. At Oxford, it had accordingly been given, as Farnell recalled, "a firm basis of philological science; so as to fend off the sarcastic criticism of opponents"—perfect for Tolkien, who had been saved from an ignominious Third in Mods by an alpha in philology, and who had no taste for 'modern' writers later than Chaucer.[53] The English School was still in its infancy by 1913, and Tolkien only discovered its existence while browsing the Examination Statutes.[54] Farnell, who also had a

---

[50] Tolkien Papers, Bodleian Library, Oxford, quoted in *Chronology* 29.

[51] Priestman (1992:27).

[52] Results were announced at Oxford on 7 April; *The Times*, 8 April 1913, 6.

[53] Though Humphrey Carpenter states that Tolkien achieved a 'pure alpha', and Joseph Wright later vouched that his mark had been $\alpha+$, in fact it was a straightforward α (see *Chronology* 777).

[54] Farnell (1934:271). *Letters* 405-6.

deep affection for things Germanic, suggested that Tolkien switch to English, and discreetly arranged for him to retain his £60-a-year Exhibition money, even though technically it was meant to fund a classicist.[55]

Tolkien's pleasure in his new course spilled over into his extracurricular life. Dull pages of amendments to Stapeldon Society rules, written out by Colin Cullis as society secretary in Hilary Term 1914, were turned over by Tolkien and their versos used to list unusual words he wanted to look up in the *Oxford English Dictionary*.[56] More productively, he presented a paper on the Norse sagas to Exeter's Essay Club in the Trinity Term of 1913, adopting (as the college's *Stapeldon Magazine* reported) "a somewhat unconventional turn of phrase, suiting admirably with his subject": probably a pseudo-medieval idiom, as William Morris used in his translations from Icelandic, and which Tolkien himself would later employ in 'The Book of Lost Tales'.[57] Yet Tolkien's curiosity still led him away from the narrow course confines. Farnell and his new tutors must have been alarmed when he spent his Skeat Prize money in spring 1914 not on funding his English studies but on medieval Welsh and books by Morris that lay well outside the syllabus.[58]

X Tolkien just before the war

It was now the year of the still unforeseen war, yet nothing as momentous as his 1913 coming of age, engagement or change of course seemed likely to befall Tolkien. Furthermore, he still showed little sign of becoming a prolific coiner of verse, prose or even imaginary languages. At best he was beginning to define the ground he would later occupy, through papers such as the one on Norse sagas or another, in March 1914, on the Catholic poet Francis Thomp-

---

[55] Farnell (1934:57). *Letters* 397, 406.

[56] *Chronology* 50.

[57] *The Stapeldon Magazine*, June 1913, 276.

[58] *Biography* 69; Tolkien (1983:192). With his £5 prize money, Tolkien bought J. Morris Jones, *A Welsh Grammar, Historical and Comparative* (Oxford: Clarendon Press, 1913) as well as William Morris's historical romance *The House of the Wolfings*, his epic poem *The Life and Death of Jason* and his translation of the Icelandic *Volsunga Saga*.

son. In this, he depicted a writer who could bridge the divide between ration-alism and romanticism, and he highlighted "the images drawn from astronomy and geology, and especially those that could be described as Catholic ritual writ large across the universe." "An attitude of humility befitting immaturity was necessary towards F[rancis] Thompson's most profound expressions of mature spiritual experience," he told the Essay Club audience (including Tommy Earp and Apolausticks members Michael Windle, Colin Cullis, R.H. Gordon and W.R. Brown). "One must begin with the elfin and delicate and progress to the profound: listen first to the violin and the flute, and then learn to hearken to the organ of being's harmony." (Cullis could not progress to the profound, saying he "found the sacerdotal imagery rather overpowering at times; he was attracted more by the simple poems of childhood"; but Gordon shared Tolkien's higher sensitivities, praising "a ringing of bells through Francis Thompson's poetry as through the Vulgate.") The successive metaphors of childlike receptivity and orchestral scale that Tolkien employs in his paper strikingly anticipate the 'Book of Lost Tales': both 'The Cottage of Lost Play', written more than two years later, and 'The Music of the Ainur', still five or so years in the future. Writing up this report of Tolkien's talk, his friend Lionel Thompson (no relation of Francis) commented: "One was conscious that he had felt himself into perfect harmony with the poet."[59] But perhaps for now Tolkien was too busy to find time to explore his own creativity or, indeed, to feel the need for such an outlet at all—what with his English work, his presidency of the Stapeldon in the Hilary Term and the Essay Club in the Trinity Term (from April to June), and his involvement in the forthcoming 600th anniversary of Exeter College.

XI Sexcentenary

The Sexcentenary was felt so significant that renovations of the college hall had been set in motion ten years previously, and had only just been completed. The previous Rector, W.W. Jackson, had handed over to Farnell in 1913 after twenty-six years service, feeling the younger man would be more capable of

---

[59] L.L.H. Thompson, report of 4 March 1914 meeting, Essay Club minutes, Exeter College Archives.

making the necessary preparations. The Stapeldon Society, under its new president, Colin Cullis, spent much of the Trinity Term 1914 getting ready, and omitted its customary habit of sending letters of congratulation or condemnation to monarchs and governments worldwide because no "international affairs of sufficient importance had occurred."[60] At the Sexcentenary Dinner on 6 June when the undergraduates entertained the Rector and Fellows, Tolkien appears to have sat with most of the friends already mentioned: Tony Shakespeare, Henry Allpass, the former Apolausticks members Lionel Thompson, Massiah-Palmer, Cullis, Harold Trimingham, Rolfe Brown, Mackreth, Osric Staples and Geoffrey Field, as well as Tommy Earp and the Classics don E.A. Barber.[61] Tolkien proposed the toast to the college societies (as befitted a member of so many).[62] On 18 June there was the 'Binge' for the Chequers Club, doubtless a successor to the elaborate Apolausticks dinners of 1912 and 1913; he drew its elegant invitations— decorated with pipes and tankards—and his own copy carries the signatures of himself and seven others who attended the five-course dinner.[63] Finally, from 23 to 25 June, there were three days of Sexcentenary events: a ball, a reunion for Old Exonians, a garden party with the Blue Hungarian Band, a service in the chapel, and a grand lunch at which the Chancellor of the University, Lord Curzon, proposed the toast of *Floreat Exon.*

XII Outbreak of war

Some months later Farnell recalled: "All our festivities were enhanced by charming weather, and our atmosphere was unclouded by any foreboding of the war-storm that has burst upon us. And now the memories of last term are as a golden vista seen across a dark and perilous flood."[64] The old world had

---

[60]   *The Stapeldon Magazine,* June 1914, 93.

[61]   Signed menu from the papers of E.A. Barber (courtesy of Neil Holford).

[62]   *The Stapeldon Magazine,* June 1914, 44-45.

[63]   Priestman (1992:25-26); *Chronology* 53 and *Guide* 956.

[64]   'All our festivities ...': L.R. Farnell, 'Sexcentenary Celebration of the College', in *The Stapeldon Magazine,* December 1914, 109.

come to an end just as the Trinity Term did, with the assassination of Arch-
duke Franz Ferdinand on 28 June. On 4 August, when Tolkien was in Warwick with Edith, Britain declared war on Germany, and three days later, Lord
Kitchener, Minister of War, called upon Tolkien's generation to fight.
Tolkien's summer vacation was personally momentous. He opted not to enlist;
a daunting choice at a time when able-bodied men out of uniform might be
verbally or even physically abused in the streets. And in a development that
may not be entirely unrelated, he wrote his first poem to have a real claim to
being part of the literature of Middle-earth, 'The Voyage of Éarendel the Evening Star', in which, tellingly, the hero spurns the chartered courses of other
celestial bodies in pursuit of something undefined and elusive, but ethereally
fair. The poem came to him as he slogged through the poetry of Cynewulf in
an Anglo-Saxon volume he had borrowed from Exeter College library.[65]

XIII Exeter at war

By October, Oxford was becoming a military camp for the first time since the
English Civil War. Quaintly, Farnell the Rector was giving lessons in the use
of the sabre. Instruction in signalling, Tolkien's later military specialism, was
given in the front quadrangle to students in the Officer Training Corps or
OTC.[66] As an editorial in the college magazine observed, "[w]e are becoming
accustomed to the tramp of troops on the Turl, to the sound of early-morning
bugles, to the sight of convalescent soldiers and Belgian refugees in the streets
of Oxford."[67] The college was now partly acting as billets for the Oxfordshire
and Buckinghamshire Light Infantrymen and various batteries of gunners;
men who stayed a day or two before moving on.[68] Several of the Fellows had

---

[65] Grein and Wülcker's multi-volume *Bibliothek der angelsächsischen Poesie*. During
this crucial period (19 June to 14 October 1914) Tolkien also borrowed John
Earle's 1892 translation *The Deeds of Beowulf* and Richard Morris's 1872 *Old
English Miscellany containing a Bestiary, Kentish Sermons, Proverbs of Alfred, Religious Poems of the Thirteenth Century,* Exeter College library register.

[66] *The Stapeldon Magazine*, December 1915, 132.

[67] *The Stapeldon Magazine*, December 1914, 103.

[68] How (1928:vii).

gone off to war and so had many of the servants, to be replaced by older men. Whereas 59 freshmen had matriculated with Tolkien in 1911, now there were only 28 new arrivals. The undergraduate population was reduced to just 75, and falling, as more and more students found their moment to enlist.

Tolkien declared: "It is awful. I really don't think I shall be able to go on: work seems impossible. Not a single man I know is up except Cullis."[69] Many of his friends would have left Exeter by now anyway after completing their degrees a year before Tolkien, who had changed courses in midstream. Harry Allpass and Allen Barnett were embarking on careers as teachers. But out of the 19 men who had signed Tolkien's Sexcentenary menu that June, fully 14 enlisted in Kitchener's Army by the end of the year, including Lionel Thompson, Massiah-Palmer, Harold Trimingham, G.S. Field, Osric Staples, John Mackreth and Rolfe Brown—former Apolausticks all. Other ex-members to join up in 1914 were R.H. Gordon, Michael Windle and W.E. Hall. Early enlisters from the college also included Austin Blomfield, preparing now to fight Germans instead of Oxford townsfolk. Lieutenant Thompson looked "very healthy and well in his new uniform," Tolkien (*Letters* 7) told Edith in October.[70] But in the evenings the quad was silent under darkened windows. He was relieved to be living for the first time out of college, at 59 St John Street where he shared 'digs' with Colin Cullis, who was debarred from military service due to poor health.[71]

XIV Military training

In lieu of enlisting in Kitchener's army, Tolkien enrolled at Oxford in the university OTC. His military training had indeed begun in the officer training corps at King Edward's School, but on matriculating at Exeter he had enrolled

---

[69]   *Biography* 72.

[70]   *The Stapeldon Magazine*, December 1914, 105.

[71]   Lewis Farnell kept a 'Rooms list' (Exeter College Archives) in which notes for 1914 include: "Cullis exc. Doctor. Earp ditto" and "Tolkien exc." It would be interesting to know whether Tolkien met Cullis's extraordinary older sister, who changed her name from Mildred to the Ældrin on the grounds that it sounded Anglo-Saxon, and who once posed for a photograph in Amazonian war-gear, complete with spear (information courtesy of the Brailsford family).

instead in a cavalry regiment, coincidentally named King Edward's Horse, which recruited residents of Britain born overseas. By 1911 the regiment had a strong following in Exeter College, with its considerable overseas contingent, and Tolkien presumably joined because of his South African birth: his fellow Apolaustick Osric Staples, also from the Orange Free State, was a member too. However, for reasons perhaps not unconnected with a thoroughly wet and wind-blown two-week annual camp on the exposed South Coast, Tolkien had been discharged at his own request in February 1913.[72] Now Tolkien was one of 25 Exonians on the university OTC's Course II, for those who wished to delay enlistment, which meant about six and a half hours' drill and one military lecture per week.[73] To those on the other course, who wished to join up as soon as possible and therefore spent considerably more time drilling, he cheekily provided advice at one Stapeldon Society meeting, as the minutes record: "Class II OTC in the person of Mr Tolkien then gave Class I and others valuable hints on drilling a Co[mpan]y entitled 'Jones best ever-ready word of command, always useful, will never wear out, *Hip hop*.'"[74] He wrote to Edith: "We had a drill all afternoon and got soaked several times and our rifles got all filthy and took ages to clean afterwards" (*Letters* 7). And yet he was grateful: "Drill is a godsend. I have been up a fortnight nearly, and have not yet got a touch even of the real Oxford 'sleepies'" (*Biography* 73).

XV Kullervo and Cohen

Reinvigorated by these activities, and with a new seriousness in keeping with the grim turn of international events, he set himself now to writing in earnest, eschewing his parodic tendencies and working on a tragic version of the story of Kullervo, from the *Kalevala*, in Morrisian prose "with chunks of poetry in

---

[72] James (1921:1-53). *The Stapeldon Magazine*, December 1911, 117-18. J.R.R. Tolkien's military service record (UK National Archives, ref. WO 339/34423). William Jervois.

[73] *The Stapeldon Magazine*, December 1914, 120.

[74] Report of 25 January 1915 meeting, Stapeldon Society minutes.

between."[75] It was a dark tale for dark times, from which seed his story of Túrin Turambar was to evolve in the following years. The tale of a brash young man, a fugitive from slavery, who unwittingly seduces his sister, precipitating their successive suicides—it seems strange that this so captured the imagination of a fervent Roman Catholic that he kept rewriting it for the rest of his life. An overriding attraction of the *Kalevala* was the sounds of the Finnish names, the remote primitivism and the Northern air. The initial appeal of the Kullervo element was perhaps its maverick heroism, youthful romance and despair: Tolkien had been through a prolonged and enforced separation from Edith Bratt. The deaths of Kullervo's parents may have struck a chord, too, with the orphaned Tolkien.

It is also possible that part of the leaf-mould for this early narrative experiment was an incident that had shaken Exeter College the previous year, at a time when the wider world had been buzzing with news of the deaths of Captain Scott and his polar expedition. One of the other Exhibitioners from Tolkien's matriculation year, and apparently his sole Exonian predecessor in reading English, had been one Sydney Abraham Cohen, from London. With Cohen, Tolkien had proposed a Stapeldon motion in 1912 that "This House deplores the signs of degeneracy in the present age." Quiet but popular, Cohen was a keen tennis player and, in the words of his friend Henry Allpass, "a hard-reading man"; he liked to work into the small hours.

One Monday evening in February 1913, Cohen invited Allpass to his rooms, and after some minutes' conversation went to his desk on the pretext of fetching a cigarette holder. He took out a revolver and for several minutes toyed with it, pointing it at his own head and declaring: "I wish I had the courage to shoot myself." Allpass told him to put the gun down but did not think him entirely in earnest; Cohen had often expressed the same thought before. Standing in front of the fireplace, Cohen suddenly raised the gun once

---

[75]   *Letters* 7 shows Tolkien was working on his 'Story of Kullervo' in October 1914. In a letter to W.H. Auden dated 7 June 1955 (*Letters* 214-15) Tolkien recalled beginning the tale in 1912 or 1913, but in making such retrospective estimates many years after the event he was often prone to assign earlier dates to texts than contemporary evidence would indicate. For a synopsis of the unpublished narrative, as well as comparisons with the *Kalevala* and the story of Túrin, see *Guide* 445-46.

more to his head and fired. The doctor who answered Allpass's summons found Cohen sitting on the sofa, gun at his feet, bleeding from a wound to his temple; his speech was unintelligible and he died a few minutes later. At an inquest in Exeter College's hall the following day, the bursar said Cohen had always seemed quite cheerful, with nothing in his manner to distinguish him from other undergraduates. Yet Allpass revealed that he had talked a deeply depressed Cohen out of killing himself two weeks previously, on the day he had bought the gun for that express purpose. Contrarily, Cohen had expressed a theory that one was justified in taking one's life when one was happy. The inquest jury, headed by Jackson (who had still been Rector at this point) and including Farnell, Barber, and other dons, returned a verdict of "suicide while of unsound mind," and the Coroner censured Allpass for failing to alert others about Cohen's suicide threats.[76] This strange and tragic incident seems likely to have been Tolkien's closest encounter with suicide at the time when he was writing his 'Story of Kullervo'.

XVI Earp

While working on the tale in late 1914, Tolkien enthused about the *Kalevala* to another friend who had been at his Sexcentenary dinner table, Tommy Earp. He refers to him in a letter to Edith as "that quaint man Earp I have told you of."[77] The Sub-Rector was more forthright about this Exeter maverick: alongside a list of exam failures, he jotted simply "A freak."[78] In fact Earp—the

---

[76] 'Suicide of an Oxford undergraduate', *The Times*, 19 February 1913, 8; 'Shooting fatality at Exeter College', *The Oxford Times*, 22 February 1913, 13. Two representatives from the Stapeldon Society were present at the inquest on 18 February and asked for the undergraduates' sympathy to be conveyed to Sydney Cohen's family. The society minutes make no reference to any of these events. News of Captain Scott's death had broken on 11 February.

[77] *Letters* 7, written probably in October 1914; signed menu from the papers of E.A. Barber (courtesy of Neil Holford).

[78] Sub-Rector's notes, Exeter College Archives. Earp's repeated failure at 'Divvers', the theological exam all Oxford students had to pass, was what ensured his prolonged tenure as an undergraduate; and he escaped military conscription by "his unique talent for twitching his eyebrows, wrinkling his nose, and waggling his

only son of an affluent Liberal MP (by then deceased)—was homosexual or bisexual, and has been described as "the last, most charming, and wittiest of the 'decadents.'"[79]

Thanks to a reference by Tolkien, T.W. Earp is immortalised in an *OED* etymology as "the original twerp."[80] The two must have disagreed about almost everything. They had jousted in Stapeldon Society debates such as the 1912 one when Tolkien with Cohen deplored modern 'degeneracy', but lost against Earp; and another in March 1914 when Tolkien, again taking a conservative stance, had supported the claim that "The cheap 'Cinema' is an engine of social corruption"—which the thoroughly modern Earp had also defeated.[81] At yet another Stapeldon standoff, Earp opposed Tolkien's motion that "This House believes in ghosts"—clearly a personal favourite—"with such wit [as Tolkien observed in the minutes] that in despite of Messrs. Hall, Sims, Crichton, R.H. Gordon, Ricketts, Waterfield, all of whom supported Mr Tolkien, he alone carried the silent votes with him and the motion was lost by 6 votes to 8." Earp, however much he may have been the target of undergraduate sniggers and taunts, was clearly a force to be reckoned with. Earlier that same session, as Tolkien's minutes record, Earp had been elected to the "Senior Public Oratorship (to which are attached the duties and perquisites of Chief Jester or Buffoon)." The evening was remembered in Earp's own synoptic 1949 memoir as a personal triumph against his (unnamed) tormentors at Exeter: he felt that he had been "made 'Public Orator' as an excuse for being ragged, but manage[d] to turn the tables, a turning-point in my life." Tolkien's minutes for the following Monday pay tribute to Earp's further progress: "The

---

ears: when called up he exercised this to such horrifying effect that the Tribunal found him unfit for service" (Dodds 1977:41).

[79] At least Earp was bisexual or homosexual in the early 1920s, when he was one of the lovers of the aspiring poet Roy Campbell. Peter F. Alexander, 'Campbell, (Ignatius) Royston Dunnachie', *Dictionary of National Biography*, vol. 9, 858. In a letter to his son Christopher on 6 October 1944 (*Letters* 95), Tolkien notes, euphemistically or otherwise, that Earp "went about" with Campbell in the 1920s. See also www.etymonline.com/index.php?term=twerp.

[80] *Letters* 95.

[81] Reports of meetings on 4 March 1912 and 2 March 1914, Stapeldon Society minutes.

house turned cheerfully to the pièce de résistance of the meeting when Mr
Earp, a blushing débutant, arose and perpetrated some scores of excellent and
topical jests."[82]

The war forced Earp, who never enlisted to fight, to look beyond Exeter
College for company, and now—just as Tolkien was beginning his own
metamorphosis—this formerly prickly oddball was busily transforming himself
into a magnet for Oxford's other artistic and unconventional souls.[83] Soon he
would be playing host in his rooms on Beaumont Street (round the corner
from St John Street) to a new undergraduate poetry circle, the Coterie, which
included Aldous Huxley and Tolkien's future Leeds colleague Wilfred Roland
Childe, and which provided the first English audience for 'The Love Song of J.
Alfred Prufrock', read by T.S. Eliot himself.[84] Before that, Earp was also president of the Coterie's predecessor, the Psittakoi, when Tolkien addressed it on
28 May 1915 on the subject of a volume of verse by Rex Freston, *The Quest of
Beauty and Other Poems*, just then published by Basil Blackwell.[85] But more

---

[82] J.R.R. Tolkien, reports of meetings on 20 and 27 October 1913, Stapeldon Society minutes.

[83] Earp's synoptic memoir records his "return to war-time Oxford and start of con-
tacts outside Exeter—beginning of my later character."

[84] Earp papers; Dodds (1977:40). T.S. Eliot was at Oxford from October 1914 to
June 1915.

[85] Contrary to Scull and Hammond (*Chronology* 65), Freston matriculated in 1912,
a year later than Tolkien. He is buried in the same military cemetery as R.Q. Gilson of the T.C.B.S. Freston's poems have been much derided as examples of blind
patriotic fervour, but it would be unwise to guess at what Tolkien's view of them
may have been. The Psittakoi was a group founded by E.R. Dodds and another
University College undergraduate with a passion for French symbolist literature
(Baudelaire, Laforgue, Mallarmé) and modern English poetry (James Elroy
Flecker, Rupert Brooke); the group consisted of "like-minded enthusiasts." Despite these preferences, Dodds writes in his memoir, "Of their meetings I recall
only that one of the speakers was an Exeter man called Tolkien. Whether he
talked to us about the habits of hobbits I cannot now remember. I believe the addiction to hobbitry goes a long way back in his life, but to us I suppose it is more
likely that he discoursed on Norse sagas." The Psittakoi was shortlived, starting no
earlier than autumn 1912 and being replaced by the more ambitious wartime
'Coterie', founded by Earp and active from at least 1915. It is unclear whether
there was any connection between Dodds's Psittakoi and Oxford's post-war Psittakoi Society, founded by Beverley Nichols; see Connon (1991:73).

importantly, by late 1914, when almost all of Tolkien's other friends had vanished from the college, it was the aestheticist Earp who proved a willing listener to panegyrics about the Finnish epic, and the two dined together, notably just before Tolkien read 'The Voyage of Éarendel' out loud at "an informal kind of last gasp" for the Essay Club in November.[86]

XVII College societies during the war

In this way, urged on by Farnell the Rector, Tolkien and his few fellow undergraduates strove to maintain the college societies, the heartbeat of Exeter life. The Stapeldon Society, a shadow of its former self, sent letters of support to King Albert of Belgium and Winston Churchill, First Lord of the Admiralty.[87] On a note of rather surreal normality, Tolkien was tasked with pursuing the long-standing question of the redecoration of the Junior Common Room, the undergraduates' meeting place, with Austin Blomfield's father, Sir Reginald, the architect responsible for the Sexcentenary renovation of the college hall and later for the Menin Gate at Ypres. But the students were warned that war would mean going short on luxuries such as redecoration, and the Sub-Rector (now E.A. Barber) told Tolkien that student entertainments were unduly wasteful and must be banned.[88] Tolkien poked fun at the freshmen for not taking baths, "no doubt," he said, because they were "economising with the best of intentions in this time of stress"; he elaborated on the joke with "an incisive demonstration of Bursarial logic [...] half the College were unwashed, therefore the baths should be closed down, so that the other half might become likewise." When one wit demanded that a key to the baths—a safe indoor retreat—be placed in a glass case for use in Zeppelin raids, Tolkien and Cullis opposed the motion, which was lost "possibly owing to hon. members' fears that they would be crowded out by the Rectorial party."[89]

---

[86]   'Éarendel' was read to the Essay Club on 27 November 1914; *Letters* 7-8.

[87]   J.R.R. Tolkien, report of 20 October 1914 meeting, Stapeldon Society minutes.

[88]   J.R.R. Tolkien, report of meeting Stapeldon Society minutes, 27 October 1914; *The Stapeldon Magazine*, December 1915, 132.

[89]   Colin Cullis, report of 25 January 1915 meeting, Stapeldon Society minutes. On another occasion, Tolkien tried to engage the interest of his peers in a debate on a

Thus high spirits helped to alleviate the darkening of the days, and much fun was also had over a municipal decision to tear up Oxford's tramlines. Earp declared that this constituted the destruction of a valuable link with the past, and the Stapeldon Society petitioned the town clerk for the honour of receiving a tramline, or part of one, "fashioned as Mr Tolkien aptly suggested in the shape of a link with the past."[90] When the request was actually granted, and seven feet of iron arrived at the college, the undergraduates were delirious:

> The bubbling flow of wit now culminated in an Arizonean war-whoop. Immediately after the First Year were despatched for the tramline. The carnival procession then set out headed by the officers elect (who were not carried on the tramline). The House following the venerable relic and showing a respect for it profound not to say excessive. At each corner of the quad Mr Rogers whooped. On arrival at its 'summer home' the emblem was christened Duschy Wow-wow by the President-Elect breaking a champagne bottle against it.[91]

At another meeting, in November 1914, one of the American students, Henry Furst (regarded by the Sub-Rector as "a worthless and dangerous fellow"), regaled the Stapeldon Society with an astounding but vainglorious account of how he had ventured into the university town of Louvain in Belgium after its capture by the Germans. "Mr Furst then gave an account of his heroic performance in Louvain. He and his journalistic friend arrived just as the city was in flames. Most opportune. They met four girls in the market place—lovely girls. Also opportune. A German soldier gave Mr Furst a canary, which got loose and being a continental canary made for the warmest place, a burning house whence it was rescued by Mr Furst amid cheers from a Belgian peasant, a private of the Landsturm and Mr Daw [sic]. The President then presented Mr Furst with the Order of the Iron Cross as a token of esteem from the

---

pet subject: "This House approves of spelling reform" (J.R.R. Tolkien, report of 3 November 1914 meeting, Stapeldon Society minutes).

[90] Colin Cullis, reports of 25 January and 8 February 1915 meetings, Stapeldon Society minutes.

[91] Colin Cullis, report of 8 March 1915 meeting, Stapeldon Society minutes.

House."[92] (A letter to *The Times* from the journalist friend, A.J. Dawe, has rather more to say about the situation in Belgium: the two civilian adventurers saw houses torched, their occupants shot dead as they fled, and children walking through piles of corpses.)[93] Later in the meeting that heard Furst's account, Tolkien spoke against the topical motion "This House deprecates an ideal of nationalism". Perhaps unsurprisingly in the light of what German national pride was doing to Belgium, his pro-nationalist arguments did not sway the House, which backed the anti-nationalist motion by a two-thirds majority.[94]

XVIII National myth, Finnish and Qenya

Yet Tolkien's ideal of nationalism had nothing to do with imperial might trampling small nations. It placed him entirely on the Belgian side, against the aggressor Germany. As he expressed the ideal at the time, "I don't defend 'Deutschland über alles' but certainly do in Norwegian 'Alt for Norge' [All for Norway]."[95] To him the nation's greatest goal was not power over others, but cultural self-realisation. Indeed, a key part of the appeal of the *Kalevala* for him was the fact that it was a *national* myth, the embodiment in poetic language of one cohesive culture's imagination and values. Right now the Finnish national myth brought into focus his personal yearning for a parallel national mythology for England, glimpsed earlier in his motion urging the importance of a cultural belief in ghosts.[96] A few days after the debate on nationalism, he once

---

[92] J.R.R. Tolkien, report of 10 November 1914 meeting, Stapeldon Society minutes.

[93] A.J. Dawe, 'The crime of Louvain. Vivid account by an eye-witness. A ruthless holocaust. The real horrors of the war', *The Times*, 3 September 1913, 4.

[94] J.R.R. Tolkien, report of 17 November 1914 meeting, Stapeldon Society minutes.

[95] Letter from Tolkien to C.L. Wiseman, 16 November 1914; Tolkien family papers, Bodleian Library, Oxford, quoted in Garth (2003:51).

[96] Presenting his paper on the *Kalevala* to the Exeter College Essay Club in February 1915, Tolkien declared that the "mythological ballads" that comprise the Finnish epic "are full of that very primitive undergrowth that the literature of Europe has on the whole been cutting away and reducing for centuries with different and earlier completeness in different peoples." In the early 1920s he added: "I would that we had more of it left—something of the same sort that belonged to the English."

more borrowed Eliot's *Finnish Grammar* from the college library, and immersed himself in it through the Christmas vacation.

Looking at these apparently disconnected and ephemeral events with the benefit of hindsight, it is possible to see how they now directed him towards the key discovery of his creative life, as he described it later: "that 'legends' depend on the language to which they belong; but a living language depends equally on the 'legends' which it conveys by tradition." Evidence of the truth of this lay all around him, in the urgent word-coining and rumour-mongering that are part of war. The discovery offered a new life for his creation: he would invent not only a language, as he had done in various rudimentary ways in the past, but also the mythological world in which it existed.[97] Thus both Qenya and the Eldar came into being, and with them Middle-earth. The absence of so many of his friends, combined with the approach of Finals (always a good time to find ways of escape from study), and a wartime need to seize the day, doubtless all contributed to the sudden flowering of Tolkien's creativity in 1915.

XIX Opening up

Alongside pieces such as 'The Voyage of Éarendel the Evening Star' and 'Kôr', which have since been published posthumously by Christopher Tolkien as part of his *History of Middle-earth*, during his final undergraduate year Tolkien also wrote at least one poem which, to judge from its title alone, reflected directly upon the current war: 'Ferrum et Sanguis: 1914', written three days before Christmas.[98] A key part was played in this "tremendous opening up of everything," as Tolkien described it, by his former friends from King Edward's School, the T.C.B.S, who circulated his poetry among themselves and com-

---

Sundial Society minutes, Corpus Christi College Archives, Oxford. Tolkien family papers, Bodleian Library, quoted by Scull and Hammond (*Chronology* 57, 115).

[97] Tolkien later stated (*Letters* 231): "It was just as the 1914 War burst on me that I made the discovery that 'legends' depend on the language to which they belong; but a living language depends equally on the 'legends' which it conveys by tradition."

[98] *Chronology* 58.

mented on it.[99] However, Exeter College provided an immediate audience, with Tolkien reading to the Essay Club not only 'The Voyage of Éarendel' but also, in March 1915, 'Sea Chant of an Elder Day' (a revised version of a poem probably first written three years earlier), as well as an essay on the *Kalevala* the previous month in which Tolkien outlined some of the passions and artistic convictions that also underpinned his own creative work.[100] The college even makes an appearance of sorts in his lexicon of Qenya, which provides names for a handful of places of special significance to Tolkien in England, or *Tol-eressea*, the Lonely Isle, as he now mythicised it. Thus *Kor* is Warwick, where Edith lived, and *Taruktarna* is Oxford itself; but *Estirin* or Exeter merits a lexicon entry not because Tolkien had an affinity with the Devonshire city but, plainly enough, because it gave his college its name.[101] And Tolkien's 'quaint' friend T.W. Earp proved his value by overseeing the earliest publication of a Tolkien fantasy, the much-derided 'Goblin Feet', as editor of *Oxford Poetry 1915*.[102]

XX Goodbye to all that

Tolkien's time as an undergraduate came to an end in a flurry of borrowings from Exeter College library—the *Cambridge History of English Literature* as well as introductions to Dryden, Keats and Shakespeare: titles which show clearly the areas of his course which he had neglected. For a week, starting on Thursday 10 June, Tolkien sat his final exams, or 'Schools', with another twenty-four candidates in English from across the university; despite all his early indolence and his recent creative distractions, he was one of the four who

---

[99]   *Letters* 10.

[100] *Shaping* 214; *Chronology* 59, 115. Tolkien had previously read his paper 'The Finnish National Epic' (alternatively titled 'On 'The Kalevala' or Land of Heroes') to Corpus Christi's Sundial Society.

[101] Tolkien (1998:36, 48, 89, 94). *Tol-eressea* and *Kor* are so spelt in the lexicon (not as elsewhere *Tol Eressëa, Kôr*).

[102] Cole and Earp (1915:71). Earp noted in his synoptic memoir that he had become "more or less permanent editor of *Oxford Poetry*—also, with notable ill-success, of the *Isis* and *Varsity*"; Earp papers.

achieved First Class Honours.[103] Then, yielding to pressures he had resisted for almost a year, he packed up the home he had shared with Colin Cullis at St John Street and 'bolted' into the army.[104] Until the war was over, he seems to have returned to Oxford only once—six days before he married—for his long-delayed degree ceremony on 16 March 1916.[105] That day he started an uncharacteristically personal poem, 'The Wanderer's Allegiance', which addresses Oxford in wartime, a shadow of the joyous, carefree, scholarly, youthful university Tolkien had known up to 1914:[106]

> along thy paths no laughter runs
> While war untimely takes thy many sons [...]

The lost fellowship of college life is invoked amid the tragedy of the war, the past now unnervingly present in a visionary moment, as "old days come to life again," restoring light to the darkened rooms of the undergraduates who have enlisted to fight:

> I see thy clustered windows each one burn
> With lamps and candles of departed men.
> (*Lost Tales II* 295-96)

The image anticipates by nearly three decades one of Tolkien's most celebrated sequences, 'The Passage of the Marshes' in *The Lord of the Rings*, where once again candles burn supernaturally, lit by soldiers who have gone to war unre-turning. Within three months, Tolkien himself was fighting in the Battle of the Somme.

XXI Post-war Oxford

After Armistice Day in 1918 Tolkien, still an army officer but now officially free to seek employment, asked to be stationed at Oxford "for the purposes of

---

[103] *The Times*, 3 July 1915, 6.

[104] *Letters* 53.

[105] How (1928).

[106] Quotations are from the November 1916 revision, retitled 'The Town of Dreams and the City of Present Sorrow', in *Lost Tales II* 295-96.

completing his education."[107] He moved back into St John Street, this time with Edith and their one-year-old son John, and found work as a lexicographer on the *Oxford English Dictionary*. Soon he was supplementing his income by giving tuition, mainly to women students, and pillaging Exeter College library for general reference works on English language and literature as well as texts of Chaucer and *Sir Gawain and the Green Knight*.[108] He remained an honorary member of the college and continued to involve himself in its societies. Its undergraduate population had fallen to just seven in 1918, almost all of them foreigners and none eligible for war work despite their repeated applications; but students were now flooding back from the armed forces, and new fresh-men were arriving too, "acutely aware of stepping into the shoes of dead men," in the words of one historian.[109]

XXII Exeter's war dead

Because they came from the class that provided the army with its junior offi-cers, the war had cut a swathe through Tolkien's friends, both the close and the casual, both from school and from Exeter College.[110] Of the 57 who had matriculated here in his year, 23 died as a result of the war—two in every five. Out of 771 Exonians who had served in all, 141 had been killed—equivalent to the college's entire intake of students over two-and-a-half years at pre-war matriculation rates. In due course, Sir Reginald Blomfield furnished the chapel with a war memorial on which all their names are recorded. Four fifths of these had died in France or Belgium, including nine at the Battle of Loos in 1915 and ten on the Somme in the first month of the battle there in 1916.[111] Of the 17 undergraduates who had dined with Tolkien at the Sexcentenary dinner on the eve of the war, eight were dead by the end of 1919 either as a result of war or the Spanish Influenza epidemic that came on its heels.

---

[107]   *Biography* 98.

[108]   Exeter College library register.

[109]   How (1928:viii). Winter (1994:18).

[110]   "123 of Exeter's 141 casualties (87%) were second lieutenants, lieutenants or captains [...]" (Maddicott 1998:49).

[111]   Maddicott (1998:49-50).

Of the Apolausticks, *Allen Barnett* had indeed survived his two years' service with the U.S. Army, and had returned to Kentucky to teach; he was still corresponding with Tolkien in the Second World War, and sending him food parcels in the austere late Forties.[112] Captain *G.S. Field* of the Royal Berkshire Regiment survived wounds in 1916 and later returned home to Reading to join his father's law practice as a solicitor. Captain *Harold Trimingham*, who served first with the Queen's Westminster Rifles and then with the new Tank Corps, was also wounded twice but found time in 1917 to marry, ultimately heading back to Bermuda to teach. *C.A.H. Fairbank*, son of the royal surgeon at Windsor, was twice wounded while serving in the Royal Field Artillery on the Western Front, but rose to the rank of major and was decorated for valour before going to work as a solicitor in Cumbria. Also promoted to major was *Lionel Thompson*, who served in the Cheshire Regiment in France and Belgium but survived relatively unscathed to become Deputy Master and Comptroller of the Royal Mint in London, and to see old age.

And the others? One, *W.E. Hall*, who had not appeared in the May 1912 photograph, was already dead before Tolkien left Exeter College: killed in action in the Dardanelles on 22 or 23 May 1915. Thompson marked the rest off on his copy of the photograph. Two had been reported missing in action during the Battle of the Somme: *John Mackreth* (d. 15 September 1916), who had served, like Tolkien, as a signaller, and *R.H. Gordon*, who had fought in the Liverpool Regiment (d. 8 August 1916). *Rolfe Brown*, serving with the Artists' Rifles, had been reported missing in action at Passchendaele on 30 October 1917. *Osric Staples*, who had come to Oxford all the way from the Orange Free State, was killed on 25 September 1915 fighting in the Royal Scots Fusiliers at Loos, France, the first major assault involving Kitchener's army of volunteer soldiers. The same day left *Michael Windle* dead on the same battlefield—"long remembered among us," as *The Stapeldon Magazine* put it, "as the keenest of oarsmen, hardest of workers, and a tall, splendid young officer of the finest type."[113] On the eve of the assault, Windle had written home:

---

[112]   Grotta (1978:111).

[113]   Obituary, *The Stapeldon Magazine*, December 1915, 151-52. Another Old Exonian, George Allen Maling (matriculated 1907), was awarded the Victoria Cross for "conspicuous bravery and devotion to duty" during a subsidiary action at Fauquissart on the day Windle and Staples died at nearby Loos.

> We moved up here last night, and all day long I have been listening
> to the biggest cannonade I've yet heard. I wish I could give you
> some idea of it. The sound that preponderates is like the regular
> thump of a steamship's engines. But across this from time to time
> comes the thunder-clap of a gun being fired, or a shell exploding,
> while the shells as they pass moan like the wind in the trees.

His classical education had not deserted Windle as a 2nd lieutenant with the
Devonshire Regiment:

> Thucydides is a gentleman whose truth I never appreciated so thor-
> oughly before. In his description of the last great effort of the
> Athenians to break out of Syracuse he tells how the officers lectured
> and encouraged their men right up to the last moment, always re-
> membering another last word of counsel, and wishing to say more,
> yet feeling all the time that however much they said it would still
> be inadequate. Just the same with us now. We've all lectured our
> platoons, but something still keeps turning up, and after all we can
> only play an infinitesimal part in Armageddon!

The letter, published in *The Times* a few weeks after his death, was supplemented there by a piece of Windle's poetry, a lament for the lost past.[114] The
first student to arrive at Exeter on an Exhibition established to help the sons or
brothers of the college's war dead was his younger brother, H.A.J. Windle.[115]

Even with Armistice, the losses among Tolkien's college friends were
not over. After active service with the Northumberland Fusiliers in Salonika,
France, Egypt, Palestine and Gallipoli, *Massiah-Palmer* went on to act as a
deputy assistant director of war graves registration and enquiries; but in February 1919 he died in London from Spanish Flu, which had come on top of a
case of typhoid he had contracted back in Salonika. He left a wife and young
daughter. Even *Colin Cullis*, unfit to fight, who had spent the war working as
an interpreter, did not long survive the war: he died in London of pneumonia,
brought on by the same terrible flu epidemic, just after Tolkien was demobi-
lised in July 1919.[116] Cullis seems to have been particularly mourned by

---

[114]   *The Times*, 16 October 1915, 3.

[115]   H.A.J. Windle matriculated in 1926 and died in 1975 (Maddicott 1998:53).

[116]   Colin Cullis's death certificate.

Tolkien, but war and its pestilential aftermath had now taken fully half of the 14 Apolausticks members whose names we know—and half of the dozen who had posed together against the vine-grown college window for the club photograph in May 1912.

Of other Exonians I have named, the Catholic Tony Shakespeare lived into old age after a career as a Birmingham solicitor; the aesthete T.W. Earp went on to an influential career as an art critic but squandered, some felt, a much richer potential; the pugilistic Austin Blomfield followed his notable father into architecture; the Louvain adventurer Henry Furst remained mad, bad, and dangerous to know, yet left a string of literary translations from Italian.[117] But at Gallipoli on 12 August 1915, Staff Captain Trevor Oliphant disappeared along with his entire battalion, the 5th Norfolks.[118] Second Lieutenant Henry Allpass, who had witnessed the 1913 suicide of Sydney Cohen, was reported missing on the Somme battlefield in September 1916, and his name is engraved on the Thiepval Memorial there, along with those of John Mackreth, R.H. Gordon and 70,000 other British and Commonwealth soldiers whose bodies were never identified.[119]

XXIII Tolkien's legacy

In a recent account of his college's part in the First World War, the Exeter history don John Maddicott (1998:51) writes:

---

[117] At the tail-end of the Second World War, Furst even fought for Mussolini's Fascists in the defence of the Republic of Salo (Michael Mewshaw, 'Montale as Couplet', *The Nation*, 29 March 1999; www.thenation.com/doc/19990329/mewshaw).

[118] "Long after the war, a strange story popped up, when two Gallipoli veterans declared they had seen the Norfolks march into a strange cloud, that engulfed them, then lifted and drifted away, leaving nobody behind" (http://user.online.be/~snelders/sand.htm).

[119] Most grievous to Tolkien were the deaths of his former schoolfriends, R.Q. Gilson and G.B. Smith of the T.C.B.S. In 1965 Tolkien wrote that by the end of the First World War all but one of his 'close friends' were dead; the survivor, whom he did not name, was the other remaining T.C.B.S. member, Christopher Luke Wiseman (1893–1987).

Those who served did little publicly to record their experiences, and Exeter turned out no Graves or Sassoon or Blunden; though it did produce one or two of those many subalterns, brought up on Horace and Propertius, who wrote nostalgically about home, family and country in the innumerable volumes of minor verse which were a more characteristic product of the war.

Allpass was one such minor poet; another was H.R. Freston, who had been killed in action at La Boisselle on the Somme in January 1916. But of course there is another Exonian soldier-writer whom Doctor Maddicott passes over: J.R.R. Tolkien, an author in a category of his very own, who left no published crop of First World War poems *per se*, whether sadly nostalgic or bitterly ironic. Yet Tolkien's writings were shaped by the war.

At Exeter College during the war, T.W. Earp had "set himself the task of keeping the Oxford tradition alive through the dead years" (in the words of Robert Graves), preserving the minute-books of many societies which had become entirely dormant but were now being revitalised.[120] Afterwards, Oxford was heaving with young men eager to revive the life of the mind. The Essay Club elected Tolkien once more to the post of Critic in June 1919, and on 10 March 1920 provided the first public audience for a story from his legendarium. Among those listening were Nevill Coghill and Hugo Dyson, later both members of the Inklings. Coghill, who was rather over-awed by Tolkien's collegiate and military seniority, and by his budding reputation as a philologist on the *Oxford English Dictionary*, had been deputed to invite him to speak. He recalled the encounter later:[121]

> And he said, in his abrupt and very quick-spoken manner, 'Yes, certainly.' It was extraordinarily difficult to hear what he said sometimes, because he spoke so rapidly, and without biting off words at the end. And so I said, 'Well, what will be the title of your essay,' and he said, hastily, 'The Fall-of-Gondolin.' And I said, 'I beg your pardon.' He said, 'The Fall-of-Gondolin.' So I said, 'The Fall of Gondolin?' 'Yes, that's right.' So I wrote it down, never having heard of Gondolin you see, and I spent a week, then, trying

---

[120]   Graves (1960:257).

[121]   From 1974 radio documentary *The Road Goes Ever On*; with thanks to Douglas A. Anderson.

to swot up in Bodley what Gondolin was, but there was no mention of it anywhere, you see.

This was Tolkien's first prose mythological narrative, an epic of war which he had written in a cathartic outpouring in hospital and on leave after his return as an invalid from the Somme at the end of 1916. The minutes for the meeting that followed from Coghill's invitation suggest a mixture of amazement and bemusement among the Essay Club literati:[122]

> As a discovery of a new mythological background Mr Tolkein's [sic] matter was exceedingly illuminating and marked him out as a staunch follower of traditions, a treatment indeed in the manner of such typical Romantics as William Morris, George Macdonald, de la Motte Fouquet etc. We gathered likewise that the reader's acquaintanceship with Scandinavian saga and legend was not a little. [...] The battle of the contending forces as represented by the Gongothlin [sic] and the followers of Melco was very graphically and astonishingly told, combined with a wealth of attendance to detail interesting in extreme.

It is curious to see here no attempt to relate the mythological war to the real one; yet this oversight has been true of many responses to Tolkien ever since.

Nevertheless, Tolkien could hardly have become the writer he did but for his experiences of war, as I have argued at length in my Postscript to *Tolkien and the Great War*: his writings, although never directly about those experiences, were fundamentally shaped by them. Those experiences encompassed not only his time as a soldier, in training camp, battle or hospital, but also his final year as an undergraduate—the first year of the Great War, when Middle-earth was born. Apart from his four months on the Somme in 1916, when work was virtually impossible, he continued for the rest of his life on the creative path he had begun at Exeter College. The full equation of war's loss also, of course, involved the prelude of peace, in which Tolkien had made so many friends at school and university who were to be cut down in their prime. It is difficult to read the lament of the poet of Rohan for the dead of the Pelennor Fields, in *The Lord of the Rings*, without thinking of the fates of those

---

[122] Report of 10 March 1920 meeting, Essay Club minutes.

care-free young men who lined up with Tolkien for a summer's photograph in 1912.

JOHN GARTH is the author of *Tolkien and the Great War: The Threshold of Middle-earth*, which examines the development of Tolkien's *legendarium* in the context of his experiences during the First World War. For the book, Garth retraced Tolkien's steps on the Somme and examined the military service records of Tolkien and his friends, their private correspondence, the war diaries of their battalions, and many other official and personal archives. *Tolkien and the Great War* was awarded the Mythopoeic Society's Scholarship Award in Inklings Studies in 2004.

References

Abbreviations used:

Artist and Illustrator: see Hammond and Scull 1995

Biography: see Carpenter 1977

Chronology: see Scull and Hammond 2006

Family Album: see Tolkien 1992

Guide: see Hammond and Scull 2005

Letters: see Carpenter 1981

Lost Tales II: see Tolkien 1984

Shaping: see Tolkien 1986

Allpass, Harry Blythe King, 1920, *Oxford, St Bees and the Front, 1911-1916,* London: T. Werner Laurie.

Baden Clay, Robin, 2001, 'The Powell Pedigree: 500 years of Family History', www.pinetreeweb.com/bp-family-tree-500-years.htm

Carpenter, Humphrey, 1977, *J.R.R. Tolkien. A Biography,* London: George Allen & Unwin.

--- (with the assistance of Christopher Tolkien) (ed.), 1981, *The Letters of J.R.R. Tolkien,* London: George Allen & Unwin.

Cole, George Douglas Howard and Thomas Wade Earp (eds.), 1915, *Oxford Poetry 1915,* Oxford: Blackwell's.

Connon, Bryan, 1991, *Beverley Nichols: A Life,* London: Constable.

Dodds, Eric R., 1977, *Missing Persons: An Autobiography,* Oxford: Clarendon Press.

Farnell, Lewis, 1934, *An Oxonian Looks Back,* London: Martin Hopkinson.

Garth, John, 2003, *Tolkien and the Great War: The Threshold of Middle-earth,* London: HarperCollins and New York: Houghton Mifflin.

Graves, Robert, 1960, *Goodbye to All That,* London: Penguin.

Grotta, Daniel, 1978, *The Biography of J.R.R. Tolkien, Architect of Middle-earth,* (second edition, first edition 1976), Philadelphia: Running Press.

Hammond, Wayne G. and Christina Scull, 1995, *J.R.R. Tolkien: Artist and Illustrator,* London: HarperCollins.

---, 2005, *The Lord of the Rings. A Reader's Companion,* London: HarperCollins.

Hibbert, Christopher (ed.), 1988, *The Encyclopaedia of Oxford,* London: Macmillan.

How, Archibald B., 1928, *Register of Exeter College Oxford 1891-1921,* Oxford: Blackwell.

James, Lionel, Lt Col DSO, 1921, *The History of King Edward's Horse (The King's Oversea Dominions Regiment),* London: Sifton, Praed and Co.

Maddicott, John R., 1998, 'An infinitesimal part in Armageddon: Exeter College and the First World War', *Exeter College Association Register*, Oxford: Exeter College, 46-55.

Priestman, Judith, 1992, *J.R.R. Tolkien: Life and Legend*, Oxford: Bodleian Library.

Scull, Christina and Wayne G. Hammond, 2006, *The J.R.R. Tolkien Companion and Guide. Chronology*, London: HarperCollins.

Strong, Leonard Alfred George, 1961, *Green Memory*, London: Methuen.

Thompson, Paul, 1991, *The Work of William Morris*, Oxford: Oxford University Press.

Tolkien, John and Priscilla, 1992, *The Tolkien Family Album*, London: HarperCollins.

Tolkien, John Ronald Reuel, 1983, 'English and Welsh', in *The Monsters and the Critics and Other Essays*, edited by Christopher Tolkien, London: George Allen & Unwin, 162-97.

---, 1984, *The Book of Lost Tales: Part II* (volume two of *The History of Middle-earth*), edited by Christopher Tolkien, London: George Allen & Unwin.

---, 1986, *The Shaping of Middle-earth: The Quenta, the Ambarkanta, and the Annals together with the earliest 'Silmarillion' and the first Map* (volume four of *The History of Middle-earth*), edited by Christopher Tolkien, London: George Allen & Unwin.

---, 1998, *Qenyaqetsa: The Qenya Phonology and Lexicon*, (*Parma Eldalamberon* 12, edited by Christopher Gilson, Carl F. Hostetter, Patrick Wynne, and Arden R. Smith), Cupertino.

Topliffe, Lorise, 1992, 'Tolkien as an Undergraduate', *Exeter College Association Register*, Oxford: Exeter College, 32-38.

Winter, Jay M., 1994, 'Oxford and the First World War', in Brian Harrison (ed.), 1994, *The History of the University of Oxford*, vol. 8, Oxford: Clarendon Press, 3-25.

Wynne, Patrick and Arden R. Smith, 2000, 'Tolkien and Esperanto', *Seven: An Anglo-American Literary Review* 17:27-46.

The Word as Leaf:
Perspectives on Tolkien as
Lexicographer and Philologist

PETER GILLIVER, EDMUND WEINER, AND JEREMY MARSHALL

Summary

Three editors working on the *Oxford English Dictionary* Revision Programme consider aspects of Tolkien's involvement with the Dictionary and the influence of lexicography on his creative use of the English language. Peter Gilliver looks at Tolkien's personal relationship with two of the OED's chief editors, William Craigie and Henry Bradley, and his work on Middle English texts with Kenneth Sisam. Edmund Weiner explores the way in which even the driest textbooks of academic philology could act as a spur to Tolkien's linguistic creativity. Jeremy Marshall contributes a note on Tolkien's distinctive use of the irregular plural *dwarves*.

Introduction

By the end of the First World War, the editors of the *Oxford English Dictionary* (then still known simply as the *New English Dictionary*) were having a hard time. Their leading light, Sir James Murray, had died in 1915 at the age of 78, still doggedly working his way through the letter T in the damp seclusion of his scriptorium in North Oxford. Most of the younger and abler members of staff had vanished on active service or for other war work, and in 1918 one of the three remaining editors, C. T. Onions, was summoned to the Admiralty to serve in naval intelligence. His colleagues, William Craigie (Oxford University's professor of Anglo-Saxon) and Henry Bradley, desperately needed qualified assistants; in fact Craigie had noted as early as 1916 that the project needed another assistant with expertise in Old and Middle English. Fortunately, one of Craigie's former students was to return to Oxford in late 1918 in search of work. Convalescing from an illness which had forced him home from the trenches, and with a wife and small child to support, he was understandably grateful for the offer of employment on the staff of the OED, and his linguistic credentials were well known to Craigie, who had tutored him in Old Norse. His name was Ronald Tolkien.

Over the following months, Tolkien established himself as a versatile and diligent member of staff, working on a wide range of words beginning with W (including *walrus, waistcoat, wan,* and *wold*). This involved detailed work on the histories of these words, both within English, and in the Germanic or other foreign languages which preceded it. By late 1920, when he left the project for a new job as Reader in English Language at Leeds University, he had made a notable contribution. He had also gained a great deal of experience in dealing with the English language, and he would later say that he "learned more in those two years than in any other equal period of my life" (*Biography* 101).

At the same time that Tolkien was spending his days in English lexicography and philology, he was, of course, spending much of his spare time on a kind of parallel philological project: the creation of two interrelated Elvish languages, with extensive vocabularies and grammars, together with the elaboration of the 'Lost Tales' of Elves and Men which would underpin them. He was making notes on English and Germanic runes and inventing his own runic and cursive scripts; he was devising calendars; in fact, he was developing the whole cosmology and legendarium of Arda.

We are all editors engaged in the *Oxford English Dictionary's* present-day revision programme. From that perspective, we recently produced a short book, *The Ring of Words,*[1] looking at Tolkien's relationship with the Dictionary, and how this sheds light on his creative use of the English language. Here we will, rather approximately, follow the pattern of that book, in which Part I discusses Tolkien as lexicographer and philologist, Part II looks at linguistic aspects of his creative writing, and Part III is a collection of anecdotal information about individual words. Peter Gilliver, as a historian of the Dictionary, looks at Tolkien's personal relationship with two of the OED's chief editors, William Craigie and Henry Bradley, and also his work on Middle English texts in conjunction with Kenneth Sisam, during and after his time at the Dictionary. Edmund Weiner then looks at the way in which not only narrative literature, but even the dustiest tomes of academic philology, could act as a spur to Tolkien's linguistic creativity. Finally, Jeremy Marshall contributes a brief note

---

[1]   See Gilliver, Marshall, and Weiner (2006).

on a single word from Tolkien's distinctive English vocabulary: the irregular plural *dwarves*.

Part I
(Peter Gilliver)

Many of you will be familiar with Andrew Lang's series of *Fairy Books*, in which he retold for an English-speaking audience some of the folk-tales of other cultures. As Tolkien read Lang's stories when he was a boy, it was almost certainly through them that he first came indirectly under the influence of William Craigie. Several of the *Fairy Books* contain tales translated from various Scandinavian languages, and Lang acknowledged many of these as the work of Craigie, as, for example, a story called 'Prince Ring' in the *Yellow Fairy Book* of 1894, translated by Craigie from the Icelandic. Folklore was just one of Craigie's interests—in fact he began to write about folklore while he was still an undergraduate at Oriel College, Oxford, in 1892. He was meant to be studying Classics, but he managed to squeeze in quite a lot else, including Celtic and Scandinavian languages, despite the fact that there were no Scandinavian lectures in Oxford, following the sudden death of the University's Reader in Icelandic, Gudbrand Vigfusson, only a few months after Craigie had arrived in Oxford. In fact Craigie went on to become one of the foremost Icelandic scholars of his generation; he published numerous books and articles on Icelandic language and literature, including a Supplement, completed near the end of his life, to Vigfusson's *Icelandic Dictionary*.

By the time that Tolkien came up to Exeter College in 1911, also to read Classics, Craigie had been appointed Taylorian lecturer in the Scandinavian languages at Oxford; and when Tolkien, who like Craigie had found himself distracted by the allure of languages other than Greek and Latin, subsequently switched to the School of English Language and Literature, he was in the fortunate position of having Craigie as his tutor in Old Norse. Craigie was also of course the third editor of the OED, and he no doubt told Tolkien all about the great work of English philology that was going on in the Old Ashmolean (what is now the Museum of the History of Science in Broad Street). There was also James Murray, the first and oldest of the Dictionary's editors; whether Tolkien met Murray we don't know, although he would have regularly passed his house on the way to study—and have tea—with the remarkable Joseph Wright, who also lived on the Banbury Road, and who was also a lexicographer (and whose *Primer of the Gothic Language* had of course first awakened Tolkien's interest in philology).

But to return to Craigie, who would have been working on words beginning with the letter V when Tolkien went off to war. By 1916 he had begun to think about the letter W; of the remaining letters of the alphabet, this had the highest proportion of words of Germanic origin. He thought it would be a good idea if someone could be found to do preparatory work on this material: someone with the necessary expertise in Old and Middle English. Tolkien may have come to mind, but he of course was away fighting with the Lancashire Fusiliers. In fact when Craigie and his team of assistants finished V, it was decided that they had better go back and do the letter U, which had been allocated to James Murray's team, but which they had not begun to tackle when Murray died in 1915; so that when the war came to an end in November 1918, Craigie was just beginning to contemplate the vast—and on the whole not very interesting—collection of words beginning with *un-*.

The prefix *un-* presented an old problem for the OED, but on an unprecedented scale. The historical principle on which the OED was based required each word that the Dictionary included to be dealt with separately, with a selection of illustrative quotations beginning with the earliest known example. The problem with *un-* was not only that it was more productive than any other English prefix—it could be, and had been, combined with just about every English word that you could think of—but that by the time the lexicographers got to work on it, there had been the longest possible time during which evidence for all the *un-*words could accumulate. Craigie already knew that coping with this material would be a challenge, but he had no idea of how difficult it would turn out to be. Keeping the Dictionary within reasonable bounds in terms of space and time had always been a problem, but with *un-* the ideas of Craigie, as editor, about the amount of space that was needed to deal with the material adequately, brought him into conflict with the publishers of the Dictionary, Oxford University Press, as never before. It was not until 1926 that the last part of *un-* finally saw the light of day; during those eight years, Craigie's arguments with OUP would lead to him first abandoning the OED entirely for a year, while he went round the world on a lecture tour, and then detaching himself from the project by moving to Chicago to take up a post as Professor of English there—where he also started work on another great historical dictionary, this time devoted to American English, which eventually appeared in four volumes from 1938 to 1944.

In 1918, however, when Tolkien returned to Oxford, this great crisis lay in the future. When Tolkien called on his old tutor, in the hope of finding academic work, Craigie suggested that there would be work available on the OED: not on the words beginning with U that he himself was working on, but on the letter W, for which he had realized two years earlier that extra help would be needed, of just the kind that Tolkien's studies and aptitudes suited him for. W was being worked on by another team of lexicographers, headed by Henry Bradley, who, now that James Murray was dead, was the senior editor of the Dictionary. Bradley was another remarkable man: like James Murray he never went to university, but during his twenty years working as a corresponding clerk to a cutlery firm in Sheffield managed to teach himself numerous foreign languages, and came to Murray's attention in 1884 when he wrote an exceptionally insightful review of the first section of the OED to be published. Murray was so impressed that he asked Bradley to come and work on the Dictionary, and five years later he was made an independent editor, with his own team of assistants; the same happened to Craigie in 1901, and also to the fourth editor, Charles Onions, in 1914.

In some ways it is hard to say who had more impact on Tolkien's career, Craigie or Bradley. It was Craigie who offered him the job on the OED, and it was Craigie's "kindness [...] to a jobless soldier in 1918" that he remembered with gratitude over 40 years later in his valedictory address as Merton Professor of English. And in fact it was thanks to Craigie that Tolkien returned to Oxford when he did: the post of Professor of Anglo-Saxon which Tolkien secured in 1925 only became vacant because Craigie gave it up to go and work in Chicago. But it was Bradley who worked closely with him during his time at the OED. He will have learned some of the tools of the trade from the other assistants working alongside him, such as the classicist Walter Worrall, the longest-serving of all the OED lexicographers; and no doubt he also discussed things with Craigie, who may well have been glad to take a break from words beginning with *un-* to discuss a point of Norse etymology with his former pupil. (I like to think that maybe at some point Tolkien saw on Craigie's desk the two quotations he had illustrating the word *unassessable*, a word which was ultimately omitted from the Dictionary; and that decades later some buried memory of this lay behind Bilbo's words "O Smaug the unassessably wealthy";

though of course this could be coincidence.) But most of what Tolkien learned of lexicography will almost certainly have come from Henry Bradley. He was of course Tolkien's boss, and the person who corrected his draft dictionary entries; the two men clearly formed a strong relationship, and Tolkien continued to correspond with him after he left Oxford to take up a post at Leeds. When he died, only a couple of years later, Tolkien wrote an obituary for the Modern Humanities Research Association which shows the warmth of his affection for the man, as well as his respect for the scholar. A particularly striking passage recalls him as Tolkien must often have seen him, sitting at his desk in the 'Dictionary Room' of the Old Ashmolean, "momentarily held in thought, with eyes looking into the grey shadows of the roof, pen poised in the air to descend at last and fix a sentence or a paragraph complete and rounded, without blot or erasure, on the paper before him" (Tolkien 1923:5). As we make clear in *The Ring of Words*, Tolkien's own method of writing a definition often involved numerous rewrites, so he must have been particularly impressed by the clarity of thought which allowed Bradley to write one in one go.

But the two men may have been drawn together in other ways. Bradley also had a particular interest in the Goths, and had written an important popular book about the people; he had also been a fellow of Exeter College, although by the time Tolkien was working with him he had migrated to Magdalen. He was also a close friend of the poet Robert Bridges, and was much involved with Bridges in the setting up of the Society for Pure English, which concerned itself a great deal in the aesthetics of words—something in which I think Bradley may have had more of an interest than any of the three other editors of the first edition of the OED. He may also have shared Tolkien's interest in handwriting: Robert Bridges (1928:55) records how he sometimes "exhibited a penman's tricks, writing microscopically or backwards." I have seen occasional examples of such doodles on the slips of paper on which Bradley's Dictionary entries are written. Here perhaps I should mention another remarkable fact about Bradley, namely that he originally learned to read upside-down, looking at the family Bible open on his father's knees.

I'd like now to look at a third OED figure whose relationship with Tolkien continued long after he departed for Leeds. Not Charles Onions, the fourth editor of the Dictionary, although of course he was still in Oxford when Tolkien returned here in 1925, and was among other things a member of the Coalbiters, the informal club founded by Tolkien to read Icelandic sagas. A

New Zealander called Kenneth Sisam, who had also been one of Tolkien's undergraduate tutors—and who in 1915 worked briefly on the OED as one of Henry Bradley's assistants—went on to become a significant figure in the doings of OUP. By the time Tolkien joined Bradley's team, Sisam was in London, working for the Ministry of Food; but he was also working on an important project for OUP, an anthology of late Middle English texts for student use. The book needed a glossary, and in June 1919, when it became apparent that Sisam was going to be too busy with his war work to complete the glossary as well as the main text, Tolkien was asked if he would help. In fact Tolkien didn't complete the glossary until 1922, and it ended up being far larger and more elaborate than had been originally planned; but during this time Tolkien was also consulted about another OUP project, to publish a new series of editions of Middle English texts, for general use. The idea began to be discussed in the autumn of 1920, when Tolkien had moved to Leeds; various people were consulted about the project, including Onions in Oxford and Sisam in London. One of the things about which there seems most disagreement was the matter of whether the spelling, which in Middle English manuscripts is very variable, should be normalized in any way; and, perhaps surprisingly, Tolkien was in favour of doing so. John Johnson, a senior figure in OUP at this time, wrote in a letter to the historian Henry Davis in January 1921 that

> [t]here is a split which cannot be breached as to treatment, Onions & Tolkien fierce for normalization, Sisam & Nichol Smith [i.e. David Nichol Smith, Goldsmith's Reader in English at Oxford] as fierce against. [...] The breach has its good side as the spirit of contrariety will bring Sisam (who had abandoned M.E. in favour of commerce) into the field again.[2]

A letter from Tolkien to Johnson, written in February 1921, indicates how strongly he felt:

> I could write an essay (on the typewriter!) on the ethics and objects of 'normalization'—but I really cannot at the moment do anything

---

[2]   Oxford University Press Archives (hereafter OUPA), file CP53/992: 8 Jan 1921 John Johnson to H.W.C. Davis. Material from the OUP archives is reproduced by permission of the Secretary to the Delegates of Oxford University Press.

positive on my own [...]. All ME. would I think benefit by it:—
some texts—for example merely, *MS. C* of *Owl and Nightingale*
[...]—could be done with comparative ease. [...] But I feel before
even poking my nose into other matters I must knock down this
mole-hill glossary (grown into a mountain by accumulated domestic distractions)—I have an added personal motive: I badly need
the book for use here, to partly supplant Cook's Literary ME
Reader. If any one tries to teach with that book as I am temporarily
obliged to do—he *must* see the need of normalizing texts [...] for
persons whose approach is literary. Normalized it would be a very
excellent selection and eminently useful (it would need better
glossing to be really good)—but, as it is, it is monstrous. No one
seems to get anything but confusion of mind from it. Of course
texts of the Sisam kind with glossary and notes [...] are not so
bad—most of the trouble then falls on the 'glossarist', who spends
endless time (and span) recording forms that could be eliminated
and still leave the printed text perfectly Middle English (and intelligible to the scribes and authors if resuscitated).[3]

This final parenthesis is of course whimsical, but it does suggest that, to
Tolkien's imagination, the medieval figures who wrote these texts were real
enough.

The 'mole-hill glossary' commissioned to accompany Sisam's four-
teenth-century anthology, which eventually appeared in 1922, was a good
example of Tolkien's ability to make a task take longer than expected. In this
case the glossary which resulted is a very fine piece of scholarship, and one
whose enduring value arguably justifies the time it took; but I would like to
tell you about another joint project which Tolkien undertook for OUP, beside
which the Sisam-Tolkien project seems distinctly hurried. In the autumn of
1922 the suggestion was made that the Press should publish another Middle
English anthology, this time of selections from Chaucer's poetry and prose;
and Tolkien and his colleague from Leeds, George Gordon, agreed to divide
the work between them, with Gordon preparing the texts, and Tolkien once
again compiling the glossary, apparently leaving the introduction and
explanatory notes to be sorted out later. The project was overseen for OUP by
Sisam, who in July of 1923 heard from Gordon that Tolkien was hoping to

---

[3]   OUPA, file CP53/992: 14 Feb 1921 JRRT to Johnson.

have the glossary finished by October of that year.[4] This soon proved to be optimistic, and it was only in January of 1924 that Tolkien returned his first batch of corrected proofs, pleading the lack of a housemaid and the fact of having been the victim of a theft as an explanation for the delay. Sisam sympathized about the lack of a maid, commenting to Tolkien that he himself had had "a constant flow of temporaries, who are barely well enough known for the dog to stop biting them before they depart."[5] He sent another batch of proofs on 1 February, with a letter containing more excuses:

> My domestic troubles become a tragic farce. I have had my younger boy laid up with appendicitis [...] though he suddenly and miraculously got well on the eve of an operation. He is now about again—also, at last, we have found a servant (how long for, is ungrateful to enquire) so things are reviving again. Wone þe bale is alre hecst, þonne is þe bote alre necst, quod Alfred.[6]

At this point Sisam, who seems to have been overseeing the project for OUP, wrote to George Gordon expressing his concern that Tolkien "is occupied with *Gawayne*, influenza, thieves etc," and that there was as yet no sign of an introduction or notes on the texts, let alone the glossary. 'Gawayne' is of course Tolkien's work on *Sir Gawain and the Green Knight*, in collaboration with E.V. Gordon (no relation to George). Gordon replied that Tolkien had indeed had "a hellish time", but agreed to do what he could about the introduction.[7]

But still things went along too slowly for Sisam, who in March wrote to Nichol Smith:

> I do not think it will be possible to allow Tolkien to hold up the *Clarendon Chaucer* as he is holding up everything else with which

---

4 OUPA, file CP57/1041: 27 July 1923 Gordon to Sisam. All subsequent letters are from this file except where noted.

5 OUPA: 8 Jan 1924 Sisam to JRRT.

6 OUPA: 1 Feb 1924 JRRT to Sisam. The passage in Old English may be translated: 'When woe is greatest, relief is nearest, quoth Alfred.' Although many poverbs were popularly ascribed to King Alfred, this one is not one of them: Tolkien appears to have copied it from *The Owl and the Nightingale*, the Middle English poem mentioned above page 64.

7 OUPA: 26 Feb 1924 Sisam to Gordon; 28 Feb 1924 Gordon to Sisam.

he is connected. If he would put the same time into working that he devotes to writing excuses we might make some progress. [...] I think we must find another coadjutor for Gordon. After the most faithful promises he will not get on with the *Gawayne* nor let E.V. Gordon go on alone. The *Chaucer* is too important a book to have hanging about for years; and from the plain business point of view we shall have to consider whether it is possible to wait for a man who is so permanently in a sea of troubles, and is not very active in taking arms against them.[8]

In May Sisam wrote to Gordon that Tolkien had agreed to give up his part of the work. But this seems only to have been temporary, as there is a postcard from Tolkien in the file dated 23 October 1924 promising to "cram Ch. into any cracks of time there are left." In December Sisam wrote to Tolkien suggesting a new deadline of the end of the year for the glossary, and the end of January for the remaining notes. He commented that "the glossary must be short [...] The book simply won't stand the cost of a long glossary, and it will bore the readers who are not supposed to be interested in philology."[9] Within less than a week Tolkien had sent the manuscript of the glossary to Gordon, who again asked Sisam not to rush his colleague, who was "pretty well exhausted getting clear of *Gawayne* & playing servantless father to the new baby."[10] In fact the glossary turned out, perhaps unsurprisingly, to be considerably longer than planned; Sisam left it to Tolkien and Gordon to sort out how to shorten it. On 5 February 1925, after the deadline for the notes had expired, Sisam wrote again to Tolkien: "Praeterivit dies illa: Dies irae adpropiat (?)"[11] By early March Tolkien had managed to compress the glossary, and he and Gordon had produced an introduction, but there was still no sign of the notes; Sisam gave him a new deadline of the end of May.

---

[8]   OUPA: 21 Mar 1924 Sisam to Nichol Smith.

[9]   OUPA: 5 Dec 1924 Sisam to JRRT.

[10] OUPA: 8 Dec 1924 Gordon to Sisam.

[11] OUPA: 5 Feb 1925 Sisam to JRRT. The Latin text reads: 'That day has passed: the day of wrath approaches.'

The file then breaks off for several years. On 21 November 1930 Tolkien wrote a letter to Sisam which suggests that he wasn't the only one who could be dilatory:

> I must clear off *Chaucer*. I am not the sole or even chief culprit in this matter. And all the work so far done has been done by me. I have made one more effort to get back my draft of notes from my 'collaborator'! So far without success. His elevation [to the position of President of Magdalen] is some excuse [...]. I have returned again to the attack and demanded my stuff back—two years old now—with comments, from its prison in Magdalen.

It would seem from the next letter in the file, dated 22 January 1931, that Tolkien had completed a draft of the notes, which had been sent to Gordon to abbreviate, but that he had failed to do so; Tolkien reported to Sisam that he had now made good progress with the task of compression, and promised "I will finish it off, if it is physically possible, before the summer."[12] No such luck: by the autumn there was still no sign of the completed text, and Sisam's boss, Robert Chapman, Secretary to the Delegates, took a hand. In late October he wrote to Tolkien: "I understand something of your skepticism and bouleverse-ment. But you agree that we must in this crisis place Nation before Poetry & produce the book tant bien que mal, quand meme."[13] He reported to Nichol Smith: "I have growled and wagged my tail at the Bosworth Professor, who promises to swallow his scruples and perform." For good measure he also wrote to Gordon asking whether he could finish the book off.[14] A year later Tolkien again wrote to Chapman that the Chaucer anthology "must be fin-ished or I shall lose for ever the good will of the Clarendon Press."[15] To judge from his account of the materials, there had been little progress: the glossary was done, the notes largely complete but far too long. But by this stage OUP was in fact wanting more out of him than Chaucer, as Tolkien goes on to

---

[12] OUPA: 22 Jan 1931 JRRT to Sisam.

[13] OUPA: 26 Oct 1931 Chapman to JRRT.

[14] OUPA: 26 Oct 1931 Chapman to Nichol Smith; 30 Oct 1931 Chapman to Gordon.

[15] OUPA: 25 Oct 1932 JRRT to Chapman.

discuss a number of other possible books, observing "I have [...] learned a good deal in the past few years, and feel that the time is approaching when I not only ought to write out of deference to custom and what is expected of professors, but might even do so with utility." A new start was made on the Chaucer materials, with Tolkien reporting to Sisam in December that Nichol Smith was helping him to shorten the notes;[16] but then the file stops again, only to be resumed in October 1936 with a letter from Chapman to Gordon:

> The type [of the *Clarendon Chaucer*] has been standing for more than ten years. [...] I am afraid the chance of [Tolkien's] finishing the job is negligible. Your own part, I believe, is done. | Nothing (I know) would induce Sisam to do it himself. But he says that if E.V.G. does not care to do it, he thinks young Bennett of Merton could.[17]

Gordon's response was to offer to "have one more shot at Tolkien"; but a week later he reported that Tolkien "will have another try."[18] But the project once again faltered, and in fact no progress was reported before the outbreak of the Second World War.

In 1946 the name of J.A.W. 'Jack' Bennett was again put forward as someone who could finish the book; but Sisam poured cold water on the idea: "I should like to leave the C. E. Chaucer to lie fallow for a long time: Tolkien is still a professor, and it would only raise unhappy memories. I put it on record that I don't much like the selection we set up and finally distributed. There is too much early poems, and too little Canterbury Tales."[19] Another three years passed; in 1949 Tolkien was given a sabbatical, which he realized could be an opportunity to finish the project at last...but he was also at work on a new edition of *Gawain*, and on an edition of *Pearl* which Gordon had left unfinished at his death in 1942. At last he began to wonder whether it would be better to hand all the materials over to somebody else—a suggestion which OUP jumped at, although in fact it took another two years for the materials

[16]   OUPA: 18 Dec 1932 JRRT to Sisam.

[17]   OUPA: 26 Oct 1936 Chapman to Gordon.

[18]   OUPA: 28 Oct 1936 Gordon to Chapman; 5 Nov 1936 Gordon to [Chapman].

[19]   OUPA: 29 May 1946 Sisam to A. L. P. Norrington.

finally to be delivered to OUP. In June 1951 Tolkien wrote: "I deeply regret the whole affair. The material contains much that is fresh, and a prodigious amount of labour [...]. But I was given the very sticky end of the stick, and need say no more."[20] Over the next few years OUP searched intermittently for a suitable person to work the materials into a publishable state, but to no avail. Tolkien's reputation with Sisam now reached rock bottom, as is evident from this letter of 1953 about two other projects which were massively behind schedule:

> Tolkien is a rogue. He has had Middle English Studies held up for 20 years waiting for an assented[?] text of *Ancrene Riwle* which he is to edit; and his time is given to fairy stories. If his M. E. translations ever come in, they are sure to be good. But he was to bring me them all ready for printing the very next day some time around 1942, so I fear they are not imminent.[21]

The story of the Chaucer anthology reaches its final chapter with a letter of October 1960, written from the Scilly Isles where Sisam was now in retirement: "The finishing of the Clarendon English Chaucer would be a difficult & delicate job with so much done or part done. To write the Introduction would be hardest: one can't easily use another man's notes for a job he flinched from. No hurry, and if in about a month's time you cared to send me the material, I could report on its state & possibilities."[22] The materials do seem to have been sent off to Sisam, but I haven't been able to find out what became of them. The project was dropped; OUP published many editions of and books about Chaucer during Tolkien's lifetime, but this was not to be one of them. In fact an Oxford Glossary to Chaucer did appear in 1979—edited, as it happens, by Tolkien's friend and colleague Norman Davis, who succeeded him as Merton Professor of English at Oxford.

Something clearly went wrong with this publishing project, which started out with such promise but eventually petered out nearly four decades

---

[20] OUPA: 8 June 1951 JRRT to D. M. Davin.

[21] OUPA, file CP53/992: 18 June 1953 Sisam to Davin. The 'Middle English translations' were a proposed collection of modern English versions of Middle English texts, including *Gawain*. The word 'assented' is unclear.

[22] OUPA: 12 Oct 1960 Sisam to Davin.

later; it is hard to avoid the conclusion that Tolkien was at least partly to blame for this.

The real problem is perhaps revealed in his final 1951 letter, in which he asks for the manuscript material to be returned to him if the project is abandoned, since it contains "a good many notes which, though useless for the purpose […], I should find useful."[23] It seems that when Tolkien started to write, he couldn't help writing about what *he* thought was worth writing about, rather than writing what he had been asked to write.

Part II
(Edmund Weiner)

The aim of this section of our paper is to illustrate the idea that Tolkien's creative imagination frequently caught fire from apparently dry, dull, and un-inspired linguistic items—words or names encountered in a context that most people would have passed by without the arousal of curiosity or excitement, but which launched Tolkien on a journey of exploration. Perhaps the leading examples are Old English *ent* (which is discussed in Gilliver et al. [2006:119-21]) and *Earendel* (which is outside its scope). A subsidiary theme is that, as we have shown in *The Ring of Words*, many items in Tolkien's English vocabulary have more than one etymological parent, and the way in which the two or more parent forms contributed to the word varies considerably.

My first illustrations come from narrative literature. The contexts which I am quoting as having influenced Tolkien are not devoid of imaginative quality, but they are on a far lower level of inspiration than anything he wrote, and for most people today they are not compelling reading. My first source is Charles Kingsley's *Hereward the Wake*, first published in 1866. It is set in the eleventh century but only occasionally catches the imagination in the way Tolkien's writings do. It contains, however, a number of features which, taken together, suggest that it was read by Tolkien, perhaps when quite young.

Among the names of characters there are **Biorn**, "son of the fairy bear" (compare the dual nature, human and ursine, of Beorn), **Brand**, **Herluin** (cf. Hirluin), Dirk **Hammerhand** (cf. Helm Hammerhand). Among place names

---

23   OUPA: 8 June 1951 JRRT to Davin.

are the Forest of **Brocheliaunde**, where "fairies are seen bathing in the fountains" (Broceliande, which underlies the name Beleriand, Tolkien would of
course have encountered in the Arthurian legend too), and **Deeping Fen**
(compare Deeping-coomb, though a very different place topographically).
Particularly interesting is an incident in which a party is marooned on the
island of **Flat Holme** in the Severn Estuary, for Tolkien has an episode in *The
Notion Club Papers* where Vikings attacking Porlock escape to a place he calls
'Broad Relic'. This is a Tolkienian modernization of *Bradanreolice* (the element *-reolice* not actually being the word 'relic'), which was the Old English
name for Flat Holme. Tolkien's episode and the *Hereward* one both originate
in the *Anglo-Saxon Chronicle* (compare *Sauron Defeated* 277, 278 with *Lost
Road* 80). We also read about "the staves of the **Olifant**, the magic horn"
(compare the use of the archaic form *oliphaunt* in *The Lord of the Rings*) and
there is an episode involving the **war-arrow** (compare the red arrow in *The
Lord of the Rings*: Morris also has one in *The House of the Wolfings*). Not all of
these are necessarily direct sources for Tolkien's usages. Rather I suggest that
he probably read the book early in life and later unconsciously drew on his
memories of the book for his own creations, some of which fused with things
he had met in other contexts.

   Hereward the Wake also contains a number of unusual words that I
would suggest stayed in Tolkien's memory and resurfaced later on in his writings. The most significant of these is **orc**, which is a word of multiple parent-
age,[24] Old English *orcneas* being the major and material source, but the
relatively rare modern English *orc* the minor and formal source: *Hereward* may
have been where Tolkien first encountered the latter. Kingsley uses the word
hollin for 'holly' (*Hollin*, of course, is the English equivalent of the Elvish
place name *Eregion*, from *ereg* 'holly tree'). Kingsley also uses the word **horse-
boy** (as does William Morris: see below) which appears in *The Lord of the Rings*
as the orcs' nickname for the Rohirrim. Finally, he uses two very unusual
words: **springald**, which (we suggest in *The Ring of Words*)[25] may underlie the
name of the dance *springle-ring*, and the verb **ruffle**, which is found in *War*
(285): "You ruffling young fool."

---

[24]   See Gilliver et al. (2006:174-75).

[25]   See Gilliver et al. (2006:193).

William Morris and Eiríkr Magnússon translated Snorri Sturluson's *The Story of the Kings of Norway called the Round World (Heimskringla)*: Volume I was published in 1893. We know that Tolkien was a keen reader of Morris and it seems very likely that he read not only his invented Germanic romances but also his translations of Icelandic literature, which we know he studied in the original language. A number of important words and names in his writings may well have been sparked by reading these.

Firstly, Gandalf. It is a commonplace that the Old Norse name *Gandalfr* is found along with the dwarves' names in *Völuspá*, but *The Hobbit* is not the first context in which this name was anglicized. *Gandalf* already existed in Morris's *Heimskringla* translation as an anglicized form of *Gandalfr*, the name of a human leader (neither dwarf nor wizard): "That same autumn he went with an army to Vingulmark against King **Gandalf**" ('The Story of Half-dan the Black', chapter i, page 78) and "The first man of these was King **Gandalf**" ('The Story of Harald Hairfair', chapter i, page 92).

Secondly, Treebeard. This name is peculiarly formed. What kind of a compound is it? Wouldn't the (admittedly ungainly) compound 'Beardtree' make more sense? It could perhaps be justified by an appeal to its Sindarin equivalent, *Fangorn*, which depending on the age (in Middle-earth) of the formation, might be 'Tree of beard' or 'Beard of tree'. But like *Gandalf* it had already been used by Morris in the translation of *Heimskringla*. It occurs as an anglicization of the Norse name *Tréskeggr*, a compound of *tré* 'wood' and *skeggr* 'beard', which is there used as a derisive alteration of the nickname of the Viking Thorir Wood-beard:

> When he came to the Orkneys there lay before him two ships of the vikings Thorir Wood-beard and Kalf Scurvy. Einar fell to battle with them straightway, and won the victory, and they both fell. Then was this sung:
> > **Tree-beard** to the trolls he gave there
> > Scurvy there Turf-Einar slaughtered.
> ('The Story of Harald Hairfair', chapter i, page 123)

The last line translates *Þar gaf hann* **Tre-skegg** *trollom / Torf-Einarr drap Skurfo*, and it embodies a very etymological translation of *Tre-skegg* (using English 'tree' as the equivalent of Norse *tré*). Compare the translation made by Vigfusson and Powell (1883):

He gave Woodbeard to the Fiends, yea Turf-Einarr slew Scurf.
('The Story of Harald Hairfair, chapter i, page 92)

Note the association of Treebeard and trolls, which accords with the fact that in the early drafts of *The Lord of the Rings* the ents were originally not distinguished from the ettins or trolls.[26]

In *The Ring of Words* we discuss an idiom consisting of a compass point followed by the adverb *away*, as in *south-away*.[27] I think it likely that Tolkien picked this up from Morris, who uses it copiously in this translation, e.g. "He sent his son Hallad **west-away**" ('The Story of Harald Hairfair', chapter xxvii, page 122), "He sailed north all up to Northumberland, and thence **north-away** to Scotland" ('The Story of Olaf Tryggvison', chapter xxxi, page 261), "King Olaf stood **north-away** along the land" (ibid. chapter lxv, page 309). We also discuss the ethnonym *Swerting*, which is another word with more than one parent. On the surface it is a well-formed derivative of Old English *sweart* 'dark-skinned'; but it already existed as an anglicized form of the Norse name *Svertingr* in this translation: '**Swerting** Runolfson' ('The Story of Olaf Tryggvison', chapter ciii, page 354).

Finally in this text we have a probable source for the term and concept **wolf-rider**. It occurs, not in the main narrative, but in a snippet of Old Norse poetry in a note at the back of the book. The English compound is not found, but it seems likely that the idea for it crystallized around this passage of Old Norse poetry. Tolkien could have encountered the verse at any time while reading the Eddaic corpus, but it seems quite possible that he first met it here:

> *Heþinn fór einn saman heim ór scógi iólaaptan oc fann trollkono; sv*
> *reiþ vargi oc hafði orma at taumum*
> Hedinn went alone together home from the wood Yule-eve and
> found (met) a troll-wife: she **rode** on a **wolf** and had snakes for
> reins.[28]

It is especially suggestive that the word used for 'wolf' is *vargr*, the inspiration for Tolkien's **warg**, which of course denotes the kind of wolf that is ridden.

---

[26]   See Gilliver et al. (2006:120).

[27]   See Gilliver et al. (2006:171-72).

[28]   Explanations, page 405, quoting *Helgakviða Hjörvarðssonar*.

Somewhat earlier, the same writers (Eiríkr Magnússon and William Morris) translated *Völsunga Saga*. Again, I think it possible that Tolkien's imagination was seeded by some items here. The Germanic people known as the Lombards are *Langbarðar* in Old Norse, which Morris anglicizes by an etymological transposition (*lang-* into 'long' and *barðar* into 'beards') as *Long-beards*: "So they went into the hall of King Alf, and there abode them the **Longbeards**, and Franks, and Saxons" (chapter xxxiii, page 126). This, by a kind of scholarly joke, may have suggested the name of one of the two tribes of dwarves, first mentioned in *Lost Tales II*. Similarly we find Old Norse *Myrcvið* in the Atli poems rendered by Morris as *Murkwood*, which of course for Tolkien must have been reinforced by the respelt form *Mirkwood* used in *The House of the Wolfings*: "And that noble wood Men name the **Murkwood**" ('Song of Atli', page 224). In *The Ring of Words*[29] we contrast Tolkien's compound *shield-maiden* with the archaizing form *shield-may*, found in this translation. But in fact Morris also uses the form adopted by Tolkien, *shield-maiden*: "At last folk saw a great company of **shield-maidens**, like burning flames to look on, and there was come Sigrun, the king's daughter" (chapter ix, page 31). In this work also Morris uses *horse-boy* as a contemptuous term:

> Another time came Regin to talk to Sigurd, and said—'A marvel-lous thing truly that thou must needs be a **horse-boy** to the kings, and go about like a running knave.'
> (chapter xiii, page 43)

I turn now to two works of instruction, a dictionary and a grammar. For most people, an unusual word encountered in the dry context of a textbook or dictionary would be unlikely to take root in the memory, and even less likely to send up creative shoots later on, but with Tolkien it was different. The most insignificant or out-of-the-way word could be the catalyst for a character, a place, a scene, or a plotline. As we point out in *The Ring of Words*, there are at least three such items in Cleasby and Vigfusson's *Icelandic–English Dictionary* (1874). The first occurs in the entry for *dag-mál*, which is glossed "properly 'day-meal', one of the divisions of the day, usually about 8 or 9 o'clock a.m." Interestingly, Tolkien doesn't use the word in the Norse sense, but makes it the main evening meal, which is pretty well the same as Old Norse *náttmál*

---

[29]   See Gilliver et al. (2006:71-2).

'night-meal'. The second occurs in the entry for *ellefu-tíu*: "'**eleventy**' (i.e. one hundred and ten), frequent in reckoning by duodecimal hundreds": this is the only instance of the word so far discovered outside *The Lord of the Rings*. The third occurs in the entry for *viðvindill*, which (though it really means 'ivy') is suggestively and poetically translated as 'wood-**windle**' and may have been one of the contributing influences on the name of the River Withywindle. (Incidentally the word **unlight** occurs in this dictionary as the gloss to *ú-ljóss*, but this is an adjective, not the noun.)

Finally, I would like to consider Joseph Wright and Elizabeth Mary Wright's *Old English Grammar*. Considering that Tolkien was taught by Wright, there is little doubt that he studied the book. To me it is suggestive that the final chapter (chapter xvi, pages 287-313), dealing with word-formation, contains among its large collection of Old English complex words a number of items which can be regarded as underlying or influencing words shaped by Tolkien in his creative works. As a student of Old English literature he would have encountered them in other places, but I believe there are too many in this one place for coincidence. I think that as he wrote *The Lord of the Rings* (and other works) he unconsciously drew on a hoard of interesting Old English words stored away in memory long before at the time when he had studied these pages. The significant items are as follows: '**māþm**, treasure' (288), '**glēd**, live coal' (cf. the entry for *glede* in Gilliver et al. 2006) (288), '**orþanc**, skill' (291), '**oreald**, very old' (cf. *Orald*, another name for Bombadil) (291), '**samwīs**, dull, foolish' (292), '**undēop**, shallow' (293; cf. the *Undeeps*), '**emnet**, plain' (296), '**sæcyning**, sea-king' (300), '**entisc**, of giants' (304), '**dēagol**, secret' (306), '**ælfscīene**, beautiful as a fairy' (306), and '**dūnlendisc**, hilly' (307; cf. *Dunlending*).

Tolkien "had been inside language," said C. S. Lewis. More to the point, he got inside individual words. He expanded two-dimensional words on the page so as to create three-dimensional things and people for them to refer to. His was an imagination that started with a word and ended with a world.

Part III
(Jeremy Marshall)

Shortly after the publication of *The Hobbit*, on 15 October 1937, Tolkien wrote to his publisher Stanley Unwin about his press reviews:

> No reviewer (that I have seen), although all have carefully used the correct *dwarfs* themselves, has commented on the fact (which I only became conscious of through reviews) that I use throughout the 'incorrect' plural *dwarves*. I am afraid it is just a piece of private bad grammar, rather shocking in a philologist; but I shall have to go on with it. Perhaps my *dwarf*—since he and the *Gnome* are only translations into approximate equivalents of creatures with different names and rather different functions in their own world—may be allowed a peculiar plural. The real 'historical' plural of *dwarf* (like *teeth* of *tooth*) is *dwarrows*, anyway: rather a nice word, but a bit too archaic. Still I rather wish I had used the word *dwarrow*.
> (*Letters* 23)

He wrote along the same lines in a letter that was published in the *Observer* on 20 February 1938,[30] and in the introduction to the subsequent revised editions of *The Hobbit*.

But exactly how 'incorrect' was his use of *dwarves*? I would like to take up the defence of Tolkien the creative English writer against Tolkien the pedantic philologist, who (along with Tolkien the encyclopedist and Tolkien the philosopher) constantly threatened to overwhelm his more instinctive and poetic imaginings. He was perfectly at liberty to adopt a minority spelling—in this as in other instances—even if it was because he liked it and for no other reason, and his elaborate smokescreen about the distinctiveness of his mythological dwarves was really not necessary.

It is true that only one example of *dwarves* is included in the *Oxford English Dictionary*[31] prior to *The Hobbit* of 1937. It is from the *Monthly Magazine* in 1818, in a reference to "the history of Laurin, king of the dwarves" (a tale associated with the medieval German romantic sagas of Dietrich of Bern).

---

[30]   *Letters* 31.

[31]   The section containing 'dwarf' was originally prepared for publication in July 1897, according to Berg (1993:123).

However, this sparsity of evidence is slightly misleading. The form is actually attested in the work of several 19th-century and early 20th-century poets, notably William Bell Scott (an Edinburgh-born poet and painter who died in 1890 at the age of almost 80) and Edward Bulwer-Lytton (who is now remembered chiefly for his novel *The Last Days of Pompeii*). Here is a selection of examples. Some are suggestive of pygmies or midgets rather than anything mythological; this from Philip James Bailey's 'A Spiritual Legend' (in Bailey 1855):

> In various countries variant roots of men,
> Giants and dwarves and Æthiop manikins,
> And pygmies.

And this from Lytton's 'The Siege of Constantinople' (in Bulwer-Lytton 1868):

> Four black dwarves
> Like toads, green-turban'd, and in scarlet scarves,
> The four familiars of the fair witch-queen.

But other instances have a more overtly folkloric flavour: here from the fifth part of William Bell Scott's *The Year of the World*:

> The laborer overjoyed,
> Carried the tidings to Sarmatian wastes,
> And through Norwegian forests, where swart dwarves
> Forge arms for maniac warriors.

and here from the tale of 'Marietta's Needle' in Lytton's *Glenaveril*:

> 'Hearken! all ye,' the Gnome King cried, 'that scent
> The slightest savour of the smallest grain
> Of metal, whose congenial element
> Lurks hidden in the hard rock's inmost vein,
> Or wandering strays about earth's surface, blent
> With baser matter! Search with might and main!
> Nose all this soil, and say if here there be
> One particle of iron hid from me!'
>   And the Dwarves answered, 'There is gold, gold, gold!'

Here is one from C. M. Doughty's slightly indigestible *The Dawn in Britain*:

> brown and black elves, whom Luridan leads,
> Ground-demons' king, heard deep earth-bellowing sound;
> From seven stages of dark under-world.

> Dwarves rise up in the floor, that in fast rocks,
> Like maggots, wonne [i.e. dwell]

and two from his *Mansoul*, the second, interestingly, also using another un-usual word familiar from Tolkien:

> A Prince is he, amongst them, óf mild mood.
> His memory of lore likewise, a treasury was;
> Of many generations of fayfolk.
> Helmbright, great duke of dwarves and hammermen.

and

> Dun elves and grey, stern woodwards of those paths;
> Kindred, woodwoses named, of mountain dwarves.

Perhaps most dramatically, here is William Bell Scott again, from his juvenile poem 'The Incantation of Hervor' (in Scott 1875), with dwarves once more characterized as the makers of weapons:

> And she ran forth to the battle-ground
> Muttering still the magic runes.
> 'Father Angantyr, wake, awake!
> Thine only daughter, Suafa's child,
> Doth charge thee to wake up again,
> And give her the gold-hilted sword
> Forged by the Dwarves for Suafarla.'

Tolkien seems to have been using this plural spelling himself practically from the first mention of dwarves in his earliest surviving writings, during or even before his time with the OED, judging from the material published in the first volume of *The History of Middle-earth*.[32] But, far from being a purely private piece of bad grammar, by the time of the publication of *The Hobbit*, this ir-regular plural had even made its first appearance in a relatively respectable dictionary: among the collection of dictionaries I have been able to consult, the earliest to acknowledge the existence of *dwarves* is *Webster's Second Interna-tional Dictionary* of 1934, which marks it as 'rare'. It seems to have been on the point of becoming less rare!

---

[32]   In the outlines of the 'Lost Tales' and in the 'Gnomish Lexicon' (*Lost Tales I* 236, 261).

The only usage guide I have found to discuss the plural of *dwarf* explicitly is the *Cambridge Guide to English Usage* by the Australian linguist Pam Peters. In this, it is stated that

> the first form **dwarfs** is preferred by all dictionaries for the plural of *dwarf*. Database evidence from CCAE [the Cambridge International Corpus of American English] and BNC [the British National Corpus] underscores this, showing that it's the preferred form for both American and British writers, by more than 25:1 [...] The number of words with *–ves* plurals is steadily declining, and there is no reason to count *dwarf* among them, on the strength of very sporadic uses of *dwarves*.
> (Peters 2004:167)

Her first statement is hard to substantiate with complete confidence. In most dictionaries, it is hard to tell whether alternative plurals have been presented in order of preference, or simply in alphabetical order: after all, even two variants of equal frequency have got to be listed one before the other. The marking of 'rare' was dropped in *Webster's Third International* (1961), and both plurals subsequently appeared without comment in *Webster's Seventh Collegiate Dictionary* (1963), and (from a different publisher) in *Webster's New World Dictionary* (1970), though the *Random House Unabridged* (1966) ignored the variant spelling completely. British dictionaries followed on rather later: both plurals appeared—without any comment on usage—in John Sykes's sixth edition of the *Concise Oxford Dictionary* (1976), in the subsequent edition of the *Pocket Oxford Dictionary* (1978), and in the new *Collins English Dictionary* (1979). The form *dwarves* never made it into the old *Chamber's 20ᵗʰ Century Dictionary*, but it appeared, with the label 'rare', in *Chambers English Dictionary* (1988), and with the label 'less often' in its successor, *Chambers 21ˢᵗ Century Dictionary* (1996). In all of these dictionaries it is listed second, with any indication of preference being rather implicit than stated.[33]

So why did Tolkien think it at all reprehensible to have used this plural, established as it was in poetic usage, and by the time he published *The Hobbit*

---

[33] Bizarrely, it does appear first, before *dwarfs*, in *The Encarta World English Dictionary* (1999). I think this must be regarded as an aberration.

in 1937, actually listed in a major American dictionary? He described it as a
'philological' matter, and Peters sums it up concisely:

> *dwarfs* is sounder in historical terms because the *f* in its spelling is
> relatively recent, unlike others whose *–ves* plural goes back to Old
> English.

In other words, *dwarf* originated in English with a *–gh* ending (or some ap-
proximation of it) and, in strictly philological terms, using *dwarves* as the plural of *dwarf* is about as logical as using **lauves* as the plural of *laugh*. Tolkien's
remark about the 'real historical plural' is more fully explained by a note in the
OED's etymology: the Old English singular word *dweorgh* or *dweorh* became
modern English *dwarf,* following regular sound changes (which also give us the
final consonant of *enough* and the *f* of *draft*), while the plural *dweorghas* gave
rise to medieval forms such as *dwerwes,* the modern form of which would be
dwarrows.

Peters suggests that "*dwarves* seems to have arisen on the analogy of
wharf / wharves, where the plural with *–ves* connects with its antecedents."
Given the context, though, I think *wharf* seems highly improbable as the
source of the analogy. As Tolkien implies by his comment in the letter to the
Observer ("*dwarves* goes well with *elves*"),[34] the relevant comparison is indeed
surely with *elves,* an old established *–ves* plural which was bound to be not only
at the forefront of Tolkien's mind, but also in the minds of most of the
19th-century writers who found themselves writing of *dwarves*. And of course,
as Tolkien was also aware, analogy is itself a long-established process of
linguistic change, and is not inherently 'bad grammar'. In fact, the use of a
regular *–fs* plural for any word with an old *–ves* plural, such as *roofs,* is simply
the application of analogy in the opposite direction.

It was on the basis of analogy that Tolkien went on to take the
Chaucerian adjective *elvish* as his model to produce *dwarvish,* a strictly unnecessary innovation, yet seemingly a happy one, though it is still very rare outside
the Tolkienian sphere, and is as yet unacknowledged by the lexicographers.

Did Tolkien's usage have any lasting effect on the word's use? Clearly,
Peters thinks not, since she regards the occurrence of *dwarves* as 'sporadic' and

---

[34]   *Letters* 31.

the inflectional form in general as in decline. Except in the case of writers who are explicitly discussing Tolkien's works, evidence on the matter of influence can only ever be equivocal. As far as modern use is concerned, two electronic text collections I looked at did indeed have a preponderance of *dwarfs*, but rather than Peters's 25:1, they showed—mainly in specifically poetic writing— ratios of between 10:1 and 7:1. From Tolkien's own generation, I found only a solitary use by John Masefield (from 'Reynard the Fox' in Masefield 1946):

> the hill's south spur,
> Grown with dwarf oak and juniper,
> Like dwarves alive

But for poets working from the 1960s onwards, such as the Americans Robert Duncan (*The Opening of the Field*, 1960) and Jack Spicer (*Collected Books*, 1975) and, in the U.K., Ted Hughes (*The Musk Ox*, 1981), the word seems to have become entirely natural, and it is hard to perceive the decline to which Peters refers.

In one parallel case, we can definitely point to Tolkien as the originator of a pattern of use. On the strength of his writing, the *Supplement to the OED* noted the revival of the word *elven* in compound words such as *elven-king, elven-tongue*, and *elven-wise*.[35] The editors present it as a revival of the Old English plural noun *elvene*, but comparison with Tolkien's invented parallel *dwarven* suggests that it might be better regarded as an adjective, modelled on Old English adjectives such as *golden* or *wheaten*, with echoes also of archaic verbal adjectives such as *carven*. But, as with *dwarvish*, no dictionary has yet listed *dwarven*, and it is even more narrowly restricted to Tolkienian writing.

Whether Tolkien's 'bad grammar' will remain a persistent feature of the English language it is too early to tell, but perhaps there will be a footnote in the OED's future 'Third Supplement', though this book exists, as yet, only as a passing reference in *The Notion Club Papers* (*Sauron Defeated* 224-25).

---

[35] See Burchfield (1980).

PETER GILLIVER, JEREMY MARSHALL, & EDMUND WEINER
All three are editors on the *Oxford English Dictionary*. Peter Gilliver
gave a paper at the Tolkien Centenary Conference at Keble College
in 1992, and is working on an official history of the OED. Dr
Jeremy Marshall is a former president of the Oxford C.S. Lewis
Society. Edmund Weiner formerly lectured in English at Christ
Church, Oxford, and is now a fellow of Kellogg College. Their
book *The Ring of Words: Tolkien and the Oxford English Dictionary*
was published by OUP in April 2006, and is likely to be considered
one of the essential books on Tolkien.

References

Abbreviations used:

Biography: see Carpenter 1977

Letters: see Carpenter 1981

Lost Road: see Tolkien 1987

Lost Tales I: see Tolkien 1983a

Lost Tales II: see Tolkien 1983b

Sauron Defeated: see Tolkien 1992

War: see Tolkien 1990

Bailey, Philip James, 1855, *The Mystic and Other Poems*, London: Chapman & Hall.

Berg, Donna L., 1993, *A Guide to the Oxford English Dictionary*, Oxford: Oxford University Press.

Bridges, Robert Seymour, 1928, 'Henry Bradley. A Memoir', in *Collected Papers of Henry Bradley*, Oxford: Clarendon Press, 1-56.

Bulwer-Lytton, Edward, 1868, *Chronicles and Characters*, London: Chapman & Hall.

---, 1885, *Glenaveril, or The Metamorphoses*, London: John Murray.

Burchfield, Robert W. (ed.), 1980, *A Supplement to the Oxford English Dictionary*, vol. I: A–G, first edition 1972, corrected edition 1980, Oxford: Clarendon Press.

Carpenter, Humphrey, 1977, *J.R.R. Tolkien. A Biography*, London: George Allen & Unwin.

--- (with the assistance of Christopher Tolkien) (ed.), 1981, *The Letters of J.R.R. Tolkien*, London: George Allen & Unwin.

Cleasby, Richard and Gudbrand Vigfusson, 1874, *Icelandic-English Dictionary*, Oxford: Clarendon Press.

Doughty, Charles M., 1906, *The Dawn in Britain*, London: Duckworth & Co.

---, 1923, *Mansoul or The Riddle of the World*, London: Jonathan Cape & The Medici Society.

Gilliver, Peter, Jeremy Marshall, and Edmund Weiner, 2006, *The Ring of Words: Tolkien and the Oxford English Dictionary*, Oxford: Oxford University Press.

Kingsley, Charles, 1954, *Hereward the Wake*, first edition 1866, London and Glasgow: Collins Classics.

Masefield, John, 1946, *Poems*, London and Toronto: Heinemann.

Morris, William, 1889, *A Tale of the House of the Wolfings and all the Kindreds of the Mark*, London: Reeves & Turner.

Murray, James A. H. et al. (ed.), 1933, *The Oxford English Dictionary*, completed and re-issued, Oxford: Clarendon Press.

Peters, Pam, 2004, *The Cambridge Guide to English Usage*, Cambridge: Cambridge University Press.

Scott, William Bell, 1846, *The Year of the World*, Edinburgh: William Tait.

---, 1875, *Poems*, London: Longmans, Green & Co.

Sturluson, Snorri, 1893, *The Stories of the Kings of Norway called the Round World (Heimskringla)*, vol. I, translated by William Morris and Eiríkr Magnússon, London: Quaritch.

The Story of the Volsungs and Niblungs, with certain songs from the Elder Edda, translated by Eiríkr Magnússon and William Morris, edited by H. Halliday Spurling, London and Felling-on-Tyne: Walter Scott Publishing Co., 1888.

Tolkien, John Ronald Reuel, 1923, 'Henry Bradley: 3 Dec., 1845 – 23 May, 1923', *Bulletin of the Modern Humanities Research Association* 20 (October 1923):4-5.

---, 1983a, *The Book of Lost Tales: Part I* (volume one of *The History of Middle-earth*), edited by Christopher Tolkien, London: George Allen & Unwin.

---, 1983b, *The Book of Lost Tales: Part II* (volume two of *The History of Middle-earth*), edited by Christopher Tolkien, London: George Allen & Unwin.

---, 1987, *The Lost Road and Other Writings* (volume five of *The History of Middle-earth*), edited by Christopher Tolkien, London: George Allen & Unwin.

---, 1990, *The War of the Ring* (volume eight of *The History of Middle-earth*), edited by Christopher Tolkien, London: George Allen & Unwin.

---, 1992, *Sauron Defeated* (volume nine of *The History of Middle-earth*), edited by Christopher Tolkien, London: Harper Collins.

Vigfusson, Gudbrand and Frederick York Powell, 1883, *Corpus Poeticum Boreale: The Poetry of the Old Northern Tongue*, Oxford: Clarendon Press.

Wright, Joseph and Elizabeth Mary Wright, 1908, *Old English Grammar*, London: Henry Frowde, Oxford University Press.

Gilson, Smith, and Baggins

VERLYN FLIEGER

Summary

The influence of the deaths in World War I of Tolkien's close friends Rob Gilson and Geoffrey Smith on *The Lord of the Rings* was profound. Gilson was killed in the Battle of the Somme on July 1 1916. Smith died of wounds December 3 1916. Tolkien wrestled with the loss of Gilson and Smith, and with the meaning of such deaths in a war that seemed to many a meaningless stalemate. In Frodo Baggins, whose sacrifice, like Gilson's and Smith's, benefited everyone but himself, Tolkien, perhaps unconsciously, found a way to re-present his boyhood friends and honor the meaning of their lives.

Possibly the best-known line in *The Lord of the Rings* is "Well, I'm back," the simple declarative with which Sam Gamgee closes the book. Here is how it appears in context:

> Sam turned to Bywater, and so came back up the Hill, as day was ending once more. And he went on, and there was yellow light, and fire within, and the evening meal was ready, and he was expected. And Rose drew him in, and set him in his chair, and put little Elanor upon his lap.
>
> He drew a deep breath. 'Well, I'm back,' he said. (*LotR* 1031)

And on that quiet, domestic note the book and the story both are ended.

While thanks to Christopher Tolkien's work in *Sauron Defeated*, we now know that Tolkien had originally conceived an Epilogue tying up many of his story's loose ends, I think most would agree that he was wise to cut it, and end the story with Sam's return from the Grey Havens. Sam's statement echoes *The Hobbit*'s 'There and Back Again' and returns the story to hobbit simplicity after the captains and the kings depart. On thematic and structural levels, it works well, and it is fitting that Sam should have this last word. 'Well, I'm back' seems, on the face of it, to be a typically Gamgean locution—short, factual, to the point. But what exactly is the point? On the purely plot level, Sam's statement seems a bit redundant. Of course he is back, we can see that. We don't need to be told, nor do Rose and Elanor, for he is expected and the

evening meal is ready. What besides announcing his return might Sam be saying by 'Well, I'm back'? More important, what might Tolkien be saying?

Reserving answers to these questions for the moment (I will return to
them later) let us leave Sam sitting in his chair surrounded by his family, and
shift our gaze to another man, also sitting but alone out in a wood at night.
Here there is no yellow light, no warming fire, no welcoming meal. Unlike
Sam, this man, John Ronald Tolkien, is not by any means 'back', not at home.
He is in fact a long way from home, in France, in a catastrophic war, and he
has just got news of the death in battle of his close friend Rob Gilson. Most
serious readers of Tolkien's work know the story, best told in John Garth's
Tolkien and the Great War, of the Battle of the Somme, how the English soldiers came up out of their trenches on July 1, 1916, and crossed No Man's
Land under a relentless fusillade of German machine guns that mowed them
down in rows. They hadn't a chance. Twenty thousand English soldiers were
killed that day. One of them was Rob Gilson.

Who was Rob Gilson? Two years younger than Tolkien, only twenty-
two when he was killed, Rob Gilson was the son of the headmaster at Tolkien's
old school, King Edwards. My guess is that most readers are familiar with the
names of Gilson, G.B. Smith and Christopher Wiseman, and their relationship
with one another and with Tolkien, so I won't go into great detail (again, see
Garth 2003). The 'immortal four', as one of them called their fellowship (but
by that time there were only three), had been friends since schooldays. Core
members of the boyhood fellowship they called the TCBS, they were young
men with rather inchoate ambitions to change the world.

Further to contrast Tolkien's lonely isolation with Sam's firelit welcome,
we can go to his own words at that time, an account in a letter to Christopher
Wiseman of his first response to the news of Rob's death. "I went out into the
wood […] last night and also the night before and sat and thought." Tolkien
was no stranger to bereavement, having lost his father when he was barely four
years old, and his mother—a deeper and more conscious loss—when he was
twelve. But the loss of Gilson when he was twenty-four apparently raised more
perplexing questions, or perhaps he was just old enough now to face them, to
sit and think.

His letter went on:

> I cannot get away from the conclusion that it is wrong to confound
> the greatness which Rob has won [in his death] with the greatness

which he himself doubted. [...] I now believe that if the greatness which we three [surviving members] certainly meant [...] is really the lot of the TCBS, then the death of any of its members is but a bitter winnowing of those who were not meant to be great—at least directly [...] (*Letters* 9)

Why was the nature of Rob's 'greatness' or lack thereof an important question in Tolkien's mind? He went on to elaborate:

The greatness I meant was that of a great instrument in God's hands—a mover, a doer, even an achiever of great things [...]. [Rob's] greatness [...] touches the TCBS on that [...] side which perhaps [...] was the only one that Rob really felt—'Friendship to the Nth power'. [...] What I meant was that the TCBS had been granted some spark of fire—certainly as a body if not singly—that was destined to kindle a new light.

Unlike Tolkien and G.B. Smith, both of whom had ambitions to be poets, or Christopher Wiseman, who was an accomplished amateur musician, Gilson seems to have felt less intensely the 'spark of fire' to which Tolkien refers. Although by all accounts Rob Gilson was much loved by those who knew him, and though he had a keen interest in architecture and design, he was apparently regarded by the other TCBS-ites as perhaps the least artistically ambitious of the four. His great value, at least as Tolkien felt it, writing to Wiseman, was 'Friendship to the Nth power'. Rob Gilson was valuable for what he was in himself, not for any ambition to 'kindle a new light', not for what he might or might not have wanted to accomplish.

We must keep in mind that the man who sat in the wood that night, the man who wrote the letter, was not the comfortable, pipe-smoking professor of philology and world-famous writer of fantasy whose photograph is on the book covers. He was a deeply devout twenty-four year old not long out of university, in the throes of extreme mental shock, sitting alone in a dark wood trying to reason his way out of a crisis at once emotional, religious, and philosophical. He was trying to find some meaning in the apparently meaningless death of a dear friend in a useless battle that achieved nothing. His letter and two subsequent ones to Tolkien from G.B. Smith (who was himself to die from wounds a few months later—another loss for Tolkien) are poignant records of their struggle to come to terms with death—not the inevitable dying off of the previous generation which to some degree we all take for granted—but death in their own generation, violent, unnecessary, untimely death. Tolkien's letter confronts all the difficult questions—about the purpose of life and the significance of death—and gropes desperately for some comprehensible answers. It is no wonder that he went into the woods to sit and think.

In his grief and wrestling with the angel of death we can discern a mixture of emotions and reactions. First, there is survivor's guilt—Gilson is dead, Tolkien is still alive. Why, and how? The British high command placed Tolkien behind the lines on July 1, Gilson at the front. But how did that military placement fit into the greater scheme of things? Was it destiny? Providence? The luck of the draw? The words of Gandalf to Frodo, written many years later, seem drawn out of this moment. "Many that live deserve death. And some that die deserve life. Can you give it to them?" (*LotR* 58). Did Tolkien, who lived, deserve death? Did Gilson, who died, deserve life? The man in the wood, who knew he could not give it to him, found no comfortable answer.

Next there is the corollary, almost desperate need to see the point in so apparently pointless an event, to put it in the personal context of the TCBS. Was Gilson not 'meant to be great', therefore *meant* to die? Was he meant to die and therefore not meant to be great? And the inevitable next step—was Tolkien 'meant' to live in order to be great? Again, at that moment, in those circumstances, no answer. Finally, there is a probing of the unfathomable nature of God. The phrase 'bitter winnowing' carries implications not just of separating grain from chaff, but also of the hand that shakes the basket, of controlling force, perhaps even an overarching divine plan. But that is to ascribe a pretty tough attitude to the God he is struggling to understand.

It should be understood here that I am not questioning Tolkien's faith. I am not interrogating his God. I am simply trying to understand the confusion and despair out of which he was trying to puzzle his way—first while sitting in the wood and thinking, and second in writing the letter to Christopher Wiseman.

Most moving of all, however, is not Tolkien's attempt at reason, but his account of his feelings. "So far my chief impression is that something has gone crack [...] I don't feel a member of a little complete body now [...]" (*Letters* 10). This, apparently, is the shock most deeply felt, Rob's severance from the TCBS, and the effect that it will have on the fellowship. Something has 'gone crack'. Something is broken, so that Tolkien no longer feels part of a whole body, and is striving in loneliness and isolation to find coherence in the fragments that are left. A scant half year after that night in the wood, Tolkien was sent home from the Front with trench fever, and for him the war was effectively over. As it happened, only two of 'the immortal four' survived the war, Tolkien and Christopher Wiseman. Nearly fifty years later Tolkien would write in the Foreword to the second edition of *The Lord of the Rings*, "by 1918 all but one of my close friends were dead" (*LotR* xxiv). G.B. Smith's death in France from shell wounds, coming only five months after Gilson's death, was a second body-blow to the fellowship, a second severe loss for Tolkien, and one he never forgot.

Tolkien and Smith had been fellow poets, and that bond brought them especially close. When the war was over, Tolkien, encouraged by Wiseman, arranged to publish Smith's slender legacy of poetry, titled *A Spring Harvest*. I don't think it is accidental that he reached for agrarian metaphors—'bitter winnowing', 'spring harvest', with their images of wind-sifted separation and unripe grain reaped too early—to deal with these untimely losses. They convey a strong sense of youth painfully aware of its own apparent expendability in the eyes of powers beyond its control. It was at least partly in the context of these losses that Tolkien began to write his Silmarillion mythology.

Now the function of a mythology is to give meaning to existence, to put human life inside a larger frame, to address if not always to answer the fundamental questions—why are we here? What is our place in the scheme of things? Why do we live? Why do we die? As Tom Shippey (1995:84-93) has pointed out, Tolkien's concern with such questions, although superficially masked by the beauty and complexity of his invented world, links him more closely to the realistic (and pessimistic) war writers of his generation than to the later fantasists with whom he is usually grouped. It is notable that in his invented mythology Tolkien gives his invented world one race that does not die—Elves, and another that dies but does not know why—Men. Tolkien wrote to a reader of *The Lord of the Rings* that his great story, and in this he included the Silmarillion, was about death and immortality.

As Tolkien's work has ripened and his audience with it, this theme has become more and more clear. Even *The Hobbit*, the most cheerful of his books, has the two youngest dwarves, Fili and Kili, killed in battle defending Thorin Oakenshield. Moreover, they are killed uselessly since, as it turns out, Thorin himself also dies from battle wounds. The imminence of death is at the heart of

Tolkien's essay on *Beowulf* and the monsters. It informs the last half of his essay 'On Fairy-Stories', which singles out for special mention two essentials that fairy-stories offer their readers—Escape from Death, and that escape's corollary, Consolation, the joy of the Happy Ending when Death is overcome. Tolkien's major fictions give his readers all three. Death, Escape from Death, and the Happy Ending. But they also withhold them. *The Hobbit's* Bilbo Baggins comes home safe, but Thorin Oakenshield and Fili and Kili die in the Battle of Five Armies. The narrative momentum of *The Silmarillion* rides on a series of vivid descriptions of lost battles. There are a myriad deaths in *The Lord of the Rings,* all but one—that of Denethor—deaths in battle. Tolkien gives Sam the Happy Ending, but withholds that Consolation from Frodo.

A minor but important work, Tolkien's verse play *The Homecoming of Beorhtnoth,* his riff on *The Battle of Maldon,* begins with everybody dead except Tída and Totta, who were not in the battle. Searching the field for the body of Beorhtnoth, they tell over the names of those fallen and rehearse their deeds. It is a litany of deaths, most importantly that of Beorhtnoth himself, whose 'homecoming' after the battle is in a cart, delivered to the monks of Ely for burial. A bitter contrast to Sam's warm welcome. The deeper we probe into *The Lord of the Rings* the more pronounced becomes the sense of passing and loss. "For however the fortunes of war may go," says Théoden to Gandalf at Helm's Deep, "may it not so end that much that was fair and wonderful shall pass for ever out of Middle-earth?" Gandalf's answer "to such days we are doomed" (*LotR* 550) gives little consolation. A perceptive early comment by Douglass Parker (1957:609) in *The Hudson Review* notes that, "Tolkien's whole marvelous, intricate structure has been reared to be destroyed, that we may regret it […] as a necessary concomitant of being human." With the substitution of *mourn* for the milder word *regret,* Parker's statement seems to me a fitting commentary on Théoden's words.

The songs of Rohan, surely among the most moving poems in the book, are all about loss. Here is the first, chanted by Aragorn at the barrows of Edoras.

> Where now the horse and the rider? Where is the horn that was blowing?
> Where is the helm and the hauberk, and the bright hair flowing?
> Where is the hand on the harpstring, and the red fire glowing?
> Where is the spring and the harvest and the tall corn growing?
> They have passed like rain on the mountain, like a wind in the meadow;

The days have gone down in the West behind the hills into shadow.
Who shall gather the smoke of the dead wood burning,
Or behold the flowing years from the Sea returning?
(*LotR* 508)

Never has the *ubi sunt* theme of the classical poets been given more vivid life in death. Of all the Rohan poems, the most elegiac is the song of the Mounds of Mundburg, sung by "a maker in Rohan" at some unspecified time in a future far beyond the time of the book's action. Like *The Homecoming of Beorhtnoth*, it is a litany of the names of warriors fallen in the Battle of the Pelennor Fields—Théoden, Harding, Guthláf, Dúnhere and Déorwine, Grimbold, Herefara and Herubrand, Horn and Fastred, Derufin and Duilin, Hirluin the Fair and Forlong the old. They "fought and fell there in a far country," and "Long now they sleep/under grass in Gondor by the Great River" (*LotR* 849).

Looking eagerly for flaws in the surface, detractors of *The Lord of the Rings* have expressed disappointment that while lots of minor characters die (which these critics apparently consider unimportant), all the main characters in the story survive. They have not read deep enough. True, Tolkien's hobbit fellowship, unlike the TCBS, does, apparently, survive the war. None of the original four dies, and all come home. They are all, at least temporarily, 'back' in the sense of Sam's declaration. But here the similarity begins to fade. Frodo, of all of them the one who most deserves to be 'back', is never back in the way that Sam is. Unwelcomed, unappreciated, wounded, recurrently ill, recurrently in pain, he cannot stay in the Shire, for it no longer has any place for him.

Now Frodo, for all his courage and the high regard of Gandalf, is (and I think is intended to be) an ordinary hobbit. Tolkien himself conceded that "Frodo is not so interesting" as Sam (*Letters* 105). But that, I suggest, is the point of the story. Frodo is not meant to be an 'interesting' personality. Partly because he is so continually under stress, he is of all the Fellowship the least differentiated by character or temperament. He has neither the light-hearted impulsiveness of Pippin, nor the solid practicality of Merry. He is not a poet like Bilbo, not a gardener like Sam. He is not a maker, and not by any choice of his own a 'mover, a doer, an achiever of great things' or indeed any things at all. He is an ordinary person doing something extraordinary not because he wants to but because he has to.

Not unlike Rob Gilson among the TCBS, Frodo has no outstanding skills or talents except perhaps that of 'Friendship to the Nth power', best exemplified in his relationship with Sam. Although he is never in a catastrophic battle like Rob Gilson, never succumbs to his injuries like G.B. Smith, Frodo's life is, in its own way, as destroyed by war as were theirs. He is irrevocably if not fatally wounded, both physically and mentally, by his ordeal. His departure overseas to Valinor offers him no redress, only the possibility of healing *"if that could be done"* [my emphasis] wrote Tolkien (*Letters* 328), and he clearly left the outcome open.

I don't want to propose that Tolkien consciously modeled Frodo on Rob Gilson, nor that Gilson was in the forefront of his mind as he wrote. But he almost certainly was in the back of it, part of the 'leaf-mould of the mind' that Tolkien said was the source of all his work. I do want to suggest that a particular phrase about Gilson in Tolkien's letter, 'the greatness which he himself doubted', is paraphrased in Frodo's protest to Gandalf, 'I am not made for perilous quests.' It is clear from Tolkien's letter that Rob Gilson did not altogether share the sense that Tolkien certainly felt and that Smith and Wiseman quite probably shared of being 'a great instrument in God's hands'. In giving Frodo this self-doubt, Tolkien was investing him with some of the humility that Rob Gilson apparently exemplified.

Gilson's self-doubt and Frodo's plaintive 'Why was I chosen?' come from the same place in the human psyche. Gandalf's answer, "You may be sure that it was not for any merit that others do not possess" (*LotR* 61) is the precursor to Frodo's answer to Sam, many pages later. "It must often be so […] when things are in danger: some one has to give them up, lose them, so that others may keep them" (*LotR* 1029). In their sacrifice to something greater than themselves, Frodo and Rob Gilson paid a high price for their courage. Whether Rob Gilson's sacrifice bought anything lasting is a question Tolkien answered only by Frodo's sacrifice, which bought peace for Middle-earth.

When in grief and despair Tolkien wrote to Christopher Wiseman, "Something has gone crack. I don't feel a part of a little complete body now," he was feeling the amputation of Rob Gilson from the TCBS, the severance that so permanently and irrevocably divides the dead from the living. Those who are gone will never come back. In this world, we will never see them again. Tolkien recreated that 'little complete' body in *The Lord of the Rings*, but then deliberately made it go crack again. He reared a structure 'to be destroyed, that we may regret it.'

Now I want to revisit my opening questions about Sam's 'Well, I'm back'—what might Sam be saying, what might Tolkien be saying?—and offer an answer. I propose a revision—not of the writing but of the traditional reading of that sentence. What if instead of 'Well, I'm *back*,' emphasis on return, Sam said 'Well, *I'm* back,' implied evocation of those who were not back. It could just as easily have been said by Tolkien as by Sam. What might such a reading say about all those lost in Tolkien's wars—not just the war of the Ring but the war to end all wars—and the one that followed that one, when it was clear that war does not end wars? What would it say about Frodo, who came back but could not stay?[1] What would it say about Rob Gilson and G.B. Smith as well as about Fili and Kili and Thorin and Théoden and Boromir and Hama and Forlong the old? They are not back. They will never be back. Not within Time. Not within the circles of this world. Long they sleep now under grass, their graves unvisited, their lives preserved only in a song about their deaths.

But the song is important. The tradition of song and the function of song—not just as pastime or entertainment (though these clearly have real value, especially in *The Fellowship*) but also as celebration, as history, as elegy, as eulogy—these are of central importance to Tolkien's work. Again and again the motif recurs in his story. Determined to break out from Helm's Deep in a last foray, Théoden tells Aragorn, "Maybe we shall [...] make such an end as will be worth a song—if any be left to sing of us hereafter" (*LotR* 539). Pursuing the orcs at Cirith Ungol Sam thinks "I wonder if any song will ever mention it: How Samwise fell in the High Pass and made a wall of bodies round his master. No, no song [...] for the Ring'll be found and there'll be no more songs" (*LotR* 735). And it is Sam, again, who imagines hearing the song of Nine-fingered Frodo and the Ring of Doom and gets his wish at the field of

---

[1] Another real-life corollary to Frodo is Tolkien's second son Michael, described by Tolkien as "a much-damaged soldier" (*Letters* 86). As a result of "severe shock to nervous system due to prolonged exposure to enemy action" (*Letters* 439), Michael had been judged unfit for further military service. In a psychological sense, the same diagnosis could well be made for Frodo.

Cormallen, where the unnamed minstrel of Gondor makes his imaginary song a reality.

For as everyone here knows, Sam's despairing vision at Cirith Ungol is unrealized. There *is* a song. *The Lord of the Rings* is the song. And Sam's last words—whether for himself or for those who cannot come back, for Gilson, Smith and Baggins—are the end of the song.

VERLYN FLIEGER is a professor in the Department of English at the University of Maryland, where she teaches courses in Comparative Mythology and the works of J.R.R. Tolkien. Her books on Tolkien include *Splintered Light: Logos and Language in Tolkien's World*, re-published in 2002 in a revised and expanded edition, *A Question of Time: Tolkien's Road to Faërie*, given the 1998 Mythopoeic Award for Inklings Scholarship, and *Interrupted Music: Tolkien and the Making of a Mythology*. With Carl Hostetter she is editor of the critical anthology, *Tolkien's Legendarum: Essays on The History of Middle-earth*, which won the 2000 Mythopoeic Award for Inklings Scholarship. Her fantasy novel *Pig Tale* was published by Hyperion in 2002. Visit her web site at http://www.mythus.com/.

References

Abbreviations used:

Letters: see Carpenter 2000

LotR: see Tolkien 2004

Carpenter, Humphrey (with the assistance of Christopher Tolkien) (ed.), 2000, *The Letters of J.R.R. Tolkien*, (first published 1981), Boston: Houghton Mifflin.

Garth, John, 2003, *Tolkien and the Great War*, London: HarperCollins.

Parker, Douglass, 1957, 'Hwaet We Holbytla ...' *Hudson Review* 9.4:598-609.

Shippey, Tom, 1995, 'Tolkien as a Post-war Writer', in Patricia Reynolds and Glen H. GoodKnight (eds.), 1995, *Proceedings of the J.R.R. Tolkien Centenary Conference*, Milton Keynes and Altadena: The Tolkien Society and the Mythopoeic Press, 84-93.

Tolkien, John Ronald Reuel, 1979, *The Hobbit*, (first edition 1937), London: George Allen & Unwin.

---, 2004, *The Lord of the Rings*, (originally published 1954-55; one-volume 50th anniversary edition), Boston: Houghton Mifflin.

PART TWO

MYTHOS

AND

MODERNITY

Enchantment in Tolkien and Middle-earth

PATRICK CURRY

Summary

This paper begins with a few general remarks about enchantment as a human experience before turning to its importance both in Tolkien's creative life and in his principal public work, *The Lord of the Rings*. I turn for elucidation to the work of Verlyn Flieger and that of two philosophers, Ronald Hepburn and Jan Zwicky.

My intention here is to trace the effects of enchantment—largely as understood and defined by Tolkien himself—in both his creative life and the world of Middle-earth which resulted from it. I shall start by introducing the idea of enchantment itself.

I

As is well-known, Tolkien set out his own literary programme, at least in broad outline, in 'On Fairy-Stories'.[1] Not the least valuable aspect of this essay is its attempt to articulate the nature of enchantment—something which is remarkably rare, even in fat tomes with the words 'Enchantment' or 'Re-Enchantment' in their titles.[2] In contrast, intellectuals have been happy to discuss the subject of disenchantment at length. (It is central, for example, to the concerns and publications of the Frankfort School and related critical theory.)[3] Even Max Weber, who was responsible for introducing the idea of 'the disenchantment of the world' into modern discourse, had little to say about what

---

[1] See also Curry (1999).

[2] To pick just two recent examples: David Ray Griffin (2000) and Alex Owen (2004). These could be multiplied many times.

[3] Principally the work of Theodor W. Adorno, Max Horkheimer and Herbert Marcuse.

enchantment is, or perhaps was.[4] But that little, when added to Tolkien's speculations and those of a very few others, allows us to formulate a reasonably coherent and accurate idea.[5]

That idea has three parts. One is that "Enchantment produces a Secondary World into which both designer and spectator can enter, to the satisfaction of their senses while they are inside; but in its purity it is artistic in desire and purpose" (OFS 49). (The relevant contrast, which we shall not pursue here, is with magic—including modern magic, i.e., techno-science.)[6] The second part, Tolkien's definition of "the primal desire at the heart of Faërie," is fundamental: "the realization, independent of the conceiving mind, of imagined wonder" (OFS 18).

To this we can add Weber's crucial insight (in Gerth and Wright 1991:282; my emphasis) that "[t]he unity of the primitive image of the world, in which everything was *concrete magic*, has tended to split"—as a result of the process of disenchantment—"into rational cognition and mastery of nature, on the one hand, and into 'mystic' experiences, on the other." In other words, enchantment ignores the split, deepened by Descartes but inherited by him from Platonic philosophy and thence Christian theology, between spiritual and/or mental subjectivity on the one hand and material objectivity on the other; it partakes of both.

Thus an intensive delineation of enchantment includes these characteristics:

- indispensably, existential wonder—which, as such, is useless in instrumental or utilitarian terms, but by no means therefore without effects; furthermore, enchantment is
- both ineffable and mysterious, on the one hand, and embodied, even carnal, and very precisely situated on the other;
- participatory, recalling the etymological meaning of 'enchantment': to be (to find oneself) in a song (the song which one is singing or to which one is listening); and finally, it is

---

[4]   The original phrase was Schiller's.

[5]   Especially Hepburn (1984).

[6]   See Curry (1999) and Curry (2004, chapter 3).

- pluralist, in the sense that although an experience of enchantment may partake intensely of unity, completeness and infinity while it lasts, being also 'concrete' it always comes to an end. Viewed from 'outside', therefore, it is ongoing, incomplete, and potentially multiple.

An extensive delineation would include experiences of enchantment, as just described, arising out of such situations as these:

- nature (decidedly not in the abstract but particular and 'real' places, things, animals, etc.);
- love (paradigmatically erotic love, but also maternal/paternal, as well as friendship);
- ritual (especially but not only religious);
- art (all the arts, related to all the senses and faculties—including humour);
- sports (as in, feeling oneself to be in the game which one is watching…);
- food (as in, slow- as opposed to fast-food); and
- learning (in the sense of lore for its own sake).

The way this list cuts across most coherent categories to which we are accustomed signals that we are dealing here with a particular, even peculiar beast, whose distinctiveness—significant commonalities with other kinds of experience notwithstanding—should be respected.

II

Now enchantment was far from being a purely theoretical or programmatic concept for Tolkien. Two intensely personal experiences of enchantment took place in his life (to put it somewhat redundantly: enchantment by its nature is personal, *as well as* more-than-personal). Both of them massively influenced that life, including his life-work. I have taken the following accounts from Humphrey Carpenter's biography.[7]

---

[7]   But see Shippey (1982:183-85) and Flieger (1997:148-49).

The first—characteristically linguistic for someone who was, in C.S. Lewis's words, 'inside language'—took place in 1913, when Tolkien was reading the *Crist* of Cynewulf, a group of Anglo-Saxon religious poems.

Two lines from it struck him forcibly:

Eala Eardendil engla beorhtast
Ofer middangeard monnum sended.

'Hail Earendel, brightest of angels / above the middle-earth sent unto men.' *Earendel* is glossed by the Anglo-Saxon dictionary as 'a shining light, ray', but here it clearly has some special meaning. Tolkien himself interpreted it as referring to John the Baptist, but he believed that 'Earendel' had originally been the name for the star presaging the dawn, that is, Venus. He was strangely moved by its appearance in the Cynewulf lines. 'I felt a curious thrill,' he wrote long afterwards, 'as if something had stirred in me, half wakened from sleep. There was something very remote and strange and beautiful behind those words, if I could grasp it, far beyond ancient English.' (*Biography* 64)

The second experience occurred sometime in 1917-18:

On days when he could get leave, he and Edith went for walks in the countryside. Near Roos they found a small wood with an undergrowth of hemlock, and there they wandered. Ronald recalled of Edith as she was at this time: 'Her hair was raven, her skin clear, her eyes bright, and she could sing—and dance.' She sang and danced for him in the wood, and from this came the story that was to be the centre of *The Silmarillion*: the tale of the mortal man Beren who loves the immortal elven-maid Lúthien Tinúviel, whom he first sees dancing among the hemlock in a wood. [...] Of all his legends, the tale of Beren and Lúthien was the one most loved by Tolkien, not least because at one level he identified the character of Lúthien with his own wife. (*Biography* 97)

There is no need to belabour the importance of these experiences for Tolkien, and therefore for understanding his work. But it is permissible to speculate on that significance not only in a germinal, formative capacity but in relation to certain tensions—themselves perhaps creative ones; at least, betimes—which, I think, must have resulted from their juxtaposition with Tolkien's Christianity. As we have seen, enchantments, both theoretically and in Tolkien's own experience of them, include an inalienably 'concrete' dimension which could, at the very least, cast doubt on their validity from the point of view of a theological commitment to a single and universal spiritual truth. More: a counter-commitment to experiences of enchantment could throw doubt in the other direction! Now I don't say these tensions are, in principle, unresolvable psychologically or even theologically; but it would be very surprising if they were not present and/or were inconsequential.

The context for such a discussion, not necessarily helpfully but probably unavoidably, is the presence of Catholic Christianity and/or paganism in Tolkien's work.[8] In my view, notwithstanding a predilection for exclusivity stemming from the universalism just mentioned, this question can only be resolved satisfactorily by starting from the position of 'both-and' rather than 'either-or'. Then things can be noticed and said about which aspects of his fiction are more one or the other and, even more interesting, how the two passions interacted.

To return to Tolkien's two enchantments I have just reviewed, they relate principally and obviously, in the first case, to the 'star' of Venus, whose intimate association with the female pagan deity of love and beauty—but of no less religious significance for that—long predates Christianity (all of which Tolkien was perfectly well aware of);[9] and in the second instance, to a passionate, including implicitly erotic, relationship—but no less spiritual for that—between two lovers. And without for a moment denying other perspectives, Beren and Lúthien were also, *qua* lovers, under the aegis of Venus.

So how did this sort of thing, integral to both Tolkien's life and his work, relate—almost certainly in both directions—with his Catholicism? I do not intend to try to work out the details here, because there are other things I want to concentrate on, but any attempt should certainly consider his carefully complex response in 1954 to a reader's criticism of Elvish reincarnation:

---

[8] For two good papers with contrasting emphases, see Ronald Hutton, 'The Pagan Tolkien', forthcoming in the proceedings of the 'Tolkien 05' conference which took place at Aston University, 11-15 August 2005, and Stratford Caldecott, 'Christianity and Literary Culture: The Case of J.R.R. Tolkien', unpublished paper from a talk given at Regent's Park College, 15th November 2005. (See also Hutton's chapter 7, 'The Inklings and the Gods', in Hutton 2003).

[9] See *Letters* 385.

'Reincarnation' may be bad *theology* [...] But I do not see how even
in the Primary World any theologian or philosopher, unless very
much better-informed about the relation of spirit and body than I
believe anyone to be, could deny the *possibility* of re-incarnation as
a mode of existence, prescribed for certain kinds of rational incarnate creatures. (*Letters* 189)

There is also the nice distinction which Tolkien draws in his remark to Auden
in 1965 that "I don't feel under any obligation to make my story fit with formalized Christian theology, though I actually intended it to be consonant with
Christian thought and belief [...]" (*Letters* 355).

III

Let us turn now to enchantment *inside* his literary creation. Much of what we
can learn from doing so has already been discussed, but some key points become much clearer viewed from within Middle-earth.

The most important of these is the firm identification of enchantment—consistent with 'On Fairy-Stories'—as the paradigmatic experience,
property and concern of the Elves. That idea is extensively introduced, in *The
Lord of the Rings*, when Frodo is listening to the singing in the Hall of Fire in
Rivendell (*LotR* 233). But it is driven home in connection with Lothlórien,
"the heart of Elvendom on earth." This is the place, by no means coincidentally, for the most explicit discussion of enchantment within the book:

Frodo stood awhile still lost in wonder. It seemed to him that he
had stepped through a high window that looked on a vanished
world. A light was upon it for which his language had no name.
[...] He saw no colour but those he knew, gold and white and blue
and green, but they were fresh and poignant, as if he had at that
moment first perceived them. [...] On the land of Lórien there was
no stain.

He turned and saw that Sam was now standing beside him,
looking round with a puzzled expression, and rubbing his eyes as if
he was not sure he was awake. 'It's sunlight and bright day, right
enough,' he said. 'I thought the Elves were all for moon and stars:
but this is more elvish than anything I ever heard tell of. I feel as if
I was *inside* a song, if you take my meaning.' (*LotR* 350-51)

This experience constitutes just the healing reconnection with reality which Tolkien—contesting the charge of 'escapism'—describes in his essay (OFS 52-54) as "recovery" or "the regaining of a clear view."[10]

Another important point about enchantment is made by Aragorn in his rebuke to Boromir: "'Speak no evil of the Lady Galadriel! [...] There is in her and in this land no evil, unless a man bring it hither himself. Then let him beware!'" (LotR 358). This is arguably the source of the danger Tolkien had in mind when he described Faërie as "a perilous land" (OFS 9). The clear implication is that any danger to mortals from enchantment lies principally not in the latter itself but in the relationship one has with it.

The description of the Fellowship leaving Lórien—or rather, as they experienced it, Lórien withdrawing from them—brilliantly evokes the desolation of disenchantment, the unbearable end (forever, it may seem) of just what gives one's life its meaning:

> For so it seemed to them: Lórien was slipping backward, like a bright ship masted with enchanted trees, sailing on to forgotten shores, while they sat helpless upon the margin of the grey and leafless world.
> (LotR 377)

(I am reminded here of the same thing happening at the end of another book in which enchantment figures importantly and poignantly, Karen Blixen's Out of Africa (1970:381): "It was not I who was going away, I did not have it in my power to leave Africa, but it was the country that was slowly and gravely withdrawing from me, like the sea in ebb-tide." This coincidence seems to point to a truth about enchantment.)

Returning to the point about what we bring to enchantment, this condition points to the chief danger, I think, inherent in any significant involvement with enchantment: attachment, dependency, and ultimately addiction. (And the resonance here with the discourse of drugs—especially those which offer an intense version of enchantment, the ever-rising price of which often emerges later—is by no means coincidental.)[11] That, above all, is

---

[10]   See also the paper by Fr. Guglielmo Spirito in this volume.

[11]   See Aldous Huxley's still superb essay 'The Doors of Enchantment'.

what can poison the purity, beauty and intrinsic value of enchantment. For enchantment, as Tolkien wrote, "represents love: that is, a love and respect for all things, 'Inanimate' [sic] and 'animate', an unpossessive love of them as 'other'."[12]

So the corollary—which I make bold to assert would have obtained Tolkien's assent—is this: a healthy relationship with enchantment requires a *strong* ego, so to speak, with the ability to *do without it.*[13] And what is this but one aspect of the grit that Tolkien (and several of his characters) so admired: Northern courage, to coin a phrase? (If one seeks connections between 'On Fairy-Stories' and his other great essay on *Beowulf,* this is surely one.)

My point is also discernible in the history of Middle-earth. As Théoden observes rhetorically, "'however the fortune of war shall go, may it not so end that much that was fair and wonderful shall pass for ever out of Middle-earth?'" (*LotR* 550). The seal of this poignant fate is (or at least is symbolized by) the mysterious link between the One Ring—Tolkien's master trope of power- and will-driven Magic and malevolence—and the Three Rings, one of which (Galadriel's) is the guarantor of the heart of Elvendom in Middle-earth, and thence its wonder and beneficence. Sauron's hand never touched the Three. Why is it, then, that with the passing of the One, their power too wanes?

This question preoccupied me for quite a while.[14] I found what I think is the answer, however, in a passage of Verlyn Flieger's *A Question of Time.* Flieger argues convincingly that the apparent perfection of Elvish enchantment is misleading—and doubly so, given the ambivalence resulting from Tolkien's own attachment to it—insofar as human beings, unlike Elves, cannot live in, as it were, a permanent state of enchantment; and any attempt to do so is doomed. Thus,

---

[12] From MS. 9, Tolkien Collection, Bodleian Library, Oxford, quoted by Flieger (1997:247).

[13] Cf. Tolkien's related assertion that "[t]he keener and the clearer is the reason, the better fantasy will it make" (OFS 51).

[14] It was posed to me, with his usual uncomfortable perspicuity, by Michael P. Winship.

there is a concealed sting in Lórien's beauty. Its timelessness is not the unspoiled perfection it seems. Rather, that very perfection is its flaw. It is a cautionary picture, closer in kind to the Ring than we'd like to think, shown to us in all its beauty to test if we can let it go.

The Lord of the Rings is, among other things, a story about the ability to let go. The Ring is the obvious example. [...] The timeless beauty of Lórien is the deeper example. (Flieger 1997:112)

I believe this is the theme underlying and uniting the One Ring, the Three, and us. It is a theme that includes but extends far beyond Tolkien's work, the province of all religions and of none alone. Here, for example, are the reported words of the Buddha on his deathbed to his grieving friend and attendant (from the perspective of one who has transcended such suffering but spoken nonetheless, one feels, a little wearily):[15]

'Enough, Ananda, do not sorrow, do not lament. Have I not formerly explained that it is the nature of things that we must be divided, separated and parted from all that is beloved and dear? How could it be, Ananda, that what has been born and come into being, that what is compounded and subject to decay, should not decay? It is not possible.'

IV

I also recently 'discovered' a book by a Canadian philosopher, Jan Zwicky, which throws valuable light on the subject of enchantment generally, as well as specifically in relation to the work of Tolkien. (It also corroborates some of my own thinking on both counts: always welcome, in the absence of unshakeable self-confidence.)

Zwicky counterposes 'the lyric'—which is more-or-less cognate with 'enchantment'—with the technological. Thus,

---

[15] Quoted in Rupert Gethin (1998:26). I once gave a short talk to the Tolkien Society in which I suggested, tongue in cheek, of course, that Tolkien was actually a Buddhist (Curry 2001); nonetheless, there is a serious point here, which I have tried to make above.

> Lyric coherence is not like the unity of systematic structures: its foundation is a heightened experience of detail, rather than the transcendence (excision) of detail.
>
> Lyric springs from love, love that attends to the most minute details of difference; and in this attention experiences connection rather than isolation.
>
> It is poignant, and musical.
>
> Lyric value is a species of teleological value: it perceives things exclusively as ends. In this, it is genetically distinct from utility. (Zwicky 1992:120, 126, 134, 158)

In contrast, the technological is instrumentalist. It sanctions exploitation, which "occurs when a thing becomes identified with a particular role in 'the story of (Western European) (human) progress'; roughly, when it becomes a commodity; when it is used in the absence of a perception of what it is" (Zwicky 1992:222).

Recall, in this connection, Frodo's lyric experience of a tree while entering Lórien: "He felt a delight in wood and the touch of it, neither as forester nor as carpenter; it was the delight of the living tree itself" (*LotR* 351). As Zwicky says, "The experience of 'presence' precludes exploitation." But then she adds—introducing a critically important third term—"Though it does not preclude use. There is a sense of 'use' which is, we might say, *domestic*, and of a significantly different character from exploitation" (Zwicky 1992: 222; emphasis in original). To continue with the example of trees and humans, the industrial clear-cutting of whole forests, many of them ancient, is exploitation—(one is reminded of the felling of whole groves to feed the insatiable fires of Orthanc)—whereas coppicing, pollarding and selective cutting, such as surely is practiced by hobbits, is domestic use.[16]

Now life utterly without enchantment or lyric would hardly feel worth living, or even, perhaps, be livable. As Zwicky puts it,

---

[16] I am grateful to Tom Shippey for pointing out the relevance of this contrast.

Lyric springs from the desire to recapture the intuited wholeness of the non-linguistic world, to heal the slash in the mind that is the capacity for language.

But as language-using creatures, it is of our essence that that gap cannot be permanently healed. The recognition that it cannot is the source of lyric's poignancy.

Poignancy comes after yearning. It is the essential emotional colouring of lyric thought. (Zwicky 1992:230)

And, beyond a doubt, that of Tolkien's work. "It is a fair tale, though it is sad, as are all the tales of Middle-earth" (*LotR* 191). However, we humans are not Elves, so we cannot *live* in Lothlórien. As Flieger (1997:257) notes, "An important impetus for [Tolkien's] subcreation was his uneasiness with the twentieth century, his desire to escape it, and his knowledge that such escape was only partly (and then only imaginatively) possible." Or as Zwicky (1992:284, 534) puts the matter:

Lyric strives for the whole in a single gesture, yearns for a wholeness with the world that, as language-users, we cannot sustain.

It is both the sadness and strength of thought that it can see beyond what drives it, the sadness and the beauty of human being that it can comprehend the incompatibility of its essence with its most fundamental desire.

That does not, of course, mean that we must therefore be Orcs, left only with technological exploitation! This is where the concept of the domestic comes into its own (Zwicky 1992:258):

The domestic accepts the essential tension between lyric desire and the capacity for technology.

In this acceptance, it mediates.

And, she adds (Zwicky 1992:524),

Domesticity lives without absolutes—including absolute clarity.

In relation to Tolkien's great work, however, all this seems relatively clear, at least. For what are the hobbits—and thus, by Tolkien's own admission, humans[17]—if not *domestic*? And what else does the book as a whole end with— quite deliberately, we may be sure—when Sam returns home to his wife and child, evening meal and fire?[18]

As usual, Tolkien *gestures*, without the least didacticism (or in his terms, allegory),[19] to the deepest existential realities of human life, with its challenges and what we have to face them with: chiefly, courage, hope, and an appreciation of what is small and apparently insignificant; and above all, the bittersweet poignancy that is our peculiar gift.

PATRICK CURRY is a lecturer in Religious Studies at the University of Kent and the author of several books, including *Defending Middle-Earth: Tolkien, Myth and Modernity* (1997, new edition 2004), *Astrology, Science and Culture: Pulling Down the Moon* (with Roy Willis, 2004) and *Ecological Ethics: An Introduction* (2006).

---

[17]   "The hobbits are, of course, meant to be a branch of the specifically *human* race (not Elves or Dwarves) [...]" (*Letters* 158, n.).

[18]   I am grateful to Sue Bridgwater for pointing out this obvious and important point which I had somehow managed to miss.

[19]   See his 'Foreword to the Second Edition' in *LotR*.

References

Abbreviations used:

Biography: see Carpenter 1977

Letters: see Carpenter 1981

LotR: see Tolkien 2004

OFS: see Tolkien 1988

Blixen, Karen, 1970, *Out of Africa*, (originally published 1937), New York: Random House.

Caldecott, Stratford, 2005, 'Christianity and Literary Culture: The Case of J.R.R. Tolkien', unpublished paper from a talk given at Regent's Park College, 15th November 2005.

Carpenter, Humphrey, 1977, *J.R.R. Tolkien: A Biography*, London: George Allen & Unwin.

--- (with the assistance of Christopher Tolkien) (ed.), 1981, *The Letters of J.R.R. Tolkien*, London: George Allen & Unwin.

Curry, Patrick, 1999, 'Magic vs. Enchantment', *Journal of Contemporary Religion* 14.3:401-12.

---, 2001, 'On Hobbits and Elves: or, Took and Baggins Again', in Helen Armstrong (ed.), 2001, *Digging Potatoes, Growing Trees*, (volume 3), Telford: The Tolkien Society, 48-51.

---, 2004, *Defending Middle-Earth: Tolkien, Myth and Modernity*, (second edition), Boston: Houghton Mifflin.

Flieger, Verlyn, 1997, *A Question of Time: J.R.R. Tolkien's Road to Faërie*, Kent, OH: Kent State University Press.

Gerth, Hans H. and C. Wright Mills (eds.), 1991, *From Max Weber: Essays in Sociology*, London: Routledge.

Gethin, Rupert, 1998, *The Foundations of Buddhism*, Oxford: Oxford University Press.

Griffin, David Ray, 2000, *Re-Enchantment without Supernaturalism*, Ithaca: Cornell University Press.

Hepburn, Ronald W., 1984, *'Wonder' and Other Essays*, Edinburgh: Edinburgh University Press.

Hutton, Ronald, 2003, *Witches, Druids and King Arthur*, London: Hambeldon and London.

---, forthcoming, 'The Pagan Tolkien', *Proceedings of the 'Tolkien 05' Conference*, Aston University, 11-15 August 2005.

Owen, Alex, 2004, *The Place of Enchantment: British Occultism and the Culture of the Modern*, Chicago: University of Chicago Press.

Shippey, Tom A., 1982, *The Road to Middle-earth*, London: George Allen & Unwin.

Tolkien, John Ronald Reuel, 1988, 'On Fairy-Stories', in *Tree and Leaf*, (edited by Christopher Tolkien), London: Unwin Hyman, 11-73.

---, 2004, *The Lord of the Rings*, (originally published 1954-55; one-volume 50th anniversary edition), Boston: Houghton Mifflin.

Zwicky, Jan, 1992, *Lyric Philosophy*, Toronto: University of Toronto Press.

From Vico to Tolkien:
The Affirmation of Myth
Against the Tyranny of Reason

MAREK OZIEWICZ

Summary

This paper argues for a strong parallel between the work of Italian philologist Giovanni Battista Vico and the English philologist J.R.R. Tolkien. Just as Vico speaks out in protest against the predominant rationalism of the eighteenth century, Tolkien speaks out against the stifling rationalism of the twentieth. Like Vico, Tolkien suggests that humans are traditional beings who live in larger, largely unconscious structures, which it is dangerous or impossible to change. Like Vico, he asserts that myth is the language of the human psyche which is true even when it is not factual and as such constitutes the main mode of our knowledge of reality. Finally, like Vico's, Tolkien's oeuvre can be taken as one extended argument for the mythopoeic construction of human consciousness.

"Tolkien himself did not approve of the academic search for 'sources'"—with this sentence Tom Shippey opens his appendix on Tolkien's sources in *The Road to Middle Earth: How J.R.R. Tolkien Created a New Mythology*. For Tolkien, Shippey continues, any such search "tended to distract attention from the work of art itself, and to undervalue the artist by the suggestion that he had 'got it all' from somewhere else." Thus, instead of matching sources to passages, Shippey (2003:343) proposes a brief overview of "works that nourished Tolkien's imagination and to which he returned again and again." Vico's treatise is not among them. The English translation of the third *New Science*, by Thomas G. Bergin and Max H. Fisch, appeared only in 1948; of the first *New Science*, by Leon Pompa, only in 2002. If, to the best of my knowledge, Tolkien was not familiar with Vico's work, the identification of Vico as Tolkien's 'source' may thus be legitimate only in its broadest sense of 'intellectual tradition' with the two authors seen as expressing strikingly similar ideas: the former as constructing a mythopoeic theory of history, the latter as describing its one specific mythopoeic trajectory. On this perspective certain Vicean claims may be taken as, in a sense, prefiguring Tolkien's achievement

in the 'Silmarillion'—an immense chronicle-cum-mythology-cum-legen-
darium corpus of works of which *The Hobbit* and *The Lord of the Rings* are "in
a way only off-shoots, side branches" (Shippey 2000:226). Although the parallels seem coincidental, Vico's and Tolkien's projects are alike in so many
ways that the convergences beg a reflection. Considering the immensity and
scope of, respectively, Vico and Tolkien critical assessment, this paper is, obviously, a tentative curtain-raiser rather than the kind of in-depth, perhaps book-
length study the issue deserves. My work here is that of a medieval compiler
for, alongside Vico's and Tolkien's own commentaries, I will bring together
the ideas presented by some of the top scholars in Tolkien and Vico studies:
Tom Shippey, Humphrey Carpenter, Verlyn Flieger, and Patrick Curry on the
Tolkien side, and Leon Pompa, Mark Lilla, and Joseph Mali on the Vico side.

Vico and Tolkien: Careers, Works, and Reception

The two major parallels between Vico's *New Science* and Tolkien's oeuvre that
I want to focus on concern their skepticism toward modernity and their affirmation of myth. However, I propose to start with a general overview of the
two authors' careers, interests, and the public reception of their works all of
which suggest correspondences not irrelevant to any attempt to collate them.
In as much as the facts about Tolkien's life are generally known, in the following section I shall privilege information about Vico so as to reveal, as fully
as possible, in what important ways his life and thought triangulates with that
of Tolkien.

Born in 1668 in Naples, Italy, Gianbattista Vico was a son of a modest
bookseller, whose life and fate, as Isaiah Berlin has put it, "is perhaps the best
of all known examples of what is too often dismissed as a romantic fiction—
the story of a man of original genius, born before his time, forced to struggle in
poverty and illness, misunderstood and largely neglected in his lifetime and all
but totally forgotten after his death" (quoted in Lilla 1993:1). For lack of powerful friends, Vico's career was blocked at almost every turn. Although trained
in law, he was denied a post in that lucrative discipline so that for forty-two
years out of his seventy-four he remained an ill-paid professor of rhetoric at the
University of Naples and had to supplement his meager income by all sorts of
odd writerly jobs. Although he wrote copiously, he failed to engage other Italian and European scholars so that "the audience for his own philosophical

writings—on metaphysics, jurisprudence, and finally a 'new science concerning the common nature of the nations'—hardly extended beyond Naples" (Lilla 1993:1). Shortly before he died, Vico admitted in one bitter letter that "he expected nothing from his native city but the complete isolation which enabled him to work so hard" (Grafton 2001:xvi).

Tolkien's life was less afflicted for he lived on the genteel side of poverty only in his youth, and succeeded, where Vico failed, in winning the academic post that enabled him to earn his living by the pursuit of his scholarly interests. After 1925, when, at thirty-three, he was elected to the Rawlinson and Bosworth Chair of Anglo-Saxon, Tolkien's academic life was largely unremarkable and for thirty-nine years, until his retirement in 1959, he remained a professor at the University of Oxford.

Plain as Vico's and Tolkien's academic careers were, they did follow a downward slope in at least one important aspect: both authors spent their lives fighting, in vain, for philology against the onslaught of what Vico (2001:77 [par. 127]) called "the conceit of scholars" and what Tolkien (1997b:225) referred to as "misology". Vico (2001:77 [127]) defined the conceit of scholars as the assertion that "what they know is as old as the world," a conceptual fallacy of projecting one's own views, ideas, ignorance, likes and dislikes—local and subjective as they are—on all earlier literature and history, which results in distorting those works and reading into them meanings which were never there. Instead, Vico proposed that meanings closest to the original ones can be deducted from the old texts by the philological study of the clues that remained in the language of those and other texts from more or less the same historical period. This argument is exactly what Tolkien brought up in his essays—most notably, perhaps, in '*Beowulf*: the Monsters and the Critics'—and he too fought to expose the same conceit of scholars in its one specific aspect which Tolkien dubbed 'misology'. Clearly "a disqualifying defect or disease" for any student of "humane letters," misology in Tolkien's (1997b:225) opinion was the widespread fallacy of decrying language, the medium of literary expression, as unliterary and irrelevant for the study, understanding or enjoyment of literature. As "the product of ignorance and muddled thinking" (*ibid.* 234)—and thus basically "dullness and ignorance" (*ibid.* 225)—misology aggravated Tolkien especially when it was promoted "by some professional persons" as "a human norm, the measure of what is good" in the study of literature and its history (*ibid.* 225). Like Vico before him, Tolkien

believed that the *apartheid* of Language and Literature or History could produce only impoverished, if not downright distorted, understanding (*ibid.* 238).

Vico and Tolkien thus shared one major interest, or passion, which was
philology. Trained in law and rhetoric, Vico considered himself primarily a
philologist, member of a class of scholars which, in his own description, included "all the grammarians, historians, and critics who have contributed to
our awareness of peoples' languages and deeds, including both their domestic
customs and laws, and their foreign wars, peaces, pacts, travels, and trade"
(Vico 2001:79 [139]). Tolkien spoke about himself as "*pure* philologist"
thrilled by the sound of words and fascinated by history buried in them (*Letters*
264).[1] Defending philology as "confined to no period," "concerned with all
aspects of written or living speech at any time," and as "not incompatible with
the love of literature" (Tolkien 1997b:234), Tolkien, like Vico, saw its great
value for the recovery of the past and our understanding of it. "Philology," he
argued, "rescued the surviving documents from oblivion and ignorance, and
presented to lovers of poetry and history fragments of a noble past that without it would have remained forever dead and dark" (*ibid.* 235).

From Vico's and Tolkien's philological passion came the philological
methods informing their works and the works themselves,[2] for each author—

---

[1]   Tolkien's philology was, obviously, a more specialized discipline than that of
        Vico's which seems to have indefinable overspills into numerous other disciplines
        such as history, the then-unknown anthropology, law, political sciences and so on.
        Still, as Shippey's (2000:xi-xvii) description in *Author* makes clear, Tolkien was
        clearly of Vico's philological faction and his works were as deeply rooted in philol-
        ogical investigations as those of Vico's.

[2]   Tolkien admitted many times that all his stories "are and were so to speak an
        attempt to give a background or a world in which my expressions of linguistic
        taste could have a function" (*Letters* 214). In a famous letter to his son Christo-
        pher he said explicitly: "Nobody believes me when I say that my long book is an
        attempt to create a world in which a form of language agreeable to my personal
        aesthetic might seem real. But it is true" (*Letters* 264). Vico, on the other hand, as-
        serted that all previous scholars failed to see truth in myth because they looked for
        it *behind* rather than *in* its figurative language. Thus one objective of his *New Sci-
        ence* was to retrace and describe the development of the process of signification
        from the first poetic tropes—metaphor, metonymy, synecdoche, and irony—
        "which were in fact necessary modes of expression in all the early poetic nations,
        and originally had natural and proper meanings" (Vico 2001:162 [409]).

quite independently of his academic career—channeled his entire creative power into one huge project. For Vico the work of his life was the *New Science*—first edition in 1720, second in 1730 and third, final in a sense of posthumous, in 1744—in which he attempted to reconstruct the histories of ancient civilizations known to him and thereby explain the mechanisms on which human societies and institutions are based. For Tolkien the work of his life was the reconstruction of the history of Middle-earth—the legendarium spread out among several books from *The Hobbit* (1937), through *The Lord of the Rings* (1954-55), *The Silmarillion* (1977) and works unfinished at the time of his death—which was his attempt, through a philological investigation of invented languages, to make sense of the entire Western history by embedding it into a mythical past and uncovering the principles behind the rise and demise of civilizations, including the modern Western one. Significantly, both works were composed in the shadow of and as a rejoinder to what their authors saw as a major crisis of European civilization. Vico was reacting against rapid moral, political, intellectual and cultural deterioration of the period and saw himself as a champion of traditional civilization, right reason, and humanistic learning. Tolkien was responding to the traumatic events of his own times—world wars, the rise of totalitarian systems, economic instability and the collapse of culture—and, unlike most in his disenchanted and uprooted generation, spoke as a defender of "the traditions in which he was brought up," upholding certain "elementary decencies" which he saw as indispensable to the survival of the civilization as such (Shippey 2003:335). Both projects absorbed the bulk of their authors' mature lives. If, as Anthony Grafton comments in his 1997 'Introduction' to the *New Science*, already by 1710 Vico "was developing what he called a 'philosophical philology' and 'a new science'—a radically new approach to the understanding and study of human history" (Grafton 2001:xv), then the work took him at least thirty-four years. If 1930, when *The Hobbit* was begun, is taken as a breakthrough in the development of Tolkien's corpus, then the work took him at least forty-three years.[3]

---

[3]   If an earlier date is taken—for example 1913, when Tolkien began writing 'The Story of Kullervo' which was eventually to become the germ for one chapter of *The Silmarillion*—then, of course, this period is much longer (see Shippey 2000:227).

At this point it would be fitting to briefly present the two works if not for the fact that it is practically impossible; what exactly the *New Science* is cannot be answered with any more precision than what exactly Tolkien's multi-novel legendarium is. Both defy recapitulation. Both are odd, ahead of their time, unruly and, to a large extent, unfinished. However, whereas the development of Tolkien's ideas and the composition history of his mythology have been made available by Christopher Tolkien's twelve volume *History of Middle-earth* and have been excellently analyzed in studies such as those by Shippey, Flieger, and Curry, the story of Vico's is less known. A few embarrassing generalizations about the *New Science* may thus not be out of place.

Considered today as one of the founding works of modern human sciences, "as deep and original as the contemporary work that transformed the natural sciences, the *Principia* of Isaac Newton" (Grafton 2001:xi), the *New Science* consists of five 'Books', prefaced by an 'Introduction' and summed up by a 'Conclusion'. Grown to its final 1744 form over the period of twenty-four years and through three thoroughly revised editions, the treatise is a "massive decoding of ancient history, mythology, and law" (Grafton 2001:xi) interwoven with the presentation of "the main philosophical and theoretical presuppositions involved in this reconstruction" (Pompa 1990:1). Because Vico did not always distinguish the two objectives, the text is often obscure; because he spoke as a pre-modern, it is sometimes—as in the case of his fusion of history with gigantology or the biblical natural history—baffling or even naïve. As the title suggests, the work constitutes Vico's proposal of a new science of humanity intended to "reform both philosophy and philology by connecting the two enterprises" (Grafton 2001:xviii) through the integration of the rationalist, experimental-mathematical *scienza* with the poetic, experiential-historical *co-scienza* into a superior *scienza nuova* of human history (Mali 1992:3). The book has, by Vico's own account, seven principal aspects being, at the same time, a "rational civil theology of providence," "the philosophy of authority" (Vico 2001:150 [385, 386]), "the history of human ideas" (*ibid.* 152 [391]), "philosophical criticism" (*ibid.* 153 [392]), "the ideal eternal history through which the history of all nations must in time pass," "the system of the natural law of nations" (*ibid.* 154 [393, 394]), and finally the study of "the origins of universal history" (*ibid.* 156 [399]). As a summa of Vico's thought, it posits a number of theses, perhaps the most widely accepted among which are claims that understanding of history is contingent upon the researcher's "capacity to enter imaginatively into the mind of past peoples" (Pompa 1990:241), and that because human mentality develops through stages—poetic, heroic, human (Vico 2001:395 [915])—these stages also characterize the course of development of every civilization in human history. As I shall demonstrate further in this paper, Vico's book is also—and predominantly, according to Lilla and Mali—what the former calls in the title of his study "the making of an anti-modern" and the latter "the rehabilitation of myth."

Difficult to interpret in its own time, the *New Science* has continued to spawn a range of interpretations ever since it was discovered by the Romantics. His evolutionary approach to history made Vico a prophet of modern historicism praised by the French historian Jules Michelet already in the 1820s; his theory of stages through which societies must pass made Vico a forerunner of social sciences, embraced by scholars from Auguste Comte to Karl Marx; his insistence on the necessity to "feel one's way into the strange textures of past cultures" made Vico a harbinger of modern hermeneutics praised by such pioneers of the method as Karl Lamprecht and Aby Warburg (Grafton 2001:xiii); his discovery of "a true Homer" as oral literature and a work of not a single author but many rhapsodes and compilers, predated the same claims of Milman Parry and Moses Finley by almost two centuries; his emphasis on the role of imagination in the formation and functioning of human societies made Vico the prophet of Romantic intellectual-cum-spiritual awakening embraced by Samuel Taylor Coleridge, Ralph Waldo Emerson, and countless *Risorgimento* rebels (Lilla 1993:2); "Still later," says Grafton (2001:xiii), "Vico provided Benedetto Croce with the core of his attack on the positivism that the comparatist parts of the *New Science* had helped to nourish, and inspired James Joyce to devise the complex structure of *Finnegans Wake*." After Croce's groundbreaking 1911 monograph *La Filosofia di G.B. Vico* became available to European and American scholars, the study of Vico gained even more momentum. "Today," Lilla (1993:2-3) sums up, "Vico is the domesticated property of the university, where he is honored as an important forerunner of modern sociology, anthropology, psychology, and social history, and has been claimed by every imaginable school in these disciplines—by positivists, Marxists, phenomenologists, structuralists, post-structuralists, and many more."

This enthusiastic modern reception of Vico—as much as the growing appreciation of Tolkien—stand in sharp contrast to how many difficulties Vico and Tolkien had to face to get their works published, and how viciously these works were criticized when they appeared. Vico was unable to find a publisher and eventually had to self-finance all three editions—the first, for example, by selling a family ring (Grafton 2001:xv). Tolkien debated with the publishers for five years, 1949-1954, defending his original conception of *The Silmarillion* as an integral part of *The Lord of the Rings*, but had to compromise: doomed unsellable *The Silmarillion* did not appear during his lifetime, and *The Lord of the Rings*, to temperamental Tolkien's great anguish, was broken into three parts. Even then Tolkien was told that the books will lose money and was offered what, by a strange twist of fate, turned to be one of the best contracts in the publishing history of the world: fifty percent of any future income instead of the customary royalty.

When they finally appeared, *The Lord of the Rings* fared almost as badly as the *New Science*. "The whole style of the book seemed archaic and remote," says Grafton (2001:xii). "With its allegorical title page, pullulating erudition, and strange language (even some central and north Italians prefer to read Vico in English), the *New Science* was generally declared dead on arrival: out of scale, out of date, and doomed to be thoroughly out of mind." Because it was so different from anything attempted before, Mali (1992:10) suggests that Vico's work was simply "ignored rather than misunderstood or rejected by his contemporaries." Of a very similar nature were the accusations leveled against the 'lightning from a clear sky' that *The Lord of the Rings* was—its archaic language, juvenile style, hypertrophic redundancies in the plot, and overall lack of *raison d'être*. Reviewers such as Alfred Duggan (1954), Edmund Wilson and Mark Roberts (both 1956) or Phillip Tonybee (1961), and critics such as Colin Manlove (1975), Rosemary Jackson and Christine Brooke-Rose (both 1981) all used what Shippey (2000:305) calls "classic tactics of attempted marginalization,"[4] and what Attebery (1992:26) refers to as "negative evaluation, which is a matter of taste, masquerading as analysis."[5]

---

[4] See Shippey (2003:319-21) for a discussion of Brooke-Rose's criticism.

[5] For the reviews and a response to them see Shippey (2000:117, 224, 305-28) and Curry (2005). Manlove's criticism of Tolkien and fantasy in general can be found in his *Modern Fantasy. Five Studies* (Manlove 1975:152-206); Jackson's—in her *Fantasy. The Literature of Subversion* (Jackson 1981:1-10, 153-56); and Brooke-Rose's—in her *A Rhetoric of the Unreal. Studies in Narrative and Structure Espe-*

This ferocious resistance of the academia to both works was fuelled by many considerations, not the least important among which were the novelty of the *New Science* and *The Lord of the Rings* as well as their going, in an unprecedented manner, against the dominant literary tastes of their times: Vico's against the philosophical skepticism and devaluation of the humanities brought about by eighteenth-century rationalism; Tolkien's against equally stifling twentieth-century rationalism and the *Sonnenkinder* frivolous idea of literature (Shippey 2000:306ff; 2003:335-37). While Vico was ignored because he put his ideas into a scientific treatise rather than in fiction, and Tolkien was ignored because he used fantasy fiction instead of scholarly treatise (Shippey 2000:ix), in both cases the academic marginalization was belied by the widespread, enthusiastic reception of their works.[6] This popular and whole-hearted fascination with Vico and Tolkien is, in my opinion, the key to locating them within the same intellectual tradition—one to which modern people turn in search of intellectual sanity and spiritual nourishment. On this perspective, a consideration of the reasons behind Vico's and Tolkien's powerful appeal seems to me suggestive of so deep parallels between their works that all the correspondences I have given above pale into insignificance. Specifically, I believe that Vico and Tolkien—in their capacity of mythographers, historians, humanists, and philosophers—are so relevant to contem-

---

cially of the Fantastic (Brooke-Rose 1981:233-55). Attebery's assessment of Tolkien criticism can be found in his *Strategies of Fantasy* (Attebery 1992:18-42).

[6] The fact that the process took almost two hundred years for Vico and about forty for Tolkien is not evaluative and reflects how much faster ideas spread today than a century or two ago. The figures are, of course, not precise but approximate. Ignoring the many ideological fascinations that Vico incited among the Romantics, the beginnings of the real scholarly interest in his thought are usually located in the 1940s—when Croce's 1911, Amerio's 1947 and Paci's 1949 groundbreaking monographs on Vico began to exercise influence among European scholars. If this dating is accepted, the proper study of Vico begins about two centuries after the 1744 publication of the final *New Science* (see Pompa 2002:l-lvi, 'Bibliographical Note' to his translation of the first *New Science*). In Tolkien's case, three to four decades is the period that separates the 1965-68 rise of *The Lord of the Rings* to mass popularity from the emergence of works such as, for example, Curry's 1997 *Defending Middle Earth*, Shippey's 2000 *J.R.R. Tolkien. Author of the Century*, his 2003 (first edition 1982) *The Road to Middle-earth*, and Flieger's 2005 *Interrupted Music* all of which testify to the growing scholarly recognition of Tolkien's legacy.

porary readers because, in their own unique ways, they offered a viable humanist philosophical alternative to the deterministic, hegemonic, and oppressive modernity and because they affirmed the value of myth and poetic understanding in the construction of human individuals and societies.

Vico and Tolkien as Anti-Moderns

While one of the first to point out the ways in which Vico anticipated the Counter-Enlightenment was a historian of ideas, Isaiah Berlin, in his 1976 *Vico and Herder*, my primary reference in discussing Vico's anti-modernism is Mark Lilla's excellent 1993 *G.B. Vico: The Making of the Anti-Modern* which discusses all of Vico's important writings rather than just the *New Science* alone. Following Berlin, Lilla claims that Vico was the first thinker who realized that the Enlightenment project—headed by such French philosophers as Descartes, Voltaire, Diderot or Holbach and presented as liberating humans from all kinds of ignorance—will, if followed, make people slaves of "impious ambitions," "insane rationalism," and their "untamed tongue and spirit" (Lilla 1993:52). Vico sensed that the Enlightenment thinkers were, as Lilla (*ibid.* 52) puts it, "radical rationalists who dogmatically held all truths about nature and man to be universal, objective, timeless, and transparent to reason." Even before he wrote the *New Science* Vico understood that "[a]s a movement [Enlightenment philosophers] propounded essentially ahistorical philosophical and political doctrines" that are and will, sooner or later, be revealed as "utopian, inflexible, deterministic, arrogant, unfeeling, homogenizing, intolerant." In his opposition to these, Vico was a harbinger of the important current of modern thought called the Counter-Enlightenment. Because, as Lilla and Berlin assert, the debate between the proponents of Enlightenment and Counter-Enlightenment "has never been settled" and constitutes "the intellectual landscape of our own age," Vico's philosophy still stands out as a relevant, if somewhat disorderly, exposition of anti-modern attitude (Lilla 1993:4). In the last century it has also been taken as giving intellectual form to what Lilla (*ibid.* 5-6) calls "an inchoate dissatisfaction with modern life" brought about by the awareness that the Enlightenment project has, among other things, sanctioned "defacing nature in the name of scientific and technological progress, [...] destroying traditional communities in the name of cosmopolitanism and individualism, and [...] encouraging political extremism in the name of social engineering." According to Berlin, Vico is especially relevant in his seven crucial, anti-Enlightenment notions, which allow seeing the *New Science* as "the first significant effort to derive a modern philosophy of knowledge free from rationalism" (Lilla 1993:4). These notions, which Vico offered as alternatives to Enlightenment dogma, are claims

> that human nature is changeable, and that humans themselves contribute to this change; that man only knows what he creates; that therefore the human sciences are distinct from and superior to the natural sciences; that cultures are wholes; that cultures are created essentially through self-expression; that art is a major form of such expression; and that we may come to understand the expressions of other cultures, in the present or past, through the exercise of reconstructive imagination.
> (Berlin quoted in Lilla 1993:4)

The alternative, anti-modern philosophy that Vico constructed rests on his questioning of the Enlightenment assumptions that "the natural light of reason shines equally in all human beings" (Lilla 1993:5) and that humans command themselves at will and "mold their own natures freely in history by choosing their own ends" (*ibid.* 11). The first assumption Vico countered by arguing that the presumed universality of reason ignored feeling, imagination, "the traditional and prejudicial background of all human understanding" (*ibid.* 5) and thus envisioned humans as automatons whose all activities are "rationalizable along Carthesian lines" (*ibid.* 51-52). The second assumption he challenged on theological-metaphysical grounds, arguing that human beings are fallen—imperfect, vulnerable to irrational impulses, and "constitutionally incapable of acquiring full knowledge of nature" (*ibid.* 16)—so that their freedom of thought and action is circumscribed by God's providence which directs the course of creation "through the power of an irrational force (*conatus*) in individuals and irrational common senses (religion, marriage, property) in societies" (*ibid.* 11). Revealing those common senses as "the foundations of every society [...] which deserve support" (*ibid.* 10), and the providential *conatus* as a theological principle which draws individuals and societies "out of barbarism and into reason and virtue" (*ibid.* 16),[7] Vico wanted to demonstrate

---

[7]   Lilla deals extensively with *conatus* and describes it in a number of ways in which it functions in Vico's philosophy, for example as "the property of human mind

that order and authority are more conducive to human fulfillment than the so-
called 'freedom' extolled in the political and social theories of the Enlightenment, which celebrated materialism, individualism and atheism—all three
suicidal, in the long run, to human individuals and societies. His fundamental
motivation being "to defend pre-rational man and traditional society against
the acids of modernity, and especially modern thought" (*ibid.* 9), Vico thus
proposed the theory of "universal right"[8] which described God's constant presence in the human realm as not only the origin of all right but also as a power
which—indirectly and through imperfect human institutions—sees to the
development of universal right in individuals, societies, and the course of history as such. One facet of this theory, which Vico saw as describing "ideal
eternal history," was the idea of the "cycle" of universal right adumbrated in a
doctrine of *corso-ricorso*—a cyclical process of rise and fall of societies out of
"barbarism of the senses" and back into it through "barbarism of reflection"
(Vico 2001:488 [1106]).[9] Although Vico never resolved difficulties inherent in
this concept—related, specifically, to its implied historical determinism and
"pessimistic providentialism" (Lilla 1993:217)—so that it is impossible to say
whether he intended this doctrine to be taken as a factual description of the
historical process or just as a prophetic warning, drawn on the example of
Rome, to modern Europe, in Lilla's opinion the second interpretation is more
consistent with Vico's other writings (*ibid.* 218) and Vico does seem to hope
that "his *corso-ricorso* doctrine will assist rather than hinder prudent political
action against modern decadence" (*ibid.* 227).

---

that induces men to pursue virtue naturally" (Lilla 1993:75). See also Lilla
(1993:98ff.).

[8]   This attempt to lay out a universal explanation of "human virtue, natural right,
the nature of regimes, political change, and the roots of law" (Lilla 1993:71-2)
was, according to Lilla, one of Vico's most ambitious ways of translating metaphysics into political science. In its most general, the theory of universal right
posits that 1) although fallen, humans are not totally abandoned by God and
know natural right by those faculties of their minds which are animated through
conatus toward virtue and truth; that 2) these virtues are "eternal ideas that all men
[...] can share through the mind"; and that 3) "the political correlate of virtue in
the individual" is called justice and, when applied to society, becomes right—a
natural extension of human virtues to the social sphere (Lilla 1993:77).

[9]   For a discussion of this concept see Lilla (1993:204-24).

The parallels between Vico's anti-modernism as outlined in this brief summary and Tolkien's anti-modernism in his legendarium, and particularly in *The Lord of the Rings*, are extensive on the general level and grow even more so if Vico's and Tolkien's specific ideas are collated. Like Vico, Tolkien was a conservative who defended the traditionalist outlook against the modern one and whose work, like Vico's, has attracted both rebellious youths who saw it as envisioning the dawn of an era of imagination and nostalgic adults who saw it as a yearning for the world irretrievably lost. Tolkien's anti-industrialism and his defense of traditional ways of living—both as inscribed in the fantasy and myth traditions he was blending in his work and as his personal reaction to the changes that he saw technology was bringing into people's lives and English countryside—have been noted in innumerable studies. Negative evaluators of traditionalism, such as Rosemary Jackson in her *Fantasy: The Literature of Subversion*, accused Tolkien of escapism, naïveté, and chauvinism. Like Jackson (1981:155) those critics saw his books as "conservative vehicles for social and instinctual repression" which "reinforce a blind faith in 'eternal' moral values, really those of an outworn liberal humanism." Scholars sympathetic of Tolkien's medievalism and traditionalist outlook, such as Patrick Curry in his *Defending Middle-Earth*, contended, however, that the setting and values Tolkien chose give his stories internal consistency and constitute a significant part of their appeal. Tolkien is a traditionalist consciously and for a reason, Curry (1998:23) argues, for traditionalism is his way of questioning "the value of the kind of deranged, totalizing rationality" that the Enlightenment engendered. It is also Tolkien's way of presenting

> the values whose jeopardy we most now feel: relationships with each other, and nature, and (for want of a better word) the spirit, which had not been stripped of personal integrity and responsibility and decanted into a soulless calculus of profit-and-loss; and practical-ethical wisdom which no amount of economic or technological 'progress' will ever be able to replace.
> (Curry 1998:23-4)

If Tolkien can thus be seen as inviting the reader to experience, at least in imagination, "a compelling and remarkably complete pre-modern world" (Curry 1998:23)—which is a kind of humanist alternative to the contemporary world dominated by "the combination of modern science, a global capitalist economy, and the political power of the nation-state" (Curry 1998:22)—

he is not unlike Vico whose aim in the *New Science* was to defend traditional society against dehumanizing, totalitarian claims of modernity.

In this sense, and like Vico's, Tolkien's work has been revealed as "a vehicle for philosophical and metaphysical speculation" on the major problems of the contemporary world—most of them products of the scientific, moral, political, and aesthetic doctrines of the Enlightenment—which "speaks to and for the anxieties" of contemporary readers (Flieger 2002:viii). What anxieties those are has been noted in many studies: for Shippey Tolkien belongs in a group of "traumatized authors" who voiced, in fantasy, "the most pressing and most immediately relevant issues of the whole monstrous twentieth century—questions of industrialized warfare, the origin of evil, the nature of humanity" (Shippey 2003:xvii). On this perspective *The Lord of the Rings* is "a war-book, also a post-war book, framed by and responding to the crisis of Western civilization, 1914-1945, (and beyond)" (Shippey 2003:329). For Curry Tolkien's books speak to a disenchantment of the world brought about by modernity's "war against mystery" (Bauman quoted in Curry 1998:23). They nourish "an emotionally empowering nostalgia" for decentralization, democracy, community, "bioregionalism," "love of, and feeling for, place," genuine "environmentalism," and "ethics rooted [...] in spiritual values" (Curry 1998:27, 28)—in other words for qualities which are now, sixty years after Tolkien, spoken of as crucial components of the only viable alternative to global capitalism which Fritjof Capra in his 2002 *The Hidden Connections: A Science for Sustainable Living* calls "ecological sustainability" (xvii). For Flieger (2002:26), finally, Tolkien's work "is more than mere reaction" to modernity whose many developments are ugly and destructive in their effects, and "more than nostalgia" for pre-industrial past; it is rather his particular expression of an essentially spiritual longing for prelapsarian life—"humankind's longing for its own past, the childhood before the Fall" (*ibid.* 27).

It is not irrelevant that the concept of the fall plays a crucial role in Vico's and Tolkien's works. Both firmly believed that human beings are fallen and should recognize certain natural limitations of their powers and aspirations. Whenever they succumb to the hubris of pride, as Vico's Romans do with their "barbarism of reflection"—the abandonment of ancient ways in the name of reason which lures with freedom and leads into a void, anarchy or chaos because it cuts people off from traditional order and authority—as Tolkien's Elves do in *The Silmarillion* through Fëanor's possessiveness and its disastrous consequences as delineated by Tolkien himself in one of his letters (*Letters* 148)—they lose and further degeneration follows.[10] Tolkien's conception of the ages of the world, as explored, among others in Charles Huttar's 1992 'Tolkien, Epic Traditions, and Golden Age Myths,' is thus neither Hesiodic (ahistorical), nor Judeo-Christian (historical), but rather mythopoeic, as is Vico's doctrine of *corso-ricorso*, albeit Tolkien's scheme is one of constant degeneration which "has no place outright for [...] a vision" of significant betterment (Huttar 1992:104). Both Vico and Tolkien—one explicitly, the other implicitly—constructed a quasi-historical perspective in which modern Europe may well be seen, in Vicean terms, as passing through a *ricorso* of Roman decadence and decline, and in Tolkienian terms, as shored against the ruins of much older and grander civilizations (*Letters* 283). In both cases, the decadence, cyclical or linear, is directly tied to the excesses of individual liberty and to the withering of tradition. The result is, as Vico and Tolkien asserted, the progressing atomization of society accompanied by the ruthless elimination—in the name of progress—of local forms of government, economy and culture which are then replaced with "the brutal universalism and centralized efficiency" such as the one represented by the totalitarian Mordor (Curry 1998:27). Vico's and Tolkien's anti-modern stance manifests, however, not only their resistance to the philosophy of modernity which impels changes they deem destructive; it is also glaring in their affirmation of the value of myth and poetic understanding.[11]

---

[10]   In that same letter Tolkien explains the fall of the Elves and says that the first fall of men happens a long time before men come on stage (*Letters* 147).

[11]   Tolkien's anti-modern stance has given rise to various interpretations, with critics such as Curry and Attebery correctly identifying elements in Tolkien's work that overlap with those that characterize a postmodern work (Curry 1998:20-26; Attebery 1992:36-42). While Curry leaves the issue open, Attebery asserts that Tolkien cannot be called a postmodernist writer. I believe this is so for in terms of attitude and the solutions proposed, Tolkien's response to modernity is sharply different from that offered by postmodernists.

Vico and Tolkien as the Revivers of Myth

The claim that "in his *New Science* Vico sought, and ultimately achieved, a *Rehabilitation of Myth*" (2) comes from a compelling 1992 study under the same title by Joseph Mali, a monograph that I shall extensively draw on in this section. Mali's thesis is that the crucial notion that undergirds Vico's work is his definition of myth as "true narration (*vera narratio*)" and that by this definition "Vico conceived not only a new theory of classical mythology, but a *New Science* of humanity." At a time when rationalistic Enlightenment philosophers were discrediting myths as irrational superstitions—childish, trite, and untrue—and arguing that humanity would be much better off if myths were eradicated, Vico took mythology "to be *true* in itself" (Mali 1992:3): as "*vera narratio*, true narration" (Vico 2001:159 [403]). This was, says Mali (1992:3-4),

> the definitive conclusion of his inquiries into the origins of 'the history of human ideas,' in which he found out that the archaic and anonymous *mythologein*, the discourse of tradition which consists in repeating what they say, is the main mode of knowledge in which men have actually constituted their civil world (*mondo civile*). [...] He regarded the archaic myths as the 'true narrations' of this history because he saw that in our (and any other) civilization the fictions of mythology illuminate the 'real world' by constituting or 'prefiguring' all its human actions and institutions: unlike natural occurrences which display law-like, repetitive regularities which are unknowable to us because they are totally alien to our form of life, human occurrences throughout history display forms of action which are knowable to us insofar as we can recognize in them the coherent narrative patterns of the mythical stories with their well-made characters and plots. His comparative study of classical and primitive myths had led him to believe that these had formed a 'mental language common to the nations' (*una lingua mentale comune a tutte le nazioni*), that is, a symbolic language composed of concrete figures or acts which initially served as vehicles for more abstract and general concepts not yet fully conceived. Vico thought that these archaic images, which he called 'poetic characters,' were still embedded in a variety of modern cultural performances—as in linguistic common-places, religious beliefs, social customs, or political rites and institutions.

If this sounds like prefiguring Jung's collective unconscious; Wittgenstein's horizon of language as the horizon of cognition; Potebnja's and Cassirer's claims about myth as a vehicle of poetic language; Lang's and Taylor's theory of survivals of history in myth; Durkheim's idea of collective representations; or Lévy-Bruhl's notion of primitive rationality—it is, indeed, a prefiguring of all those ideas. Eleazar Meletinsky is very much correct when he says in his 1998 *The Poetics of Myth* that "Vico's philosophy of myth [...] contains in embryo [...] almost all of the main tendencies of later mythological studies, varied and contradictory as they sometimes may be" (Meletinsky 2000:7). As is the fate of geniuses who are ahead of their time, Vico was aware of the importance of his shattering realization that the ancients "spoke by means of *poetic symbols*" which were "*imaginative general categories*, or archetypes" (Vico 2001:24 [34]) and constitute the essence of myths. In fact, he stated explicitly that

> [t]his discovery provides the master-key of my New Science, but making it has cost me nearly an entire scholarly career spent in tireless researches. For to our more civilized natures, the poetic nature of the first people is utterly impossible to imagine, and can be understood only with the greatest effort. (Vico 2001:24 [34])

The effort Vico refers to is, in Mali's (1992:4) opinion, the linguistic turn: the appreciation that "the world in which men live is a world of institutions based on language" and, consequently, that the study of language as envisioned by philology should be elevated "to a universal method of understanding human beings in past or foreign cultures through [the study of] their collective symbolic figures and myths." Vico's idea that the poetic symbols of myths are alive in language, and that through language they still influence human cognition— as he says, "[p]oetic speech, which we have studied as a product of poetic logic, continued to run its course well into the historical period" (Vico 2001:163 [412])—enabled him, Mali (1992:5) continues, to "decipher the essentially mythopoeic constitution of humanity" and to claim that "practically all human creations (*cose umane*) can, and indeed must, be traced back and reappraised according to their mythical components" (*ibid.* 6). With its philological method and poetic style, the *New Science* itself thus consists, Mali says, "in the activity of *mythopoesis* itself" (*ibid.* 9). Not an attempt at creating a new myth, it is rather aimed at clarifying "the work of myth in our minds and cultures" (*ibid.* 10). Like Eliade who reiterated similar claims in his conception of *homo*

religious two centuries later, Vico believed that "modern man, being the in-
heritor of former modes of thought, speech, and behaviour, still lives by these
examples" (*ibid.* 11). In Mali's opinion Vico is thus, in an elementary sense, a
revisionist. Opposed to "the rational-liberal [and progressivist] theories of humankind and society," he assumed that "human affairs are intricate and un-
certain because they are always liable to be disrupted by chance, ignorance and
error of egotistical desires, so that what happens in history is often unforeseen
and undesired." More importantly for his rehabilitation of myth, Vico decon-
structed the Enlightenment theories of "mind, man, and society" by arguing
that human beings are

> essentially traditional, living in immemorial and largely impersonal
> structures of meaning, of which they are only dimly aware, and
> which they cannot, nor should, change by radical intellectual or
> political acts. Believing that behind all the forms of modern ration-
> alism there lurk past and continuous traditions of belief, he exposes
> in them the poetic images and habitual practices which resist pro-
> gressive, or revolutionary, categories. (Mali 1992:14)

Tolkien would have no doubts about any of that. As a philologist he knew that
humans are traditional beings, in the least by virtue of their language which
consists largely of semantic deposits of the former modes of knowing, some of
which existed before, and still exist outside, later rational conceptualizations of
reality. In fact, like Owen Barfield whose theory was encapsulated in his 1928
Poetic Diction, Tolkien believed that philology reveals mythology as "closely
associated with the very origin of speech and literature" (Carpenter 1997:41).
Thoroughly steeped in mythic traditions of Northern Europe Tolkien held, as
he admits in one letter, "that legends and myths are largely made of 'truth' and
indeed present aspects of it that can only be received in this mode" (*Letters*
147). When challenged by the then-theist-but-not-Christian C. S. Lewis that
myths are "lies breathed through silver" Tolkien built such a passionate argument against the depreciation of myth that it helped to convert Lewis to
Christianity (Carpenter 1997:43-45) whereas Tolkien, in order to cool off, had
to write his famous poem *Mythopoeia* in which he declared himself as "Philo-
mythus," the lover of myth (Christopher Tolkien, 'Preface' v). The essence of
the poem is what lies at the bottom of Tolkien's entire corpus: 1) humans live
within and are circumscribed by a teleological historical process—"At bidding
of a Will, to which we bend // (and must), but only dimly apprehend, great

processes march on [...]" (Mythopoeia 85); 2) humans are co-creators of the world through their language—"trees are not 'trees' until so named and seen" (Mythopoeia 86) and "We make still by the law in which we're made" (*ibid.* 87); and 3) the essence of human language is myth, the creation of which is much less a recording of the past than a foreshadowing of the future—"a rumour of a harbour guessed by faith" so that "Blessed are the legend-makers with their rhyme // of things not found within recorded time" (*ibid.* 88).

One important difference between Vico and Tolkien is that whereas Vico aimed to create the science of mythology—claiming that "the first science we must study is mythology, meaning and interpretation of myths," by which "we shall discover the beginnings of the sciences as well as of the nations" (Vico 2001:44 [51])—Tolkien aspired to create a new mythology. As he admitted in a famous letter:

> I was from early days grieved by the poverty of my own beloved country: it had no stories of its own (bound up with its tongue and soil), not of the quality that I sought, and found (as an ingredient) in legends of other lands. [...] I had a mind to make a body of more or less connected legend, ranging from the large and cosmogonic, to the level of romantic fairy-story—the larger founded on the lesser in contact with the earth, the lesser drawing splendour from the vast backcloths—which I could dedicate simply to: to England; to my country. It should possess the tone and quality that I desired, somewhat cool and clear, be redolent of our 'air' (the clime and soil of the North West, meaning Britain and the hither parts of Europe: not Italy or the Aegean, still less the East), and, while possessing (if I could achieve it) the fair elusive beauty that some call Celtic (though it is rarely found in genuine ancient Celtic things), it should be 'high', purged of the gross, and fit for the more adult mind of a land long now steeped in poetry. I would draw some of the great tales in fullness, and leave many only placed in the scheme, and sketched. The cycles should be linked to a majestic whole, and yet leave scope for other minds and hands, wielding paint and music and drama. (*Letters* 144-45)

The above is a good description of what the 'Silmarillion' actually is. Although Tolkien prefaces, interrupts and concludes this confession with a number of defensive remarks—"here I hope I shall not sound absurd," "Do not laugh!"—by which he was trying to assure Milton Waldman of the publisher Collins that the enterprise was, obviously, absurd, impossible, a folly of Tolkien's youth, and an issue that should not be taken against him for his "crest has long since fallen" (*Letters* 144), recent studies demonstrate that Tolkien did exactly what he had described here. Joseph Pearce's *Tolkien: Man and Myth* (1998) and Patrick Curry's *Defending Middle-Earth: Tolkien, Myth and Modernity* (first published 1997), Shippey's 2003 (first edition 1982) *The Road to Middle-Earth: How J.R.R. Tolkien Created a New Mythology* and Flieger's 2005 *Interrupted Music: The Making of Tolkien's Mythology* are all extensive explorations of why Tolkien thought that without its own mythology a culture is impoverished, what he meant by 'mythology for England,' to what extent he succeeded in the attempt, and how he was able to do so.

Inasmuch as those arguments, especially as profound as Shippey's and Flieger's, need not and, quite simply, cannot be summarized here, indisputably the most important aspect which allows seeing Vico and Tolkien as expositors and forerunners of the same tradition of the rehabilitation of myth is their insistence that understanding of the past—of history and of how people 'co-create' history in their minds—is indispensable for anyone who wishes to grasp the present or conceive of the future, especially those of the Western civilization.[12] In this, besides identifying strengths and virtues of the Christian, Western culture which, albeit deteriorated, may be revived for a viable future, Vico and Tolkien intuited how tightly myth is interwoven with history.[13] Most importantly they asserted that humans are mythopoeic beings who construct their identities and social institutions on mythic narratives which constitute their culture's collective historical memory and dream of themselves. If Vico's was a theory of history, Tolkien's was an unintended yet practical application of it, not less real for his specific history being imagined. Tolkien admitted in the 'Foreword' to *The Lord of the Rings* that he cordially disliked allegory and preferred to it "history, true or feigned, with its varied applicability to the

---

[12]   Compare, for example, Robert Conquest's argument in his 2000 *Reflections on a Ravaged Century* according to which "ignorance of history is one of the most negative attributes of modern man" (Conquest 2001:3). The result, Conquest says, is that in the twentieth-century humanity has been savaged and trampled by rogue ideologies (*ibid.* xi).

[13]   This point has recently been compellingly argued by Bruce Lincoln in his 1989 *Discourse and the Construction of Society: Comparative Studies of Myth, Ritual, and Classification* (see especially Lincoln 1992:21-26).

thought and experience of readers" (*LotR* xxiv). It does not take much to realize that the whole 'Silmarillion' is, in fact, an extended feigning-cum-rediscovering of history so understood.[14] Tolkien's idea of exploring what lies behind the fragmented surviving traditions of England, its place names, habits, customs, and 'national character' in general, was not unlike Vico's too.[15]

---

[14]
Tolkien is known to have claimed that the stories "arose in [his] mind as 'given' things" and that he always had "the sense of recording of what was already 'there,' somewhere: not 'inventing'" (*Letters* 145). A number of his other comments suggest that he did not consider his 'history' all that improbable and that, moreover, only complemented with his version of pre-history did the history of Western Europeans make sense. For Vico, who followed exactly the same formula of decoding the past to understand his contemporary Europe, the pre-history encompassed what he knew or inferred about the civilizations of the Jews, Chaldeans, Scytians, Phoenicians, Egyptians, Greeks, and Romans. One difference between Vico's and Tolkien's projects, and the natural consequence of the choice of their source material, is that whereas Vico was referring to extant historical sources, Tolkien had to invent them, besides constructing a whole history of how, through translations, linguistic inheritance and serendipity the ancient records of earlier eras survived into the twentieth century. This elaborate literary conceit of Tolkien's is explored in detail in Flieger (2005:61ff.), and in Shippey (2000:226ff.) which associates it with Tolkien's notion of literary depth as "the sense of age, of antiquity with yet greater antiquity behind it," even if imagined, which informs a literary work (*ibid.* 236). The very extent of the conceit suggests how serious Tolkien was about making 'his story' a 'history'.

[15]
Like Tolkien later and somewhat implicitly, Vico asserted that to understand how the ancients established their world is not just irrelevant curiosity but is necessary for us to understand *our* world. Since we are, for him, the inheritors of the archaic patterns of knowing and making things and since the myths which were used by the ancients to build their social world still persist in our societies and in our minds, it is essential to grasp what these myths mean. "My Science," says Vico (2001:131 [356-57]), "attempts to sift truth from falsehood in whatever popular tradition has preserved for many centuries. For as Axiom 16 states, popular traditions have been preserved for so many years by entire peoples because they have a basis in truth. The great fragments of antiquity were previously useless to science because they were squalid, mutilated, and dispersed. But once they have been cleaned, restored, and set in their proper place, they will shed new life on the past." Tolkien does exactly that both in his criticism—in '*Beowulf:* The Monsters and the Critics', for example, he defends old ways of thinking and conceptualizing experience through a poetic form distinctly different yet not less legitimate than modern ones—and in his 'fiction'.

The parallels between Vico's and Tolkien's anti-modernisms and between their reassessment of the role of myth in the life of human individuals and societies are, obviously, deeper and more intricate than what I was able to outline above. Even this brief presentation, however, suggests that the two spoke for the same tradition of Christian-humanist alternative to the reductionist and to-talizing Enlightenment, whose program has been severely, and rightly, criticized by post-modernists. Vico and Tolkien are, however, not of Lyotard's camp. Although they speak against the same excesses that post-modernists contest, they represent an older, quieter and different tradition; one that sees myth as a vehicle for truth and human beings as seeking this truth through, primarily, the activity of mythopoeia: incessant recreation and actualization of myth in their lives. On this perspective, even if he was not familiar with how the Italian philologist Giovanni Battista Vico laid the path to poetic know-ledge for humanities, the English philologist John Ronald Reuel Tolkien can be seen as making the same path available to a genre which was destined to become the most dynamically evolving literary category in the second part of the twentieth century. The deepening interest in Vico and the growing appreciation of Tolkien suggest that the path they opened is no longer narrow or overgrown but wide and beaten by innumerable feet. And every pilgrim on this road to understanding how deeply mythopoeic humans are, may well be thankful to Vico for resuscitating a nearly forgotten mode of knowledge, and to Tolkien for re-introducing the taste for this mode of knowledge into the literary world.

MAREK OZIEWICZ is Assistant Professor of Literature and Director of the Center for Children's and Young Adult Fiction at the Institute of English Studies, University of Wroclaw, Poland. He has taught courses on literature and mythopoeia since 1997, with a break in 2005 to research American fantasy on a Fulbright fellowship. He is the author of the first Polish language monograph on C.S. Lewis: *The Magical Spell of Narnia: Poetics and Philosophy in C.S. Lewis' the Chronicles of Narnia* (Universitas, 2005) and co-editor of *Towards or Back to Human Values: Spiritual and Moral Dimensions of Contemporary Fantasy* (Cambridge Scholars Press, 2006). His most recent book is *One Earth, One People: The Mythopoeic Fantasy Series of Ursula Le Guin, Lloyd Alexander, Madeleine L'Engle and Orson Scott Card* (McFarland, 2008).

References

Abbreviations used:

Letters: see Carpenter 2000

LotR: see Tolkien 2004

Mythopoeia: see Tolkien 2001

Attebery, Brian, 1992, *Strategies of Fantasy*, Bloomington, IN: Indiana University Press.

Brooke-Rose, Christine, 1981, *A Rhetoric of the Unreal: Studies in Narrative and Structure, especially of the Fantastic*, Cambridge: Cambridge University Press.

Capra, Fritjof, 2004, *The Hidden Connections: A Science for Sustainable Living*, New York: Anchor Books.

Carpenter, Humphrey, 1997, *The Inklings. C.S. Lewis, J.R.R. Tolkien, Charles Williams and Their Friends*, London: HarperCollins.

--- (with the assistance of Christopher Tolkien) (ed.), 2000, *The Letters of J.R.R. Tolkien*, (first published 1981), Boston: Houghton Mifflin.

Conquest, Robert, 2001, *Reflections on a Ravaged Century*, New York: W.W. Norton.

Curry, Patrick, 1998, *Defending Middle-Earth. Tolkien: Myth and Modernity*, (first edition 1997), London: HarperCollins.

---, 2005, 'Tolkien and his Critics: A Critique', in Thomas Honegger (ed.), 2005, *Root and Branch. Approaches towards Understanding Tolkien*, (first edition 1999), Zurich and Berne: Walking Tree Publishers, 75-146.

Flieger, Verlyn, 2002, *Splintered Light. Logos and Language in Tolkien's World*, Kent, OH: The Kent State University Press.

---, 2005, *Interrupted Music. The Making of Tolkien's Mythology*, Kent, OH: The Kent State University Press.

Grafton, Anthony, 2001, 'Introduction', in Giambattista Vico, *New Science*, (translated by David Marsh), London: Penguin Books, xi-xxxiii.

Huttar, Charles A., 1992, 'Tolkien, Epic Traditions, and Golden Age Myths', in Cath Filmer (ed.), 1992, *Twentieth-Century Fantasists: Essays on Culture, Society and Belief in Twentieth-Century Mythopoeic Literature*, New York: St. Martin's Press, 92-107.

Jackson, Rosemary, 1981, *Fantasy: The Literature of Subversion*, London and New York: Methuen.

Lilla, Mark, 1993, *G.B. Vico. The Making of the Anti-Modern*, Cambridge, Mass: Harvard University Press.

Lincoln, Bruce, 1992, *Discourse and the Construction of Society: Comparative Studies of Myth, Ritual, and Classification*, New York: Oxford University Press.

Mali, Joseph, 1992, *The Rehabilitation of Myth. Vico's New Science*, Cambridge: Cambridge University Press.

Manlove, Colin, 1975, *Modern Fantasy: Five Studies*, New York: Cambridge University Press.

Meletinsky, Eleazar M., 2000, *The Poetics of Myth*, (first edition 1998), New York: Garland.

Pompa, Leon, 1990, *Vico. A Study of the New Science*, Cambridge: Cambridge University Press.

---, 2002, *Vico. The First New Science*, Cambridge: Cambridge University Press.

Shippey, Tom, 2000, *J.R.R. Tolkien. Author of the Century*, New York: Houghton Mifflin.

---, 2003, *The Road to Middle-earth: How J.R.R. Tolkien Created a New Mythology*, (third edition, first edition 1982), New York: Houghton Mifflin.

Tolkien, Christopher, 2001, 'Preface', in *Tree and Leaf*, London: HarperCollins, 2001, v-ix.

Tolkien, John Ronald Reuel, 1997a, '*Beowulf:* The Monsters and the Critics', in *The Monsters and the Critics and Other Essays*, (edited by Christopher Tolkien), London: HarperCollins, 5-48.

---, 1997b, 'Valedictory Address to the University of Oxford', in *The Monsters and the Critics and Other Essays*, (edited by Christopher Tolkien), London: HarperCollins, 224-40.

---, 2001, 'Mythopoeia', in *Tree and Leaf*, (edited by Christopher Tolkien), London: HarperCollins, 85-90.

---, 2004, *The Lord of the Rings*, (originally published 1954-55; one-volume 50th anniversary edition), Boston: Houghton Mifflin.

Vico, Gianbattista, 2001, *New Science*, (translated by David Marsh), London: Penguin Books.

Frodo or Zarathustra:
Beyond Nihilism in Tolkien and Nietzsche

PETER M. CANDLER, JR.

He who wants to partake of all good things must know how to be small at times.[1]

Summary

This paper explores the intricate relationships between philology, creativity, creation, myths, the return to the past and the recurrence of things as discussed by Nietzsche and Tolkien.

I. The Origins of an Allusion

There seems to be no evidence that J.R.R. Tolkien ever read Friedrich Nietzsche; in fact, as commentators are often somewhat pleased to point out (playing upon a kind of myth which Tolkien himself played no small part in constructing),[2] it seems that Tolkien read very little from his own century, except for the works of his fellow convivators in the 'Eagle and Child'. It is perhaps no accident that Tolkien's reading seemed to comport with his drinking. One might even argue that there's something basically very religious about beer, and that this explains in part why the works of Tolkien bear a certain theologicity born of friendships nurtured in the public-house. Nietzsche, by contrast, was a notorious teetotaler who said that "coffee spreads darkness," an ascetic troglodyte ever in search of pure air, an anti-Christ who once be-

---

[1] Nietzsche in 'The Wanderer and His Shadow' (Nietzsche 1986, §51, 323).

[2] See the beginning of Tolkien's essay '*Beowulf*: The Monsters and the Critics' (BMC) as well as Letter 294, to Charlotte and Denis Plimmer, 8 February 1967, (*Letters* 377): "I seldom find any modern books that hold my attention." See also Shippey (2003:6).

moaned "how much beer there is in the German intellect!"[3] It is hard to imagine, however, that the name of the Hermit of Sils Maria was never invoked during those sessions at the 'Eagle and Child' in St. Giles' Street.

What, if any, manner of direct experience Tolkien had with Nietzsche, is impossible to say. It is difficult to believe, however, that his influence was not felt in some indirect way. In 1913, just two years after the last of Nietzsche's untranslated works, *Ecce Homo*, made its appearance in English, Charles Sareola wrote that "A searching estimate of Nietzsche in English still remains to be written. And there is only one man that could write it, and that man is Gilbert K. Chesterton."[4] Chesterton never wrote such a "searching estimate," but he did write about Nietzsche, largely negatively, if somewhat superficially, already in *Heretics*, published in 1905. One might be justified in inferring then a kind of Chesterton-mediated Nietzsche as influencing Tolkien, but as it stands this must remain a conjecture, however likely.

Nevertheless, the interest of this paper is not the direct or indirect influence of Friedrich Nietzsche upon the work of J.R.R. Tolkien, much less on the question of whether *The Lord of the Rings* can be seen as in any way influenced by Nietzschean themes. Rather am I interested in what must remain a kind of allusive affinity between the two thinkers. After all, they are both, by profession and by their own admission, philologists, and both are in some way or another suspicious of the mechanization of European culture. Nonetheless, both Tolkien and Nietzsche shared a problematic, if not caustic, relationship to modernity as a philosophical-cultural problem. In what sense, then, does their shared profession of philology inform their respective 'responses' or 'critiques' of modernity? Moreover, in what sense does philology, for each, offer a

---

[3] Nietzsche, 'What the Germans Lack' (Nietzsche 1990:72). Regarding beverages of a different cask, I am entirely in sympathy with David Hart's (2003:108-9) suggestion that "a theological answer to Nietzsche could be developed entirely in terms of the typology of wine." There may be more than just bombast to Nietzsche's claim that "To believe that wine *exhilarates* I should have to be a Christian—believing what for me is an absurdity" (*Ecce Homo*, Nietzsche 1992a:694).

[4] Charles Sareola, 'Nietzsche', *Everyman* (May 16, 1913, page 136). Quoted in Thatcher (1970:207).

kind of redemptive alternative understanding which modernity, however conceived, cannot deliver?

The answers to these questions are not at all straightforward. Even so, I contend that for Tolkien, philology (understood broadly as 'the love of words') returns one to the inescapably linguistic character of all revelation and truth, pointing one to a certain conception of the human being as fundamentally sacramental in its created participation in the Trinity. Thus will I argue that philology, for Tolkien, is a fundamentally positive science, insofar as it discloses the innate fecundity of 'natural' human formulations and products—a naturality which itself bespeaks a transcendence which cannot be reduced to any material cause. At the same time, I will argue that Tolkien's taxonomy of culture(s) is indicative of a certain kind of Thomist conception of human making which renders even pagan culture not as Christianity's antagonistic 'other', but instead as its surprising friend. For *poeisis* is itself profoundly disclosive of the divine—understood, of course, from the perspective of Catholic Christianity. Tolkien's 'response' to modernity, then, is to re-enshrine narrative, particularly the 'fairy tale', as the medium of Christian persuasion to beauty. That is, it is not apodictically that Tolkien seeks to make a case for Christianity; rather he 'argues' for Christianity by making an appeal to the beautiful in the form of the story, more particularly, in the form of his characters. Even in their pre-Christian forms, they anticipate the Christ who is the consummate form of the beautiful, the good, and the true. After modernity (or at least, within its death-throes) the Christian appeal is, with a certain element of charm (if not 'glamour'), to a *mythos* that is in some way more attractive because more beautiful, and beautiful because true.

Nietzsche, too, understands modernity as tending towards a kind of nihilism that permits no easy dismissal. For Nietzsche, as for Tolkien, one must appeal to a different conception of the human being in terms of a new narrative, or a different *mythos*—an alternative form of being and beauty. Nietzsche similarly refuses the demonstrative in favor, first, of the aphoristic, and later, of the poetic. For him philology renders the limits of intelligibility or credibility of a concept. In other words, Nietzsche's critique of Christianity is 'philological' at the point where he argues that, if one were to 'get at the root' of things, to find out what the 'original' meaning or concept is behind its various deceptive masks, one would then come either to some retrievable idea or, ultimately, to nothing. Philology is thus an essentially *negative* science insofar as it undoes or 'deconstructs' the real, disclosing it as fundamental *chaos*. Yet what remains after the dismantling accomplished by philology is, again, the need for the creative re-construction of *mythos*. The truthfulness of Nietzsche's account then is proportional to the beauty of his form, which is ultimately that of Zarathustra. Nowhere is the contrast between Nietzsche and Tolkien starker than in the forms of their two chief poetic creations, Zarathustra and Frodo Baggins.

II. The Sacramentality of Sub-Creation

Our chief concern here must be with what Thomas Aquinas called *recta ratio factibilium*, "right reason about things to be made," namely, Art. In Article 57 of the *Prima Secundae* of the *Summa Theologiae*, Thomas famously distinguishes *Art* from *Prudence*. Art "has the nature of a virtue," but is, properly speaking, an "operative habit."[5] Art is "right reason about things to be made," while Prudence is "right reason about things to be done." Nevertheless art "is called a virtue" because it has a relation to the good. Yet it is not perfect virtue "because it does not make its possessor to use it well."[6] The correlative distinction between making and doing, or *poiesis* and *praxis*, is as old as Aristotle's *Metaphysics* and *Nichomachean Ethics*: *poiesis* is an activity that extends to an external object, while *praxis* is an activity that remains within the agent. Thus art is not a perfect virtue, because, as *poiesis*, its activity passes into an external object, and does not, like prudence, concern the good of the artist, but only the good of the thing made. Of course, for Aquinas, "art does not presuppose rectitude of the appetite" since prudence concerns *praxis*. Nonetheless, art has to do with the goodness of the thing made—and even the imprudent can produce good art.

Aquinas is notoriously evasive when it comes to any explicit account of beauty. Despite being one of the transcendentals, beauty did not become a discrete object of study until the eighteenth century. Nonetheless, there is indeed a peculiarly Thomistic 'aesthetics', as evidenced by Umberto Eco and others, but this must be in some sense gleaned from his work, since he no-

---

[5]   Aquinas (1981), *Summa Theologiae* (henceforth *ST*), IaIIae.57.3, *res.*

[6]   Aquinas, *ad* 1.

where treats it in the same way he treats 'the good' and 'the true'.[7] Whatever the case, Tolkien, while not straightforwardly 'Thomist', is quite clearly, like Flannery O'Connor, at least 'a Thomist thrice-removed'.[8] This is evident in the way in which he understands the human activity of *poiesis* to be explicitly bound up with creation, particularly in the sense that all human making reflects the gratuity of the creation itself, forming not a discrete set of activities of an agency of purely human propriety, but rather participating in the divine creation itself.

In Question 44 of the *Prima Pars* of the *Summa Theologiae*, Thomas Aquinas says that

> [s]ome things [...] are both agent and patient at the same time: these are imperfect agents, and to these it belongs to intend, even while acting, the acquisition of something. But it does not belong to the First Agent, Who is agent only, to act for the acquisition of some end; He intends only to communicate His perfection, which is His goodness; while every creature intends to acquire its own perfection, which is the likeness of the divine perfection and goodness. (Aquinas, *ST* Ia.44.4, *resp*)

The centerpiece of Thomas' account of human making is the divine gratuity, in which human beings analogically participate in any act of making. The act of creation belongs to God alone (Aquinas, *ST* 45.5, *resp*), and bodies cannot, strictly speaking, 'create', because their making always acts upon already-existing matter, to which it gives accidental form. Hence to create is "not proper to any one Person, but is common to the whole Trinity" (Aquinas, *ST* 45.6, *resp*). Human beings, then, cannot create, but they can compose.[9] Thomas alludes here to the notion of *concreation*—although his discussion seems to tend specifically to nature, one can speak of the human agent as 'concreating' with God

---

7
    See Eco (1988).

8
    The most formative elder influence on Tolkien's boyhood was Father Francis Morgan, a priest of the Birmingham Oratory founded by John Henry Newman in 1849. One can only speculate on the influence of a figure such as Aquinas on Tolkien, but there can be little doubt that some kind of mediated Thomism was certainly in the air that Tolkien breathed—delivered, perhaps, through the pipe-bowl.

9
    See Eco (1988:173-79).

in any human making. Any act of human *poiesis*, then, is a participation in the creative agency of God—an act which is nevertheless 'creation' by analogy, insofar as human beings are, analogically speaking, 'self-subsistent beings'. Denys Turner (2004:224-35) makes this crucial point clear:

> Thomas [...] argues that anything at all in the sensible world is a sign of something sacred, and so in a general sense is a 'sacrament' even if, other than in the cases of the seven sacraments of the Christian dispensation, they lack the character of a sacrament in the strict sense, for only those seven are 'causes' of our sanctification. [...] The connection of thoughts between creation's power to disclose God and its possessing in a general sense the form of the sacramental is in Thomas incontestable.

Thus in an analogous sense, all art, as *signum*, 're-presents', rendering its object 'really present' under the form of paint, or verse, or other media. As created things, these objects are intelligible and beautiful in so far as they are 'laid up', offered as oblations to God. Hence the claim of Aquinas (*ST* Ia.44.4, *ad* 3) that "[a]ll things desire God as their end, when they desire some good thing, whether this be intellectual or sensible or natural, *i.e.,* without knowledge; because nothing is good and desirable except forasmuch as it participates in the likeness to God."

Yet these 'offerings' are not our own, but are received as gifts. Not simply gifts *for us*, but gifts to themselves and to the rest of creation. In other words, the things of this world exist not simply for our use, but have a kind of subsistence in themselves which does not require any kind of human legitimation of their existence. As Tolkien suggests, the created order is utterly gratuitous, in a way that grants to the objects of the world their proper dignity and freedom as unique singulars in their own right:

> As for 'other things' their value resides in themselves: they ARE, they would exist even if we did not. But since we do exist one of their functions is to be contemplated by us. If we go up the scale of being to 'other living things,' such as, say, some small plant, it presents shape and organization: a 'pattern' recognizable (with variation) in its kin and offspring; and that is deeply interesting, because these things are 'other' and we did not make them, and they seem to proceed from a fountain of invention incalculably richer than our own.
> (Letter 340, to Camilla Unwin, 20 May 1969, *Letters* 399)

The implication of all this is that without the doctrine of the creation, under-stood as the generous and gratuitous bringing into being of all that is and all that appears, we lose the world. This is not a question then of the created order over and against God, as it is in Nietzsche (get rid of God, recover man), but rather that without the sense of the sacramental order of creation, the things of this world themselves lose their inherent dignity as irreducible singulars. When Aquinas says that "all things desire God" he means not just rational creatures, but quite literally *all things*. Tolkien (OFS 156) might add that this includes our own sub-creations: for is not God "the Lord, of angels, and of men—and of elves"?[10] What makes human beings unique in the order of creatures is that they "collaborate with God in making" (Jones 1959:88). This is not to arro-gate to the human creature some idolatrous status but rather to declare what only the Christian gospel can say: "Let your works shine before men, that they may see your good deeds and glorify your Father Who is in heaven."[11] Or, to cite St. Augustine's celebrated dictum: "become what you are."[12]

How does this account of human sign-making help us to understand Tolkien's own treatment of a similar theme, that of story-telling, specifically the 'fairy-story'? In the first instance, Tolkien (OFS 122) says that "[t]he mind that thought of *light, heavy, grey, yellow, still, swift,* also conceived of magic that would make heavy things light and able to fly, turn grey into gold, and the still rock into swift water." Such adjectives ("there is no spell or incantation in Faërie more potent" [OFS 122]) are irreducibly human artifacts, and like all human products, they go out from their makers and assume a rich and ex-tended sense that surpasses even the intentions of the inventor. As such they are *remembered* concepts whose life is sustained by their constant use, however various. This use remains bound to certain 'rules', and it is of the nature of Faërie to suspend, as it were, those rules. Yet in that suspension they image the con-creative character of human making.

---

[10] It matters little whether or not elves 'actually exist'—to ask the question might reveal a crude materialism at work already in one's notion of 'existence', not to mention 'actuality'.

[11] Matthew 5.16, as Augustine cites it in *The City of God Against the Pagans* (1998:215, V.14).

[12] A gloss on the this same passage of Scripture.

The human sub-creative power is to mix and transpose these predicates to different objects: "we can take green from grass, blue from heaven, and red from blood" and transfer those descriptors to things with which they are not 'naturally' associated, such as putting "a deadly green on a man's face" and thereby producing a "horror". Yet the ability to wield such an "enchanter's power" does not mean that it will always be well exercised. Regardless, when one exercises this ability, one nonetheless partakes of something distinctly human—one makes signs. As Tolkien (OFS 122) says, "in such 'fantasy,' as it is called, new form is made; Faërie begins; Man becomes a sub-creator." The imagination of such poetic forms is that "aspect of 'mythology' proper to fallen humanity" which Tolkien (OFS 122) names "sub-creation," as opposed to "either representation or symbolic interpretation of the beauties and terrors of the world."

III. The Glamour of Poesis

In '*Beowulf:* The Monsters and the Critics', Tolkien argues that most contemporary critics of the poem, besotted by its ostensible 'historical' value as a source of information for the Anglo-Saxon age, have missed the fact that, as he writes, "the illusion of historical truth" in *Beowulf* is "largely a product of Art" (BMC 5). It seems that Tolkien here means 'illusion' not in the modern, pejorative sense that is also given to 'myth', but rather in its etymological origin in *in-ludere,* to be 'in-play' (Huzinga 1950:11; see also Rahner 1972). This 'illusion of historical truth' in *Beowulf* is not simply a matter of pulling back the disguising veil in order to espy the historical kernel, but is in fact one of those 'peculiar poetic virtues' of the poem itself. A crude historicism actually robs history of its own inherently illusory quality, rendering to it in fact a *less* trustworthy status as history. The 'illusion of historical truth' is therefore dangerous because it in fact may disclose a truth that is *more than* historical, and even history, for Tolkien, "often resembles 'Myth,' because they are both ultimately of the same stuff" (OFS 127).

Tolkien, as is well known, is suspicious of historical-critical methods in philological literary criticism which assume that there is some 'essence' to which one could reduce a poem. The danger in such methods is that they treat a poetic creation as an instrument, a thing that can be mined or reduced to *some other thing,* or a story that can be turned into mere use. It is ultimately a rejection of the work of art as an irreducible event in itself, which is in a sense its own end. In a profound sense, such a version of philology takes the 'fun' out of literature because it removes from it the fundamental element of play. And play, like contemplation, strictly speaking serves no purpose external to itself. Thus Tolkien concludes that "[t]he lovers of poetry can safely study the art, but the seekers after history must beware lest *the glamour of Poesis* overcome them" (OFS 127).

In 'On Fairy-Stories' Tolkien also invokes the notion of "the glamour of Elfland" which has been transformed into "mere finesse" in so much of the "flower-and-butterfly" daintiness of elves in Disneyesque post-rationalist literature. What is it about Elfland that is so 'glamourous'? Shippey writes that "the quality [Tolkien] evidently valued more than anything in literature was that shimmer of suggestion which never quite becomes clear sight but always hints at something deeper further on." Faërie, for Tolkien, is characterized as a kind of 'primal desire': "the realisation, independent of the conceiving mind, of imagined wonder" (OFS 116), "the desire of men to hold communion with other living things" (OFS 117). Indeed, Tolkien says, reflecting on his own childhood, the successful fairy-story is one that awakens such desire (OFS 134). It is precisely this sense of 'glamour', as alluring playfulness or merriment, which characterizes Faërie as the site in which the possibility of "communion with other living things" becomes as it were 'reality'. Such an eschatological hope in the restoration of creation is 'escapist' only in the sense of an escape from imprisonment. It is escape only if one means something akin to 'liberation'.

Faërie also makes possible a kind of 'literary' or 'secondary belief' which, in contrast to Coleridge's dictum that it requires a "willing suspension of disbelief," suggests that the world of Faërie is not 'false' but 'true', in the sense that it operates according to rules of play which, when violated, return one to the 'Primary World'. Only then can Faërie be entertained in suspended disbelief, because there emerges a boundary across which one looks into the 'Secondary World'—one is no longer 'within' the enchanted Secondary World. This is analogous to what Johan Huizinga (1950:11) has to say about play:

> The player who trespasses against the rules or ignores them is a 'spoil-sport'. The spoil-sport is not the same as the false player, the cheat; for the latter pretends to be playing the game and, on the face of it, still acknowledges the magic circle. It is curious to note

how much more lenient society is to the cheat than to the spoil-sport. This is because the spoil-sport shatters the play-world itself.

Such are the unhappy results what when one 'pretends' at Faërie: disbelief destroys the world of Faërie itself and causes it to fail (Huizinga 1950:11).[13]

So the world of fairy-stories is true, but not simply in a 'metaphorical' sense. The denigration of the 'secondary' linguistic world of Faërie is analogous to a modern deprecation of metaphor as mere ornamentation. As Janet Soskice has shown, what in the wake of such historicism has come to be called 'metaphorical truth' is not simply a chimera or mere fancy. For example, she writes, "We may warn someone, 'Watch out! That's a live wire,' but even if we think wires are not literally 'live' we do not add 'but of course that is only metaphorically true'" (Soskice 1985:70). The same principle seems to apply to fairy-stories. They cannot be told with that same caveat without violating the rules of Faërie to begin with. In other words, it adds nothing to say of elves that they are true *in a sense*, any more than it does to say of this world that it exists *in a sense*. For both claims are true, but not because they simply correspond to a reality 'out there'. Rather is the existence of Faërie analogical just as is the existence of the 'primary world'; for being itself, as David Burrell (2004:113-26) and others have shown, is not univocal but analogical.[14]

Because of the analogical structure of creation itself, the things of this world are, in a certain sense, 'consonant' with each other. The metaphor is apt, as Tolkien confessed to W.H. Auden that he intended *The Lord of the Rings* not to "fit with formalized Christian theology," but rather to render it "consonant with Christian thought and belief" (Letter 269, to W.H. Auden, 12 May 1965, *Letters* 355). It is worth remembering here the crucial image of creation as original music in *The Silmarillion*. This sense of 'consonance' explains why the pagan world of *Beowulf* is not Christianity's 'other'. For Tolkien, the author of *Beowulf* is groping after the truth that in itself can never be pos-

---

[13]   It must be said here that what Huizinga means by 'play' and what Tolkien means by Faërie are not at all the same as "a frivolous indulgence in pointless triviality," but rather constitute a fundamental characteristic of humanity as such. In Tolkien's case, fairy-stories are "a natural human taste (though not necessarily a universal one)" (OFS 136).

[14]   See also Hart (2003:241ff.) and Cunningham (2003:181-89).

sessed. Thus is the noble human longing characteristic of pagan antiquity the occasion, if not quite for pity, then at least for mourning. Because the creation—which includes all human sub-creations as well as works of nature— is created by God and sustained by participation in God, the creation is therefore imbued with a graced musicality which, for all its cacophonous disharmony, is capable of intimations of a transcendent harmonic likeness. As Tolkien writes, "It is this deeper likeness which makes things, that are either the inevitabilities of human poetry or the accidental congruences of all tales, ring alike" (BMC 24). Thus a poem like *Beowulf* is enchanting, in its fantastical elements, because it calls forth a likeness, a kind of recognition in the reader of something that cannot easily be thematized, but which nevertheless concerns the *telos* of all human lives. As Tolkien writes in a letter to Deborah Webster, "far greater things may colour the mind in dealing with the lesser things of a fairy-story" (Letter 213, 25 October 1958, *Letters* 288).

For Tolkien, it follows, philology is an essentially 'reconstructive' science that deals with the re-covery or dis-covery of what Tom Shippey (2003:57) calls "asterisk-reality," a world now lost to us but in a sense available through philological 're-creation':"[t]his activity of re-creation—creation from philology—lies at the heart of Tolkien's 'invention' (though maybe not of his 'inspiration'); it was an activity which he kept up throughout his life" (*ibid.*). Hence his lament over the decline of this 'noblest of sciences' from its historical dignity:

> Philology has been dethroned from the high place it once had in this court of inquiry. Max Müller's view of mythology as a 'disease of language' can be abandoned without regret. Mythology is not a disease at all, though it may like all human things become diseased. You might as well say that thinking is a disease of the mind. It would be more near the truth to say that languages, especially modern European languages, are a disease of mythology. But Language cannot, all the same, be dismissed. The incarnate mind, the tongue, and the tale are in our world coeval. (OFS 121-22)

In a famous letter to his American publisher, Tolkien wrote of his own compositions that "a name comes first and the story follows" (Letter 165, to Houghton Mifflin Co., *Letters* 219). Is this not precisely the logic of creation? Before all, God creates the world in Genesis by giving it a name. By divine *fiat* God's creating is the same as his naming. In naming 'light' God calls it into being.

This pattern is impressively reflected in Tolkien's own *enarratio* of Genesis in *The Silmarillion*. Moreover, this is equally true of ordinary human existence: we do not choose our own names any more than we choose our own stories. Because we cannot simply 'make up' our own accounts of ourselves, we remain creatures who compose but do not create, operating within the limits of what is given to us.

The theologian, as David Hart (2003:28) suggests, must attend to surfaces, which is, after all, "where all things come to pass." Tolkien's philological appeal to fairy-stories in a sense partakes of this same attention to surfaces as a counter to the characteristically modern claim that pure 'essences' can be known without linguistic mediation—a claim for which Nietzsche too has no small amount of scorn. For Tolkien, there can be no possibility of a Cartesian *mathesis universalis* nor of a Leibnizian *characteristica universalis* intelligible to all rational subjects (see Toulmin 1990). Truth itself is storied, and thus not reducible to an atomic moment or concept. It follows that for Tolkien, truth is ultimately—and not just ultimately, but before everything else—triune. It is not enough simply to say that the world is created *ex nihilo* by an eternal 'simplicity', but by a Holy Trinity who in its primordial fecundity is not threatened by any kind of 'original' violence, strife or chaos. For this reason Tolkien's 'creation myth' in *The Silmarillion* depicts a prior, though learned, harmony among the Ainur. Thus truth resists even any puerile conflation with 'being', understood as pure eternal *stasis*. Rather is truth (because identical with the 'being' of God) an eternal self-offering, self-receiving charity that renders it immune to colonization or conquest by any single notion of truth as power or violence.

IV. How to Philologize with a Hammer

It is noteworthy that Friedrich Nietzsche was not a professional philosopher. He never held a position in philosophy in his life; in fact in 1871 he made an unsuccessful bid to take up the chair of philosophy at the University of Basel vacated by Gustav Teichmüller late in the previous year (see Cate 2002:122-25). After 1879, when Nietzsche officially resigned his professorship of classical philology in Basel, he never again held an academic position, but began a decade of extraordinary literary production.[15]

Though Nietzsche's activity from 1879 to 1889 was not conducted in the role of an academic philologist, his late work illustrates how his own understanding of philology is both broader and narrower than the classical conception of the discipline. During his own lifetime, Nietzsche's relationship to the institutional philological establishment became somewhat acerbic. This is due to the fact that Nietzsche, like some others before him (see Porter 2000:8), came to question the very foundations of philological science to begin with. He argued that philology is a modern product whose possibility is ultimately grounded in nothing but itself. In this he was railing against the form of academic philology that sought to 'reconstruct' an illusory antiquity that it could then claim to have 'discovered' (see Porter 2000:6). It is not difficult to understand how Nietzsche could see that behind such a practice lay a philological will-to-power.

Yet Nietzsche's argument to this point is itself philological, in the sense that his exposure of the illusory pretensions to authenticity among contemporary philologists was itself philological. Philology, in other words, disclosed philology's own hidden presuppositions. In this sense, the discipline is much broader for Nietzsche than technical etymological genealogy or linguistic reconstruction; it is something more like *Kulturkritik*, "the apprehension of a cultural error" or "a mode of cultural mystification" (Porter 2000:4). In that sense, Nietzsche's later work, as James Porter argues, is in keeping with this conception of philology, and his critique of Christianity is the preeminent example of the genealogical unveiling (what later Nietzscheans would rightly label 'de-construction') of a 'corruption'. Consider, for example, the following account from *Daybreak*, written in 1881:

> *The philology of Christianity*—How little Christianity educates the sense of honesty and justice can be gauged fairly well from the character of its scholars' writings: they present their conjectures as boldly as if they were dogmas and are rarely in any honest perplex-

---

[15] During this period he wrote *The Wanderer and His Shadow, Daybreak, The Gay Science, Thus Spake Zarathustra, Beyond Good and Evil, On the Genealogy of Morals*, two books on Wagner, *The Twilight of the Idols, The Antichrist*, and *Ecce Homo*.

ity over the interpretation of a passage in the Bible. Again and
again they say 'I am right, for it is written'—and then follows an
interpretation of such impudent arbitrariness that a philologist who
hears it is caught between rage and laughter and asks himself: is it
possible? Is this honourable? Is it even decent?—How much
dishonesty in this matter is still practised in Protestant pulpits, how
grossly the preacher exploits the advantage that no one is going to
interrupt him here, how the Bible is pummeled and punched and
the art of reading badly is in all due form imparted to the people:
only he who never goes to church or never goes anywhere else will
underestimate that. (Nietzsche 1982:49, §84)

For Nietzsche, the philological axe, having been laid to the root of the tree of
Christianity, fells it by making belief itself unbelievable. To put it another way,
philology exposes Christianity as a 'fairy tale'. *Contra* Tolkien, 'fairy-tales'
represent, for Nietzsche, the world of puerile illusion, and philology can expose
Christianity for what it really is: make-believe:

It may be hoped man will raise himself so high that the things previously highest to him, e.g., the belief in God he has held up to
now, appear childlike, childish, and touching: indeed, that he will
do again what he did with all the myths—turn them into children's
stories and fairy-tales. (Nietzsche 2003:41, §39 [17])

For Nietzsche, "a good philologist (and indeed any philologically trained
scholar) is repulsed by false textual interpretations (e.g., those made by the
Protestant preachers in the pulpits—which is why the learned professions no
longer go to church)" (Nietzsche 2003:3, §34 [48]). At the same time,
Nietzsche eloquently acclaims philology as "that venerable art which demands
of its votaries one thing above all: to go aside, to take time, to become still, to
become slow—it is a goldsmith's art and connoisseurship of the *word* which
has nothing but delicate, cautious work to do and achieves nothing if it does
not achieve it *lento*" (Nietzsche 1982:5, §5]). A noble asceticism attends to
Nietzsche's practice of philology, which for him is very nearly a kind of spiritual discipline. However, 'delicate, cautious work' hardly characterizes one
who intends to "philosophize with a hammer." It is above all to the sounding-
out of idols that the hammer is put (Nietzsche 1990b:32), and no one is a
better practitioner of "the hardness of the hammer, the *joy even in destroying*"
(Nietzsche 1992a:765, §8) than the prophet of the *Übermensch* and the eternal
recurrence: Zarathustra.

In Nietzsche's case, all philological re-constructions are expressions of will-to-power, and one must begin by destroying these false idols. The central example of this call to arms is the imperative to destroy Christianity in order to erect hyperborean self-overcoming in its place. This is the fundamental logic of Zarathustra: *destroy in order to create*. At the same time, as Stanley Rosen has shown, Nietzsche presents his reader with a noble lie in his exhortation to a creativity which can exist only in an order in which there can be nothing new, but only "the illusory or phenomenal manifestation of the actual or noumenal fluctuations of chaos (i.e., intrinsically random motions of points of force)" (Rosen 1995:13). In other words, Nietzsche's is a world in which "there is no creation at all" (Rosen 1995:13).

In 1888 Nietzsche described *Zarathustra* to Karl Knortz as "the profoundest work in the German tongue, and the most perfect in its language" (Letter 171, to Karl Knortz, 21 June 1888, Middleton 1996:299). Whether or not he was right about this rather delirious claim, there were certainly those in Germany who would later agree with his assessment. Regardless, the figure of Zarathustra is Nietzsche's stratospheric answer to the 'life-denying' form of life promoted by Christianity. Zarathustra is the will-to-power incarnate, a prophet of the eternal recurrence of the same, and the figure in whom Nietzsche's philosophy as a whole finds its fullest expression.

It is interesting to note that Zarathustra is also a response to the nihilism of modernity, insofar as out of the ruins of the modern project must emerge a positive, 'Yes-saying' figure, the embodiment of the Dionysian spirit who will offer a way beyond such negations. Yet negation is central to the mission of Zarathustra. As Nietzsche writes of Zarathustra in *Ecce Homo*, "[t]he imperative, 'become hard!' the most fundamental certainty *that all creators are hard*, is the distinctive mark of a Dionysian nature" (Nietzsche 1992a:765). It is also curious that Nietzsche would choose the name of Zarathustra for his greatest poetic creation, since Zoroaster was the founder of a pre-Christian dualistic religion that sprang up in Persia in the 7th and 6th centuries BC. The Zoroastrian universe is a kind of proto-gnostic world of inherent strife between a god of light and one of darkness. In creating the figure of Zarathustra, Nietzsche appeals to his 'charm' as a persuasive form. One of the reasons why Christianity is so un-compelling, according to Zarathustra, is that its human 'shape' is so unpersuasive. "They would have to

sing better songs to make me believe in their redeemer: his disciples would
have to look more redeemed!" (Nietzsche 1969:116).

Herein lies the alleged truthfulness of Zarathustra: he is the anti-Christ
in the precise sense that he is the unequivocal aesthetic anti-form of Christ.
Whereas Christ, according to Nietzsche, offers the gift of eternal life,
Zarathustra offers the gift of eternal recurrence. The Zarathustrian gospel is
that of creative will which first destroys in order to create. Nietzsche is quite
conscious that he is writing a new gospel that lays claim to the true story of
being, understood as chaos. It is no accident that Nietzsche's sworn enemy is
Christianity; for whatever the inadequacy of his understanding of Christianity,
he recognizes that his own *mythos* was entirely 'other' to the Christian story. In
so doing, he at least registers the sense in which Christianity does indeed represent a *skandalon* to every pagan account of being as strife and of human virtue
as heroism. In this light, therefore, Nietzsche rightly establishes the notion of
the eternal recurrence as *the* only worthy alternative to the Christian *kerygma*.[16]

The *locus classicus* of the expression of eternal recurrence is found in
Thus Spoke Zarathustra III, 'Of the Vision and the Riddle' in which Zarathustra speaks, oddly enough, to a dwarf:

> 'Behold this moment!' I went on. 'From this gateway Moment a
> long, eternal lane runs *back*: an eternity lies behind us.
>   Must not all things that *can* run have already run along this lane?
> Must not all things that *can* happen *have* already happened, been
> done, run past?
>   And if all things have been here before: what do you think of

---

[16] Cf. my *Theology at Midnight: Friedrich Nietzsche and the Grammar of Atheism*,
Cambridge University M.Phil. Thesis (1997); and Hart (2003:103): "Nietzsche's
post-Christian counternarrative (which is itself perhaps occasionally tainted by
resentment rather than honesty) cannot be denied its power and its appeal, but it
should be recognized not simply as critique but as always already another *kerygma*.
Between Nietzsche's vision of life as an agon and the Christian vision of life as
creation—as primordial 'gift' and 'grace'—there is nothing (not even the palpable
evidences of 'nature red in tooth and claw') that makes either perspective self-
evidently more correct than the other. Each sees and accounts for the violence of
experience and the beauty of being, but each according to an irreducible mythos
and a particular aesthetics. A battle of tastes is being waged by Nietzsche, and the
metaphysical appears therein as a necessary element of his narrative's completeness." See also Hart (2003:124f.).

this moment, dwarf? Must not this gateway, too, have been here—
before? (Nietzsche 1969:178-79)

For Nietzsche as for Tolkien, the 'road goes ever on and on', but for Nietzsche
it is the road of identical repetition of the same, forever. One can see how this
teaching of Zarathustra is related to his call for the poetic creation. Nietzsche
declares in *The Twilight of the Idols* that "I fear we are not getting rid of God
because we still believe in grammar" (Nietzsche 1990b:48). Nietzsche is not
worried that there remains a discernible order or pattern in languages which
thus bespeaks some kind of intelligence at work in the human species—as a
kind of implicit proof of God's existence or philological natural theology.[17]
Rather is he rendering negatively what is rendered positively in Tolkien's account: the irreducibly linguistic *shape* of truth, the mythological *form* of being.

Nietzsche attempts, paradoxically, to articulate the 'goal' of human life
so as to repeat identically the Dionysian in the form of Zarathustra. As such,
the form of Zarathustra is entirely univocal—it can only be infinitely repeated
in the same way, without real difference:

> I shall return, with this sun, with this earth, with this eagle, this
> serpent—*not* to a new life or a better life or a similar life:
> I shall return eternally to this identical and self-same life, in the
> greatest things and in the smallest, to teach once more the eternal
> recurrence of all things. (Nietzsche 1969:237-38)

To become like Zarathustra is to reproduce a single way of being at every in-
stant: destroy, create. The form of Zarathustra, unlike the form of Christ, is
impatient of variation; one can only be like *this*; the form of Dionysus can only
eternally recur—identically, always.

In the figure of Zarathustra, Nietzsche offers an alternative poetic form
of life to the form of the Christ of Christianity (which Nietzsche understood as
an invention of St. Paul). The crucial point here that Nietzsche's confrontation
with Christianity is conducted entirely on aesthetic grounds, and that his critique of it operates at the level of 'taste'. For that reason, he says, "[t]he critic
of Christianity cannot be spared the task of making Christianity *contemptible*"
(Nietzsche 1990a:188, §57). As Hart (2003:95) writes, Nietzsche "understood

---

[17] Tolkien himself was prone to such 'reasoning to God' through the observation of
'patterns'. See letter 310, to Camilla Unwin, 20 May 1969 (*Letters* 399f.).

that Christian truth depends first upon a story, and so to meet his critique of Christianity tellingly (so to put it), one must engage it on the field of rhetoric, persuasion, and aesthetic evaluation first, and not that of 'historical science' or the discourses of 'disinterested' reason." It is interesting to note that Nietzsche's mythopoetic invention is, like Tolkien's, premised upon the centrality of *mythos* for the *polis*, and both figures are concerned about the sufficiency and availability of the mythological apparatus in their respective cultures. On the one hand, Tolkien ventured to bequeath to England a mythological treasury which it lacked; on the other, Nietzsche saw the re-instauration of a similarly German *mythos* as essential to the renewal of the 'German spirit'. Both therefore recognized the inseparability of politics from myth, but for different reasons and with very different outcomes.

V. A New Myth for England?

In *The Birth of Tragedy*, Nietzsche had written of the need for the purification of German spirit, through the return to its mythology of itself:

> We think so highly of the pure and vigorous core of the German character that we dare to expect of it above all others this elimination of the forcibly implanted foreign elements, and consider it possible that the German spirit will return to itself. [...] But let him never believe that he could fight [...] without the gods of his house, or his mythical home, without 'bringing back' all German things! And if the German should hesitantly look around for a leader who might bring him back again into his long lost home whose ways and paths he scarcely knows anymore, let him merely listen to the ecstatically luring call of the Dionysian bird that hovers above him and wants to point the way for him.
> (Nietzsche 1992b:138-39, §23)

In the same passage, he spoke of the "solemnly exuberant procession of Dionysian revelers [...] to whom we are indebted to German music—and to whom we shall be indebted for *the rebirth of German myth*" (Nietzsche 1992b:137). Whatever Nietzsche's intentions, it is clear that *Also sprach Zarathustra* did in fact become 'a new myth for Germany'—at least a 'Germany' mythologically ill-conceived—when, in 1935, "a handsomely bound copy of *Thus Spake Zarathustra* [...] had been solemnly placed, alongside *Mein Kampf* and Alfred Rosenberg's *Myth of the Twentieth Century*, in the vault of the Tannenberg Memorial (commemorating the Germans' decisive victory over the Russians in the autumn of 1914) as one of the three ideological pillars of Germany's *Third Reich*" (Cate 2003:576).

It is difficult to imagine Tolkien's 'new myth for England' inspiring anything like an Empire (much less a *Reich*), since *The Lord of the Rings* is animated by a deliberately anti-imperial spirit that celebrates all of those virtues which Nietzsche found so hideous: pity, mercy, charity. At the very least, Tolkien's creation is, albeit unlike most fairy-tales, a story of failure. It is an account of the irretrievability of a lost past whose loss threatens every present. Tolkien regarded 'Britain' as a conceptual Leviathan whose imperial pretensions would mean the dissolution of anything peculiarly English. As Nicholas Boyle (2005:255-56) argues, *The Lord of the Rings* then stands as a critique of British cultural *amnesia*:

> And a critique it must be, for a historical parallel to the success of Frodo's quest could only be, not the triumph of Britain, but its self-immolation—the dissolution of the empire and of everything built on the act over four centuries old by which England ceased to be Catholic and became Britain, a willed rejection of all the features of modernity that made mid-twentieth-century British society possible.

Modern Britain, argues Boyle, is "defined by what it has forgotten"—an example of the displacement of analogical *anamnesis* as the central constitutive activity of the *polis*.

It is entirely noteworthy in this context that the story of *The Lord of the Rings* begins and ends in the same place: the Shire (see Boyle 2005:248-66). The story, like *The Hobbit*, is an account of a journey and a return, an *exitus* and a *reditus*, but in a very important way *The Lord of the Rings* narrates very differently than does *The Hobbit* the kind of return and the place to which one returns. The Shire of 'The Long-Expected Party' is not at all the same as the scoured Shire to which the hobbits return. Now bereft of the Party Tree, neither the Shire nor Frodo are the same they were when the Fellowship first departed. The Party Tree proves to be the central token of Hobbiton's memory. One might wonder here to what extent Tolkien signals the loss of genuine festivity as the dangerous consummation of a modernity that threatens our future. "*The Lord of the Rings* is not just the story of hobbits venturing out to discover the greater world to which the Shire belongs. It is also the story of the greater world breaking in on The Shire, potentially with annihilating consequences" (Boyle 2005:262). The hobbits return to the Shire to find it changed forever, irreparably damaged and effaced and threatened with the loss of its own memory—not as nostalgia, but as *anamnesis*, that (analogous) activity which renders all human activity significant because it is the possibility of the past returning to us again and again, ever new. "The Shire, like Middle-earth in its state of decline, and indeed like modern England, is defined by what it has forgotten, and the hobbits' great expedition into the world to which the Shire belongs is a reawakening that will redefine the home from which they started" (Boyle 2005:260).

It is impossible to know whether or not Tolkien had Nietzsche in mind when constructing Middle-earth, but it is clear that Tolkien's world is every bit as anti-Zarathustrian as Nietzsche's is anti-Christian. For here there is a particularly Christian vision that illuminates an entirely pagan world, though one not bereft of an intimation of something *more than pagan*. Tolkien, curiously, draws attention to the allure of Christian imagination by coloring a world in which there is no mention of Christ whatsoever, much less of overt religiosity. It is, oddly enough, by depicting paganism, so to speak, *sub specie aeternitatis*, that he is able to appeal to the 'glamour' of Christ. In other words, Christianity is here re-imagined, not 'under the form of paint', but 'under the form of hobbits', and it is to the aesthetic 'shape' of such creatures that we must now turn.

VI. The Virtues of Hobbiton

In contrast to the univocal identity which eternal recurrence is condemned to repeat, Tolkien's Middle-earth survives the terrorism of Mordor because of the efforts of varied and sundry forms: Men, Elves, Ents, Dwarves, Wizards, and Hobbits. No single form of life is adequate as a representation of virtue—the moral shape of Middle-earth is not simply identical with the hobbits, but remains a function of a Fellowship. The form of Christ is like this: it is not identical with any single human life, but is productive of an endless variety of lives whose different shapes form the 'communion of saints' (and this is perhaps at least an indication of why the lives of the saints are so essential to Christian self-understanding). So in a sense there is a valid opposition: Zarathustra *or* the lives of the saints. They are both poetic forms, in the imitation of which consists (or does not) our good as human beings. Zarathustra can of course be disputed on the philosophical coherence of his doctrines, but this is not why Nietzsche presents him in the way that he does. What I have been calling his 'form' is but the irreducible quality or shape of his life as an object of aesthetic delight and persuasion. On those grounds he cannot simply be rejected but must, as it were, be 'out-narrated'.

Similarly, the lives of the folk of Middle-earth are not 'allegorical' in the sense Tolkien always derided, as if the Men simply *stood for* 'courage' or the Wizards for 'wisdom' or some such univocal representational scheme. There are indeed virtues peculiar to each, and even some virtues that may be higher than others, but the characters are not hypostases of such virtues. At the same time, there is something peculiar to hobbits which makes them particularly well-suited to the mission to destroy the Ring, and there is ample reason to suspect it lies in their playfulness, in the fact that, as John Milbank (1997:232, n. 16) points out, they "are both brave and cunning *because* they prize naïve festivity above the dwarfish interest in accumulation and preservation."[18] In some ways, what makes the hobbits, for Tolkien, worthy of imitation (and also at times prone to deception) is their ludic virtuosity, their dexterity in play.

This is why the ending of *The Return of the King* is so profound: Sam returns home with an ironic "I'm back" to a hot meal already prepared and waiting for him. The Party Tree has been replanted and is already showing some promising growth, and yet the Shire is not at all the same. He *is* back because he recognizes that what the new situation calls for is not nostalgic recovery but *anamnesic* re-creation, in which the Shire is 'raised' again—not just as it was, but differently. In fact it is not yet what it will be. And just as for Sam, the meal goes ever on before us, patient of our delight.

Curiously, Nietzsche's critique of Christianity has made possible such a re-imagination of its own story, and Tolkien's may be one such instance of this

---

[18] As evidence of this Milbank points to *The Hobbit* (227): "All the same Mr. Baggins kept his head more clear of the bewitchment of the hoard than the dwarves did. Long before the dwarves were tired of examining the treasures, he became weary of it and sat down on the floor; and he began to wonder nervously what the end of it all would be. 'I would give a good many of these precious goblets,' he thought, 'for a drink of something cheering out of one of Beorn's wooden bowls!'"

strange back-formation. Indeed, he has "bequeathed Christian thought a most beautiful gift, a needed anamnesis of itself—of its strangeness" (Hart 2003:126). The poetic form of Zarathustra recalls the truly unclassifiable quality of the form of Christ and how his entire 'shape'—the indissoluble totality of the whole: his begetting of the Father before all worlds, his birth, infancy, ministry, death and resurrection and ascension, none of which is isolable as a concept but available only as a story told and re-told—confounds the pagan tale of everlasting chaos. Tolkien's own pagan sub-creations perform a similar anamnesic recollection of Christianity's peculiarity in the form of hobbits—creatures who do not exactly fit into any pre-existing list, not even the Entish catalog of beings (*LotR* 464). On the other hand, hobbitic festivity is really the only form of virtue that stands the slightest chance of resisting the will of Sauron. Men, even wizards, are prey to the temptations to *use* the Ring, to attempt to reorient it to a utility to which the Ring itself refuses to submit. It is, alas, an evil object because it represents the abolition of play, the conscription of all being to usefulness, particularly in the way in which those who try to use the Ring end up being used *by it*. Yet the hobbits, more than anyone else, recognize that it is used at one's peril and, above all, that the Ring is so sinister because it is a thing that *cannot be enjoyed*.

What is the One Ring, then, but an image of Zarathustrian eternal recurrence? Unlike the other rings made by the elves, the One Ring is unadorned with any gemstone. It is a perfect unbroken circle, unaffected by the accidents of heat or external force, impervious even to the will of its bearer. It is, moreover, an image of false eternity—the identical repetition of all things with no beginning and no end. At the same time, as a symbol of evil, the Ring circumscribes a non-space, a pure privation. The essence of the Ring is its nothingness. This is why, at the end of *The Return of the King*, the Ring must be destroyed in the fires of Mount Doom, its source and origin. The Ring must return to its origin—thus effecting a *reditus* to its source which is a parody of the divine cosmological *reditus* of creation in the sense that the source and end of the Ring is consuming fire. But even this fire is mortal and will one day flame out to embers, so that the Ring is, paradoxically, defeated by that which it cannot promise to anyone: death.

As eternal recurrence, the Ring is so diabolical not because it promises immortality but because it cancels mortality itself, and in canceling death it obviates life. The One Ring, then, is the consummate token of nihilistic discourse in that it makes death a nothing, but makes it too disappear. The worst thing about the Ring is that it can't even kill, because it has already taken away death itself.[19] As Gandalf says to Frodo of the Great Rings:

> A mortal, Frodo, who keeps one of the Great Rings, does not die, he does not grow or obtain more life, he merely continues, until at last every minute is a weariness. And if he often uses the Ring to make himself invisible, he *fades*: he becomes in the end invisible permanently, and walks in the twilight under the eye of the dark power that rules the Rings. Yes, sooner or later—later, if he is strong or well-meaning to begin with, but neither strength nor good purpose will last—sooner or later the dark power will devour him. (*LotR* 47)

This is pre-eminently true of the One Ring of Power. Its great danger—which appears to be its great virtue, at least in its utility to Frodo—is that it makes its bearer invisible. Sauron himself is the ultimate example of this. He can never be seen because evil has entirely evacuated him of substance, reduced him to nothing but an all-seeing eye. If there were ever a metaphor for modern philosophy as Tolkien must have understood it, it is the disembodied, panoptic eye of Sauron.[20] And this, by the way, is emblematic of a modern disposition, which is not, it must be stressed, the desire to see the world *sub specie aeternitatis*, but rather to view it from the aspect of *nowhere*. This is the true bondage of *hubris*: not to see from eternity but to see from no-place, to simply *gaze*, to repeat univocally, the same gesture *ad infinitum*.

The Christian story is otherwise. The world can be seen, heard, tasted only *sub specie aeternitatis* because that is the only aspect from which anything could appear. This is not the same as an Archimedean point of 'objectivity' which sees merely appearances as all identical. Rather, to see 'from the aspect of eternity' is to see appearances for what they are: surfaces which bear a likeness to one another because they all share in an ontological peacefulness which they do not own or manufacture but receive as gift. They can therefore be like

---

[19] Here I am following Cunningham (2003:174ff.).

[20] Here Tolkien anticipates Foucault, but in a much more theologically profound way.

one another but truly different from one another because they are created by the One God, who in His eternal tri-unity, creates the world from nothing. As David Jones (1959:120) iterates yet again, "the works of man, unless they are of 'now' and of 'this place', can have no for ever." In the Christian account, to see the creation *sub specie aeternitatis*, then, is not to erect an optic Tower of Babel from which the neutral gaze could reduce all appearances to mere flatness (as happens when one, for example, reads a map), but rather to recognize that the aspect of eternity has not retreated from every act of vision to an inaccessible private realm (i.e., the Cartesian mind as the prototype of this pseudo-eternity). In this sense it is the prime act of *hubris* to *refuse* to see in this way, insofar as it amounts to a rejection of the truth that in all our seeing we give as much as we receive, and of the claim that our understanding is never entirely our own property, but partakes of the divine generosity, without which nothing at all could be seen.

In the epilogue to 'On Fairy-Stories', Tolkien speaks of "the Christian Story" as the preeminent fairy-story, not simply because its ending is a happy one. It is Faërie *properly speaking*, and all other true fairy-stories are only so by analogy to this one. It is in the perfect coincidence of the form of the Christian gospel with 'reality' in Tolkien's primary sense that its uniqueness lies. Tolkien is not saying that Christianity is a 'fairy-story' because it is like 'fairy-stories'; he is saying that the reason 'fairy-stories' are persuasive is because they are *like* the Christian story. This is because Faërie is not here, as it is in all other literary sub-creations, an 'other world'. Rather, "this story has entered History and the primary world; the desire and aspiration of sub-creation has been raised to the fulfillment of Creation" (OFS 156). In this story "Legend and History have met and fused" (OFS 156). It is, moreover, *true*, because its form is Christ, who is the form of beauty. For that reason "the Art of it has the supremely convincing tone of primary Art, that is, of Creation" (OFS 156). The gospel is true Faërie—its timbre is not of a happiness conferred by a simple resolution, but the joy of a present that is pregnant with a promised future.

What does this say about other stories, including pagan ones? There is no doubt that the figure of Zarathustra is quite simply anti-Christian, both in its creator's explicit intention and in his aesthetic form. Nor is there any doubt that the form of Christ represents a comprehensive 'revaluation of all values' of pagan antiquity. As Hart has shown, Nietzsche's opposition, in *The Anti-Christ*, of *Dionysus versus the Crucified*, is a true one, perhaps the only one. In

Zarathustra, "one gospel meets another" (Hart 2003:124). Zarathustra's gospel is in fact as old as Heraclitus, as Nietzsche himself acknowledges; it cannot but be, if all things eternally recur. But it is the Christian revelation that marks the truly revolutionary advent of the new in human culture. One must concede that Nietzsche is exactly right on this point—Christianity does inaugurate an account of beauty, as disclosed in the creating, crucified and risen Incarnate Word, that upsets all previous notions of the same. At the same time, from the side of Christianity, the pagan world can only be seen as the *Beowulf* poet saw it: as created, too, and desiring of God. This means that all stories, including pagan ones, are in the end *anathémata*—'things offered up'—because even ours is no final purchase on the truth. To see *sub specie aeterntitatis* is to grant to those stories their proper integrity as 'sub-creations', whether now true or false. As Hart (2003:34) writes, "whereas the story of violence simply excludes the story of peace, the Christian story can encompass, and indeed heal, the city that rejects it: because that city too belongs to the peace of creation, the beauty of the infinite, and only its narrative and its desires blind it to a glory that everywhere pours upon it." Put another way, narratively speaking at least, there is no salvation outside the church because the church has no outside. Nor is even the largest thing in the world. There is only one tale to tell, and it is what Tolkien calls the *eucatastrophe* of the Christian *evangelium*. But because creation partakes of the divine *Logos*, it is capable of potentially infinite variations and modulations upon a single trinitarian theme of ontological peace.

Slavoj Žižek (2003:48) argues that

> The message of Christianity [...] is that of infinite joy beneath the deceptive surface of guilt and renunciation: 'The outer ring of Christianity is a rigid guard of ethical abnegation and professional priests; but inside that inhuman guard you will find the old human life dancing like children, and drinking wine like men; for Christianity is the only frame for pagan freedom.

Is not Tolkien's *Lord of the Rings* the ultimate proof of this para-
dox? Only a devout Christian could have imagined such a magnificent pagan universe, thereby confirming that *paganism is the
ultimate Christian dream.*[21]

Tolkien (OFS 155-56), in turn, declares that "[a]ll tales may come true; and
yet, at the last, redeemed, they may be as like and as unlike the forms that we
give them as Man, finally redeemed, will be like and unlike the fallen that we
know." All tales may yet come true because, as Jones says, "[t]here is only one
tale to tell." But as Jones (1959:130) adds, most importantly, "the telling is
patient of endless development and ingenuity and can take on a million variant
forms." There is only one tale to tell, and it is what Tolkien calls the *eucatastrophe* of the Christian *evangelium*. But because creation partakes of the divine
Logos, it is capable of potentially infinite variations and modulations upon a
single theme, at whose heart is the story of ontological peace.

All other stories may be tales of violence (hence they are the true 'fairy-
stories', in Nietzsche's sense), but they may come true—redeemed into a form
whose appearance now may be unlike what its author expected or anticipated.
Perhaps this is because, as Tolkien adds in a footnote, the 'Art' of the Christian
story is "in the story itself rather than in the telling; for the Author of the story
was not the evangelists" (OFS 155, n. 2). So perhaps Žižek would be more
correct in saying that 'Christianity is the ultimate dream of paganism', because
only Christianity preserves paganism as paganism, because the former can
imagine difference as harmonious and non-violent in a way that pagan thought
cannot.[22]

Truth ever eludes us because it ever draws towards its inexhaustibility. If
truth is elusive, this is because it is ever 'glamorous' and playful, in the fullest
sense of *e-ludere*. The life of the Trinity is endless play, because it is peaceful
self-giving *caritas* that has no 'outside'. God never ceases from creating the
world, and all our making is but a partaking of that creativity. Sin emerges,

---

[21]   The reference is to G.K. Chesterton (1995:164). A more adequate critique of
       Žižek's provocative suggestion (and his account of 'The Doctrine of Uncondi-
       tional Joy') would require more space than I have here.

[22]   This is an egregiously over-simple summary of the argument in Cunningham's
       (2003) *Genealogy of Nihilism*.

therefore, as a refusal of divine generosity, and, as the Scriptures attest from Genesis to Luke-Acts, is an attempt to hoard what is from beginning to end sheer gratuity. Thus the virtues of Hobbiton in their aesthetic distaste of such possessiveness are worthy of imitation.

VII. Tolkien or Nietzsche?

Hackneyed proverbial wisdom holds that 'all that glitters is not gold.' In what could be a summary of Tolkienian aesthetics, however, the refrain throughout *The Lord of the Rings* reverses the syntax on this little bit of traditional wisdom. For as Tolkien has it, "All that is gold does not glitter," to which he adds,

> Not all those who wander are lost;
> The old that is strong does not wither,
> Deep roots are not reached by the frost.
> From the ashes a fire shall be woken,
> A light from the shadows shall spring;
> Renewed shall be blade that was broken,
> The crownless again shall be king.
> (*LotR* 170)

There is, it seems to me, a substantial, though subtle difference in the two adages. The traditional formulation amounts to saying something like, 'Don't be fooled by appearances because they are inherently deceptive.' Tolkien's version seems to suggest something more along the lines of, 'Attend more closely to appearances, for the truth has yet to arrive.' This is particularly true given the 'eschatological' thrust of the poem's concluding line—"the crownless again shall be king"—which points to a fullness of meaning which awaits us. Put another way, in the former case, the 'not' negates the gold, while in the latter, it negates the glittering. What is important in the first instance is the 'not gold'; in the latter, the 'does not glitter'. What Tolkien's revision of this traditional axiom emphasizes is that the un-gold-like appearance of gold points to an excess in which it is, for that very reason, *more than* gold. Tolkien might be seen here as adverting to a "plenitude of the object" (Blondel 2004:403)[23] in the sense that what an object is, is really *more than* it is. Moreover, it seems to

---

[23]   See Cunningham (2003:179ff.).

suggest that beauty is not simply epiphenomenal but attached to the very on-tological nature of beautiful things, which may not at all appear so. In other words, Tolkien's account has it that beauty is not simply a function of the senses or of perception. This is, after all, the demography of Faërie, whose inhabitants "do not always look like what they are" (OFS 113).

To make matters more interesting, the precise formulation, albeit in German, appears in, of all places, Nietzsche's *Human, All Too Human*: "*Alles, was Gold ist, glänzt nicht.*" Section 340 of 'The Wanderer and His Shadow', in R.J. Hollingdale's translation (Nietzsche 1986:392, §340), reads: "*Gold*—All that is gold does not glisten. A gentle radiance pertains to the noblest metal."

Nietzsche seems to miss the point. In saying, "A gentle radiance pertains to the noblest metal," does he not suggest that what sets gold apart as gold is precisely its gold-ly appearance? Does this not mean that gold is the 'noblest metal' *because* a 'gentle radiance' pertains to it? Or, perhaps, the implication might be, in a more Nietzschean fashion, that the gentle radiance is really all there is to the gold. What it is, is simply, and no more than, its appearance.

It may be pagan wisdom to say that 'all that glitters is not gold', but it is Christian wisdom to say that 'all that is gold does not glitter'. Even Nietzsche was capable of such an intimation. But the form of Christ is capable of 'tran-substantiating' all moments of human *poiesis*. The Word who is before all worlds, who was made flesh and dwelt among us, who creates the world: does not all creation speak, in an infinite variety of tones, keys, timbres and tongues, of that Word? Does not the Word made flesh render all flesh in some sense *articulate*? As Jones (1959:105) puts it, "[t]here is no escape from incar-nation. It's like a shunting train." This is because, as Maurice de la Taille (1940, quoted in Jones 1959:179) says, in a line David Jones is fond of quot-ing, "He placed Himself under the order of signs."

Tolkien's vision of creation centers on genuine newness, in which destruction is not necessary to creation. It is the hope of the return of the past in a non-identical newness. Only then can the Shire be received back, as it is given up in the quest to destroy the Ring. Sam's words at the end of the cycle, "I'm back" are true in a genuinely naïve sense: the casual nonchalance of the ending seems incommensurate with what has happened, yet at the same time, Sam is more 'home' now than when he left. The Shire, though now threatened with the loss of the memory of festive past—a memory which is *absolutely central* to the life of the hobbits, and to the success of the mission—must begin the long work of *anamnesis*, of rendering 'really present' those who are now absent, especially Frodo. The Shire will thus never be the same; it will always be different from what it was and bear the wounds of loss. But the hobbitic hope, like the Christian hope, is not nostalgia for a 'recovery' of a vanished past—after all, it is Gollum who is obsessed with "roots and beginnings" (*LotR* 53); instead it is the hope for the return of the past *to us*, albeit differently. At the same time, that hope gives us back our deaths; indeed, it gives back all deaths and restores them in the promise that the bodies of the dead will be resurrected—they will be returned, not as they were, but glorified.[24] The re-planting of the Party Tree is the necessary element of recalling the presence of the lost, the departed and the not-yet, which will restore the Shire once again, for without them, the Shire *is* not.

PETER M. CANDLER, JR. is Assistant Professor of Theology in the Honors College at Baylor University, Waco, Texas.

---

[24] Cf. I Corinthians 15.36-58.

References

Abbreviations used:

BMC: see Tolkien 1984a

Hobbit: see Tolkien 1991

Letters: see Carpenter 2000

LotR: see Tolkien 2004

OFS: see Tolkien 1984b

Aquinas, St. Thomas, 1981, *Summa Theologica*, (translated by The Fathers of the English Dominican Province), Westminster, MD: Christian Classics.

Augustine, 1998, *The City of God Against the Pagans*, (edited by R.W. Dyson), Cambridge: Cambridge University Press.

---, 1991, *The Trinity*, (translated by Edmund Hill, O.P.), Brooklyn, NY: New City.

Blondel, Maurice, 1984, *Action: Essay on a Critique of Life and a Science of Practice*, (first published 1893; translated by Oliva Blanchette), Notre Dame, IN: University of Notre Dame Press.

Boyle, Nicholas, 2005, *Sacred and Secular Scriptures A Catholic Approach to Literature*, Notre Dame, IN: University of Notre Dame Press.

Burrell, David B., 2004, 'From the Analogy of 'Being' to the Analogy of Being', in David B. Burrell, 2004, *Faith and Freedom: An Interfaith Perspective*, Oxford: Basil Blackwell, 113-26.

Candler, Peter M. (Jr.), 1997, *Theology at Midnight: Friedrich Nietzsche and the Grammar of Atheism*, Cambridge: University M.Phil. Thesis.

Carpenter, Humphrey, 1977, *Tolkien: A Biography*, New York: Ballantine.

--- (ed. with the assistance of Christopher Tolkien), 2000, *The Letters of J.R.R. Tolkien*, (first published 1981), Boston: Houghton Mifflin.

Cate, Curtis, 2003, *Friedrich Nietzsche*, London: Pimlico.

Chesterton, Gilbert K., 1986, *Heretics*, (The Collected Works of G.K. Chesterton, vol. 1), San Francisco: Ignatius.

---, 1988, *The Autobiography of G.K. Chesterton*, (The Collected Works of G.K. Chesterton, vol. 16), San Francisco: Ignatius.

---, 1995, *Orthodoxy*, San Francisco: Ignatius.

Cunningham, Conor, 2003, *Genealogy of Nihilism*, London: Routledge.

Eco, Umberto, 1988, *The Aesthetics of Thomas Aquinas*, (translated by Hugh Bredin), Cambridge, MA: Harvard University Press.

Eliot, T. S., 1963, *Collected Poems, 1909-1962*, London: Faber & Faber.

Hart, David Bentley, 2003, *The Beauty of the Infinite: The Aesthetics of Christian Truth*, Grand Rapids: Eerdmans.

Huizinga, Johan, 1950, *Homo Ludens: A Study of the Play Element in Culture*, Boston: Beacon.

Jones, David, 1959, *Epoch and Artist*, London: Faber & Faber.

La Taille, Maurice de, 1940, *The Mystery of Faith*, London: Sheed & Ward.

Middleton, Christopher (ed.), 1996, *Selected Letters of Friedrich Nietzsche*, Indianapolis: Hackett.

Milbank, John, 1997, *The Word Made Strange: Theology, Language, Culture*, Oxford: Basil Blackwell.

Nietzsche, Friedrich, 1969, *Thus Spoke Zarathustra*, (translated by R.J. Hollingdale), London: Penguin.

---, 1974, *The Gay Science*, (translated by Walter Kaufmann), New York: Vintage.

---, 1982, *Daybreak: Thoughts on the Prejudices of Morality*, (translated by R.J. Hollingdale), Cambridge: Cambridge University Press.

---, 1986, *Human, All Too Human: A Book for Free Spirits*, (translated by R.J. Hollingdale), Cambridge: Cambridge University Press.

---, 1990a, *The Twilight of the Idols and The Antichrist*, (translated by Michael Tanner), New York: Penguin.

---, 1990b, *Twilight of the Idols*, (translated by R.J. Hollingdale), London: Penguin.

---, 1992a, *Ecce Homo*, (translated by Walter Kaufmann), in *The Basic Writings of Nietzsche*, New York: Modern Library, 655-791.

---, 1992b, *The Birth of Tragedy*, (translated by Walter Kaufmann), in *The Basic Writings of Nietzsche*, New York: Modern Library, 1-144.

---, 2003, *Writings from the Late Notebooks*, (edited by Rüdiger Bittner, translated by Kate Sturge), Cambridge: Cambridge University Press.

Porter, James I., 2000, *Nietzsche and the Philology of the Future*, Stanford: Stanford University Press.

Rahner, Hugo, 1972, *Man at Play*, New York: Herder & Herder.

Rosen, Stanley, 1995, *The Mask of Enlightenment: Nietzsche's Zarathustra*, Cambridge: Cambridge University Press.

Shippey, Tom, 2003, *The Road to Middle-earth: How J.R.R. Tolkien Created a New Mythology*, (third edition; first edition 1982), New York: Houghton Mifflin.

Soskice, Janet Martin, 1985, *Metaphor and Religious Language*, Oxford: Oxford University Press.

Thatcher, David S., 1970, *Nietzsche in England, 1890-1914*, Toronto: University of Toronto Press.

Tolkien, John Ronald Reuel, 1977, *The Silmarillion*, (edited by Christopher Tolkien), New York: Houston Mifflin.

---, 1984a, 'Beowulf: The Monsters and the Critics', in *The Monsters and the Critics and Other Essays*, (edited by Christopher Tolkien), Boston: Houghton Mifflin, 5-48.

---, 1984b, 'On Fairy-Stories', in *The Monsters and the Critics and Other Essays*, (edited by Christopher Tolkien), Boston: Houghton Mifflin, 109-61.

---, 1991, *The Hobbit*, (fourth edition; first edition 1937), London: Grafton.

---, 2004, *The Lord of the Rings*, (originally published 1954-55; one-volume 50th anniversary edition), Boston: Houghton Mifflin.

Toulmin, Stephen, 1990, *Cosmopolis: The Hidden Agenda of Modernity*, Chicago: University of Chicago.

Turner, Denys, 2004, *Faith, Reason and the Existence of God*, Cambridge: Cambridge University Press.

Ward, Elizabeth, 1983, *David Jones, Mythmaker*, Manchester: University of Manchester.

Žižek, Slavoj, 2003, *The Puppet and the Dwarf: The Perverse Core of Christianity*, Cambridge: MIT Press.

PART THREE

MYTHOS

AND

LOGOS

Morals Makyth Man—and Hobbit

LEON PEREIRA OP

Summary

As an avowed theist there is only one world for Tolkien in reality and in fantasy: Middle-earth, that is, the world under God. Tolkien insisted that the religious elements of his works are absorbed into the fabric of the story itself: into its substance and symbolism. Thus the moral system of his legendarium is the same as our world's. One purpose of myth is to encourage good morals, by setting them in unfamiliar surroundings so as to appreciate them. Tolkien achieves this by making hobbits his protagonists. His myths are thus tales of the ordinary man, made to grow beyond his previous limited horizons. His tales exult in the earthy and ordinary, the things God himself delights in, and its hero is Samwise, a true saint.

I. Introduction

I am a Dominican friar from Blackfriars. Many of you are aware, no doubt, of the late Fr Gervase Mathew OP, the Dominican friar who was among other things a Byzantinist, medieval historian and a member of the Inklings. I propose to begin by considering the possible influences of Dominicans upon the other Inklings C.S. Lewis and J.R.R. Tolkien.

In Lewis's case, it is known that he had marked a childhood atlas in which the name 'Narnia' occurred. But would he have known of that town's patron saint? An Italian would know her as 'Beata Lucia di Narni', and she would only really have had a following among her own townsfolk and within the order she belonged to, the Dominicans. An English-speaking Dominican would have known her as 'Blessed Lucy of Narnia'. Is this where Lewis got the name(s) from? I doubt this 'connection' can be proved, but it must surely be ranked as more than coincidence!

In that same category of 'more than coincidence' belongs the chapel at Blackfriars, Oxford, completed in 1929. Tolkien would certainly have known it, and writes of serving at Mass there for Fr Gervase. This chapel has two features 'connected' with Tolkien. The first is the presence of 'orcs' in the Stations of the Cross. These were carved in the 1920s by the friar Aelred Whitacre, in the style of Eric Gill. All the Romans, the bad people, are depicted as monstrous creatures, orc-like, and all the good people, the Jews, are shown as ordinary humans. Even if there is no link between these carvings and Tolkien, both these 'orcs' and Tolkien's would have a common inspiration in the Catholic idea that virtue and holiness makes one *more* human, more free, and that vice and wickedness distorts the image of God in a human being and make him or her *less* human—perhaps even more orc-like.

The second 'connection' is a statue in the chapel by Eric Gill. It is the only statue of St Dominic ever made by Gill, and one of very few in the world where Dominic is depicted with a star upon his brow.[1] Most images of the saint show a star upon his halo. The motif of a hero or heroine with a star bound to their brow is one that recurs in Tolkien's writings. Indeed, it appears again in his last major work *Smith of Wootton Major*, first delivered in the refectory at Blackfriars in 1965. I suppose such 'connections' can never be proved, but they ought to be borne in mind by those researching the sources and inspiration of Tolkien.

The Dominicans may or may not have influenced Tolkien, but Catholicism as a whole certainly did. It not only shaped him, but also shaped his mythology. It is to that I wish to turn, paying particular attention to the morality of Tolkien's mythology.

II. The Moral System of Tolkien

The difficulty in speaking about morals is that one needs a context, in this case a *Weltanschauung*, a framework with which to interpret and to interact with the world. For example, you cannot believe that stealing is wrong without a particular understanding of the world.

Tolkien's legends are sometimes portrayed as naïve black and white depictions of good and evil, with the 'good guys' clearly on one side, and the 'bad' clearly on the other. This is not true, as I hope to show you.

Before talking about good guys and bad guys, we must talk about good and bad, and what makes something good and another thing bad. Tolkien does not subscribe to a moral system I call 'Nominalist Prescriptivism'.

---

[1]   To date I know of only three.

Nominalist Prescriptivism is a system most parents are tempted to use with their children. Essentially it runs as follows:

'Don't do X.'
'Why?'
'Because X is bad.'
'Why is X bad?'
'Because I say so!'

Although this system is what many secular people imagine Christianity espouses, it is actually a more fitting description of morality as understood and as taught by Islam (and certain medieval Franciscans).

Tolkien, as we know, was not a Muslim, and he would not have been enamoured by a list of dos and don'ts which were not in themselves amenable to *rational* enquiry. Why? Because, I want to suggest, he was a devout Catholic and his worldview was Catholic.

Tolkien's system begins with a look at the world around him. When a young student wrote to Tolkien asking him 'What is the purpose of life?', he replied by beginning with the human contemplation of objects in the primary world. You look at the world around you and see that things exist.

> Human curiosity soon asks the question HOW: in what way did this come to be? And since recognizable 'pattern' suggests design, may proceed to WHY? But WHY in this sense, implying reasons and motives, can only refer to a MIND. Only a Mind can have purposes in any way or degree akin to human purposes. So at once any question: 'Why did life, the community of living things, appear in the physical Universe?' introduces the Question: Is there a God, a Creator-Designer, a Mind to which our minds are akin (being derived from it) so that It is intelligible to us in part. With that we come to religion and the moral ideas that proceed from it.
> (Letter 310, *Letters* 399)

Tolkien's morality, as you can see, is bound closely with being, with the existence of things. This is very Catholic, very Thomistic. It may seem like Tolkien is leaping from existence to purpose to God to religion and morality, but this is an extremely dense and contracted passage. Tolkien does not waste time with solipsism. A solipsist, in case you've forgotten, would believe that he or she can only *really* know the contents of their own mind. I once heard a lecturer—who shall remain nameless—say that the best cure for a solipsist was either to slap them or to make love to them.

Tolkien does not fall into a solipsist's rut. The existence of things leads to their contemplation, which leads to questions about God, religion and morals. Questions about how things are lead almost naturally to questions about why things are, that is, to questions about purpose. Any question of *'purpose'* or teleology for humans must inevitably refer to morals. Tolkien writes:

> So morals should be a guide to our human purposes, the conduct of our lives: (a) the ways in which our individual talents can be developed without waste or misuse; and (b) without injuring our kindred or interfering with their development.
> (Letter 310, *Letters* 399-400)

Although it is not immediately obvious to some readers, Tolkien's mythology cannot be understood apart from religion. For Tolkien questions of *purpose* can only be answered by a theistic mind, that is, one which knows its place and boundaries in the world. If one rejects purpose then one is left with the absurd. Tolkien would have agreed with Camus who wrote, *"L'absurde conduit soit au désespoir, soit au divin."* ('The absurd leads one either to despair or to the divine.') Tolkien explains it himself in this way:

> If you do not believe in a personal God the question: 'What is the purpose of life?' is unaskable and unanswerable. [...] Those who believe in a personal God, Creator, do not think the Universe is in itself worshipful, though devoted study of it may be one of the ways of honouring Him. [...] To do as we say in the *Gloria in Excelsis*: Laudamus te, benedicamus [2] [*sic*] te, adoramus te, glorificamus te, gratias agimus tibi propter magnam gloriam tuam. We praise you, we call you holy, we worship you, we proclaim your glory, we thank you for the greatness of your splendour.
> (Letter 310, *Letters* 400)

Tolkien thought of *The Lord of the Rings* as a profoundly Christian book (*ibid.*), a "fundamentally religious and Catholic work" (Letter 142, *Letters* 172), which he says is "about God, and His sole right to divine honour" (Let-

---

[2] This should of course be 'benedicimus'. I do not know if the error is Tolkien's or his editor's; I suspect it is the latter's.

ter 183, *Letters* 243). That Tolkien believed this should not be surprising, because that is how he saw the primary world of reality, and consequently, that is how a sub-created secondary world will be viewed by what he calls "a mind that believes in the Blessed Trinity" (Letter 131, *Letters* 146). Tolkien expected his work to be more or less consonant with Catholic theology and thought, without being an allegory of them. He remarked, "Theologically [...] the picture [is] [...] less dissonant from what some (including myself) believe to be the truth. [...] I have deliberately written a tale, which is built on or out of certain 'religious' ideas, but is *not* an allegory of them" (Letter 211, *Letters* 283).

The issue of God and religion is not peripheral to an understanding of Tolkien and his work. In fact it is essential. You do not need to be Catholic to understand Tolkien, nor do you need to believe what he believed in order to grasp his meaning, but you must understand what he believed in order to appreciate his writings, especially the world of Middle-earth.

III. Tolkien's *Weltanschauung*

So how *did* Tolkien see the world? Tolkien's world-view of the primary world, that is the world we live in, shapes the form given to the secondary world of his legendarium. "Middle-earth," Tolkien says, "is not an imaginary world. [It is] the *oikoumené*, the abiding place of Men, the objectively real world [...]. The theatre of my tale is this earth, the one in which we now live, but the historical period is imaginary" (Letter 183, *Letters* 239).

The setting of this legendarium is pre-Christian, but in many ways it also seems pre-pagan. Certainly there is no worship of the forces of nature, no idols. But neither is there much in the way of an explicit monotheism among the inhabitants of Middle-earth. A pagan mindset would expect a world run by fate, and this is what we see in Tolkien's world. A prime example of one who fights fate and loses is Túrin Turambar, who calls himself 'master of doom', the master of his fate. Nevertheless Túrin fails in struggle against fate, and in death he is remembered as 'master of doom, by doom mastered'.

Although this seems like a purely pagan worldview, Tolkien has added many layers to his secondary world. His world is decidedly Christian and Catholic, and there is no fate, pure and simple. What it has is providence. Fairly often in a work like *The Lord of the Rings* Tolkien hints at divine providence using a formula like 'for this or for some *unknown* reason' or 'such and such was *meant* to be'. Túrin's tragedy is not due to the irresistible tide of fate, but an illustration of the folly behind a mentality such as William Ernest Henley's 'I am the master of my fate: I am the captain of my soul', or worse, Frank Sinatra's 'I did it my way'.

Middle-earth is shot through with providence. Concerning reviews of *The Lord of the Rings*, Tolkien commented, "The only criticism that annoyed me was one that it 'contained no religion'" (Letter 165, *Letters* 220). For Tolkien, "*The Lord of the Rings* is of course a fundamentally religious and Catholic work [but] [...] I have not put in, or have cut out, practically all references to anything like 'religion' [...] [T]he religious element is absorbed into the story and the symbolism" (Letter 142, *Letters* 172).

Although Tolkien does not explicitly mention God in *The Lord of the Rings*, God is "The Writer of the Story (by which I do not mean myself), 'that one ever-present Person who is never absent and never named'" (Letter 192, *Letters* 253). God, he says, "retains all ultimate authority, and [...] reserves the right to intrude the finger of God into the story: that is to produce realities which could not be deduced even from a complete knowledge of the previous past" (Letter 181, *Letters* 235). This 'intrusion' is what he calls the 'order of Grace'. The implicitness of religion within his story is to be found especially in the few instances of prayer in his magnum opus: namely thanksgiving (cf. *LotR* 676) and petition (cf. *LotR* 195, 720 and 729). Tolkien remarked, "These and other references to religion in *The Lord of the Rings* are frequently overlooked" (*Companion* 180). It should come as a shock, I believe, that Tolkien genuinely seemed to believe that God was the real author, even of *The Lord of the Rings*.

Although this statement sounds like an exaggeration or a pious fantasy, Tolkien makes such a claim precisely because of his worldview. God is the "Great Author" (Letter 163, *Letters* 215) the "Teller" of the "Tale" (Letter 212, *Letters* 284), Ilúvatar, 'Father of All' and primeval story-maker. Just as creatures join with the Creator in their own co-operative act of sub-creation, so too Tolkien, as father and story-maker, joins in a divine action with his own finite sub-creative act, the recounting of his *legendarium*. As one of Tolkien's characters, Aulë, says to Eru (God): "[T]he making of things is in my heart from my own making by thee; and the child of little understanding that makes a play of the deeds of his father may do so without thought of mockery, but because he is the son of his father" (*Silmarillion* 38).

God, the Primary Author, cannot really be kept out of the sub-creation, the story told by his creature, the Secondary Author, Tolkien. Nevertheless Tolkien weaves God into the fabric of the story, like the canvas rather than the painting on it. God is best revealed in and through the story, just as a canvas is revealed by the brush-strokes on it. Tolkien remarked, "I have purposely kept all allusions to the highest matters down to mere hints, perceptible only by the most attentive, or kept them under unexplained symbolic forms" (Letter 156, *Letters* 201). Almost all the explicit references to 'religion' have been removed, as Tolkien believed that they were fatal to myth *qua* myth. "For reasons which I will not elaborate," he said, "that seems to me fatal. Myth and fairy-story must, as all art, reflect and contain in solution elements of moral and religious truth (or error), but not explicit, not in the known form of the primary 'real' world" (Letter 131, *Letters* 144).

Religion is "absorbed into the story and the symbolism." Tolkien agreed with a self-styled unbeliever with "dimly dawning religious feeling" who wrote to him and observed that Tolkien had created "a world in which some sort of faith seems to be everywhere without a visible source, like light from an invisible lamp" (Letter 328, *Letters* 413). This 'light' (from God) is not the author's; it "does not come from him but through him" (*ibid.*). But the 'light' must also be with the reader if he or she is to perceive the light coming through the author (cf. *ibid.*). For Tolkien his story is not only implicitly religious, its creation by the author and enjoyment by the reader are only truly possible by the agency of the divine 'light'. "Otherwise," he says, "you would see and feel nothing, or (if some other spirit was present) you would be filled with contempt, nausea, hatred" (*ibid.*). Tolkien opines that those who have 'contempt, nausea, hatred' for his work have a different spirit in them—sufficiently different from the divine light!

IV. Hobbito-centrism

Having sketched the outline of the form of Arda, let's look at how morals work in this world. Myths are concerned with truth: for Tolkien it is the truth about Man as a creature before the one God and about how he must act within this world. Tolkien gives as one purpose of his myths "the encouragement of good morals in the real world by the ancient device of exemplifying them in unfamiliar embodiments, that one may tend to 'bring them home'"

(Letter 153, *Letters* 194). Not only is myth effective in moral instruction but, he opines, "[t]here is indeed no better medium for moral teaching than the good fairy-story—by which I mean a deep-rooted tale, told as a tale, and not a thinly disguised moral allegory" (OFS 73).

How does Tolkien 'bring home' good morals? In his major work, *The Lord of the Rings*, the focus is not Men, but Hobbits. Hobbits represent what is not immediately familiar, and their characterization acts as a literary device to 'bring home' what is often overlooked. One has to step outside and look back to appreciate what is otherwise familiar and overlooked. As Tolkien wrote, "I imagine the fish out of water is the only fish to have an inkling of water" (Letter 52, *Letters* 64).

Although the setting is unfamiliar, the morality within this secondary world is just like that of the primary world. Tolkien noted that Gollum's failure to repent (thanks to Sam) "seems to me really like the *real* world in which the instruments of just retribution are seldom themselves just or holy; and the good are often stumbling blocks" (Letter 165, *Letters* 221).

Most readers have a predilection for the Elves; they are a glimpse of the preternatural beauty and dignity of prelapsarian humans. And yet the story of *The Lord of the Rings* was, he says, "planned to be 'hobbito-centric', that is, primarily a study of the ennoblement (or sanctification) of the humble" (Letter 181, *Letters* 237). Tolkien says:

> This last great Tale [...] is seen mainly through the eyes of Hobbits: it thus becomes in fact anthropocentric. [...] [T]he last Tale is to exemplify most clearly a recurrent theme: the place in 'world politics' of the unforeseen and unforeseeable acts of will, and deeds of virtue of the apparently small, ungreat, forgotten in the places of the Wise and Great [...]. A moral of the whole [...] is the obvious one that without the high and noble the simple and vulgar is utterly mean; and without the simple and ordinary the noble and heroic is meaningless. (Letter 131, *Letters* 160)

A theme running through both *The Hobbit* and *The Lord of the Rings* is pity and mercy shown by the hobbits, in particular to Gollum. The slimy creature Gollum, in order to regain his ring and to eat, had no qualms about killing Bilbo. The ring conferred invisibility upon Bilbo, yet Gollum stood in his way, and here he faced a stark choice.

A sudden understanding, a pity mixed with horror, welled up in Bilbo's heart: a glimpse of endless unmarked days without light or hope of betterment, hard stone, cold fish, sneaking and whispering. All these thoughts passed in a flash of a second. He trembled. And then quite suddenly in another flash, as if lifted by a new strength and resolve, he leaped. (*Hobbit* 82-83)

The pity of Bilbo is initially lamented by Frodo in a conversation with Gandalf:

'[Gollum] is as bad as an Orc, and just an enemy. He deserves death.' (*LotR* 59)

When he finally encounters Gollum, Frodo also pities him, much to Sam's disgust.

'Very well,' he answered aloud, lowering his sword. 'But still I am afraid. And yet, as you see, I will not touch the creature. For now that I see him, I do pity him.' (*LotR* 615)

In a letter Tolkien explains, "[S]lowly Frodo awakes [Gollum's] long-buried better self: he begins to love Frodo as a good and kind master" (Letter 131, *Companion* 746). This Pity is crucial to the story. "*[P]ity* – a word to me of moral and imaginative worth: it is the Pity of Bilbo and later Frodo that ultimately allows the Quest to be achieved" (Letter 153, *Letters* 191). And elsewhere, Tolkien says, "Frodo's own 'salvation' is achieved by his previous *pity* and forgiveness of injury" (Letter 181, *Letters* 234). Tolkien remarked that those who misunderstood *The Lord of the Rings* "tend to forget that strange element in the World that we call Pity or Mercy, which is also an absolute requirement in moral judgement (since it is present in the Divine nature). In its highest exercise it belongs to God" (Letter 246, *Letters* 326).

At one stage in the story, Gollum, planning betrayal, returns to Frodo and Sam and finds them asleep.

Gollum looked at them. A strange expression passed over his lean hungry face. The gleam faded from his eyes, and they went dim and grey, old and tired. A spasm of pain seemed to twist him [...]. For a fleeting moment, could one of the sleepers have seen him, they would have thought that they beheld an old weary hobbit, shrunken by the years that had carried him far beyond his time, beyond friends and kin, and the fields and streams of youth, an old starved pitiable thing. (*LotR* 714)

Sam stirs awake, and seeing Gollum crouching there, assumes an evil intention in him and addresses Gollum accusingly. The moment of Gollum's repentance passes, and he sets himself again to betray them to Shelob (the giant spider). Tolkien remarks on this, "For me perhaps the most tragic moment in the tale comes [...] when Sam fails to note the complete change in Gollum's tone and aspect. [...] His repentance is blighted and all Frodo's pity is [...] wasted. Shelob's lair becomes inevitable" (Letter 246, *Letters* 330). Nevertheless, even Sam learns pity for Gollum eventually.

> It would be just to slay this treacherous, murderous creature, just and many times deserved; and also it seemed the only safe thing to do. But deep in his heart there was something that restrained him: he could not strike this thing lying in the dust, forlorn, ruinous, utterly wretched. He himself, though only for a little while, had borne the Ring, and now dimly he guessed the agony of Gollum's shrivelled mind and body, enslaved to that Ring, unable to find peace or relief ever in life again. But Sam had no words to express what he felt. (*LotR* 944)

Even Sam's pity becomes part of a grander plan. The survival of Gollum is what enables the Quest to be fulfilled, because Frodo fails at the end. Their forgiveness of Gollum opens the way for his great betrayal, which ultimately saves their lives because both Gollum and the Ring perish. Here the grace of God intervenes; the true "Writer of the Story" (i.e. God) took over (Letter 192, *Letters* 253).

For Tolkien, this moment of the story, when Frodo fails and Gollum betrays him, this "'catastrophe' *exemplifies* [...] the familiar words: 'Forgive us our trespasses as we forgive them that trespass against us. Lead us not into temptation, but deliver us from evil'" (Letter 181, *Letters* 233). Regarding this last petition, he said:

> A petition against something that cannot happen is unmeaning. There exists the possibility of being placed in positions beyond one's power. In which case (as I believe) salvation from ruin will depend on something apparently unconnected: the general sanctity (and humility and mercy) of the sacrificial person. I did not 'arrange' the deliverance in this case: it again follows the logic of the story. (Letter 191, *Letters* 252)

Frodo was in a position where "he is in a sense doomed to failure, doomed to fall to temptation or be broken by pressure against his 'will': that is against any choice he could make or would make unfettered, not under duress" (Letter 181, *Letters* 233). Thus Frodo does fail (cf. Letter 191, *Letters* 252), and 'apostatized' (cf. Letter 181, *Letters* 234).

Tolkien wrote, "But at this point the 'salvation' of the world and Frodo's own 'salvation' is achieved by his previous *pity* and forgiveness of injury. [...] By a situation created by his 'forgiveness', he was saved himself, and relieved of his burden" (*ibid.*). As in the petition from the Lord's Prayer quoted above, Frodo's pity is answered by Divine Pity, the 'highest exercise' of this virtue possible (cf. Letter 246, *Letters* 326). Tolkien believes that the following verse from Scripture is also relevant:

> Therefore let any one who thinks that he stands take heed lest he fall. No temptation has overtaken you that is not common to man. God is faithful, and he will not let you be tempted beyond your strength, but with the temptation will also provide the way of escape, that you may be able to endure it.
> (1 Corinthians 10.12-13; cf. Letter 191, *Letters* 252)

The intrusion of God here in the story may be surprising, but that is the nature of such intrusions. God, says Tolkien, "retains all ultimate authority, and [...] reserves the right to intrude the finger of God into the story: that is to produce realities which could not be deduced even from a complete knowledge of the previous past" (Letter 181, *Letters* 235). Frodo could not have succeeded in his quest without divine grace (cf. Letter 246, *Letters* 326, footnote †).

> Gollum was pitiable, but he ended in persistent wickedness, and the fact that this worked good was no credit to him. His marvellous courage and endurance, as great as Frodo and Sam's or greater, being devoted to evil was portentous, but not honourable. [...] The domination of the Ring was much too strong for the mean soul of Sméagol. But he would have never had to endure it if he had not become a mean sort of thief before it crossed his path.
> (Letter 181, *Letters* 234-35).

It is true that Gollum had been a 'mean sort of thief' before he encountered the Ring, but had he repented before Shelob's lair, Tolkien believed the story might have turned out quite differently.

The interest would have shifted to Gollum, I think. [...] Certainly at some point not long before the end he would have stolen the Ring or taken it by violence. [...] But 'possession' satisfied, I think he would then have sacrificed himself for Frodo's sake and have *voluntarily* cast himself into the fiery abyss. [...] [T]he only way to keep it and hurt Sauron was to destroy it and himself together—and in a flash he may have seen that this would also be the greatest service to Frodo. (Letter 246, *Letters* 330)

The contrast to Gollum is Samwise Gamgee ('Sam'). For Tolkien the figure of Frodo is not as interesting as Sam: "Cert[ainly] Sam is the most closely drawn character, the successor to Bilbo of the first book, the genuine hobbit. Frodo is not so interesting, because he has to be highminded, and has (as it were) a vocation" (Letter 93, *Letters* 105). And a vocation, for a Catholic of Tolkien's generation, would have meant only one thing in this context: the priesthood. Frodo is the high-minded priest. Instead, "the chief hero" (Letter 131, *Letters* 161) for Tolkien is Sam.

Sam starts off in the story as a rustic hobbit, "lovable and laughable" (Letter 246, *Letters* 329). Sam is different from other hobbits in that he has "a vision of beauty, and a reverence for things nobler than [himself]" (*ibid.*). He displays bravery, but it is closer to being rashness (cf. *LotR* 606). He remains possessive of Frodo and overly suspicious of Gollum, becoming jealous of the latter's growing love for Frodo (cf. Letter 181, *Letters* 235). Sam remains thoroughly loyal to Frodo. Tolkien writes, "Sam was cocksure, and deep down a little conceited, but his conceit had been transformed by his devotion to Frodo" (Letter 246, *Letters* 329).

Sam is pre-Christian, and it is easy to overlook his deep religiosity simply because of his being pre-Christian. Religiosity does not consist in doing what are commonly understood to be religious acts. Religiosity for Tolkien the Catholic is one simple thing: love. Sam, by his love for Frodo, is the very model of a deeply-religious layman, not unlike Tolkien himself. Love is not only at the heart of true religion, it is its *essence*. St Augustine (*Sermon on 1 John 7.8.*) remarked, "Love, and do what you will" which some have piously altered to read, 'Love *God*, and do what you will'. But Augustine said simply 'love'. God is not merely the object of love, he is its *subject*. We can love because God loves us and loves *in* us. God is doing the loving in us, and for us. Sam's love for Frodo shares in that divine love, is made possible by that divine love, and *is* that same divine love. Sam, the pre-Christian hobbit, is a very holy and religious creature.[3]

Sam is explicitly cast as Bilbo's real heir. When Frodo is stung by the giant spider Shelob, Sam rescues him with the same Ring and sword that Bilbo had used against the giant spiders of Mirkwood. Like Bilbo he has no real thought of running away to save himself. When he uses the Ring, he feels the allure of its corrupting power.

> In that hour of trial it was the love of his master that helped most to hold him firm; but also deep down in him lived still unconquered his plain hobbit-sense: he knew in the core of his heart that he was not large enough to bear such a burden, even if such visions were not a mere cheat to betray him. The one small garden of a free gardener was all his need and due, not a garden swollen to a realm; his own hands to use, not the hands of others to command. (*LotR* 901)

Sam's growth in virtue and vision is captured by Tolkien in two scenes which act as 'book-ends'. Near the beginning of *The Lord of the Rings*, Sam has been caught eavesdropping on Gandalf and Frodo, and is told to accompany Frodo on his journey. His reaction is like a child's, full of enthusiasm and fear. "'Hooray!' he shouted, and then burst into tears" (*LotR* 64). Towards the end he has grown in character tremendously to become the story's 'chief hero'. His deepest desires come true, but at the cost of sacrifice and suffering. "'All my wishes have come true!' And then he wept" (*LotR* 954). His reaction, to weep, remains the same, yet this is a very different Sam who weeps.

The priest-like Frodo becomes a saint, but not Sam. Merry and Pippin display valour in battle, but not Sam. Sam grows in wisdom and virtue, and returns to the Shire, to an ordinary life, but he returns as an extraordinary man, becoming a leader of his people. His name means "halfwise, simple" (*LotR* 1136, Appendix F), but he becomes "Samwise [...] who should rather be called Plain-wise" (*Sauron Defeated* 118). Sam marries his sweetheart Rose, and becomes Frodo's heir.

---

[3]   I cannot emphasise enough that being truly religious is not about doing overtly 'religious' acts. It is about loving. The failure to grasp this is the reason some cannot fathom Tolkien's claim to have written a religious and Catholic book, *viz. The Lord of the Rings.*

After watching Frodo leave Middle-earth, Sam, the hero of the story, returns home. Commenting on the draft version of the novel, Charles Williams noted that "the great thing is that its *centre* is not in strife and war and heroism (though they are understood and depicted) but in freedom, peace, ordinary life and good liking" (Letter 93, *Letters* 105). Tolkien himself wrote, "[T]he story began in the simple Shire of the hobbits, and it must end there, back to common life and earth (the ultimate foundation) again" (Letter 131, *Companion* 748).

This ending fits well with the image of Sam as the ordinary man, albeit heroic. Tolkien originally concluded his story with an epilogue set fifteen years after Frodo's departure. It shows Sam, one and whole, with his wife Rose, and it ends with a hint of things to come. Frodo had departed westward, but here Sam is facing east, that is, firmly towards his life in Middle-earth with his wife and children. Tolkien remarked, "I think the simple 'rustic' love of Sam and his Rosie (nowhere elaborated) is *absolutely essential* to the study of his [...] character, and to the theme of the relation of ordinary life (breathing, eating, working, begetting) and quests, sacrifice, causes, and the 'longing for Elves', and sheer beauty" (Letter 131, *Companion* 749).

That Tolkien should think simple rustic things essential or primary should not surprise us. As a Catholic he believed that God spent thirty-three years on earth, the fulfilment of the hope voiced in a later work, *Athrabeth Finrod ah Andreth*. Eru (God) has indeed entered Arda (the world) and spent most of his earthly years occupied with the simple things: eating, drinking, working, breathing and laughing. And if it's good enough for Eru Ilúvatar, it's good enough for Samwise Gamgee.

FR. LEON KURIAKOS PEREIRA OP is a Dominican friar and priest of the English province. He was born in Malaysia and grew up in Singapore. After studying Medicine at the University of Leeds and working as a doctor, he joined the Order of Preachers (Dominicans) as a novice at Edinburgh. He studied philosophy and theology at Oxford University, and moral theology at the Angelicum in Rome. His dissertation in Rome was entitled *Hobbitual Grace: Myth and Morality in the Writings of J.R.R. Tolkien.*

References

Abbreviations used:

Companion: see Hammond and Scull 2005

Hobbit: see Tolkien 1999a

Letters: see Carpenter 2000

LotR: see Tolkien 1995

OFS: see Tolkien 1997

Sauron Defeated: see Tolkien 2002

Silmarillion: see Tolkien 1999b

Augustine, *In Epistolam Ioannis ad Parthos, tractatus decem*, chapter 7, section 8 in Jean-Paul Migne (ed.), 1844-65, *Patrologia Latina*, volume 35, column 2033. For an English translation see Philip Schaff (ed.), reprint 1991, *The Nicene and Post-Nicene Fathers*, First Series, volume 7, page 504, Edinburgh: T & T Clark.

Carpenter, Humphrey (with the assistance of Christopher Tolkien) (ed.), 2000, *The Letters of J.R.R. Tolkien*, (first published 1981), Boston: Houghton Mifflin.

Hammond, Wayne G. and Christina Scull, 2005, *The Lord of the Rings. A Reader's Companion*, London: HarperCollins.

Tolkien, John Ronald Reuel, 1995, *The Lord of the Rings*, (second edition; first edition 1954-55), London: HarperCollins.

---, 1997, 'On Fairy-Stories', in *The Monsters and the Critics and Other Essays*, (edited by Christopher Tolkien), London: HarperCollins, 109-61.

---, 1999a, *The Hobbit*, London: HarperCollins.

---, 1999b, *The Silmarillion*, London: HarperCollins.

---, 2002, *Sauron Defeated* (volume nine of *The History of Middle-earth*), edited by Christopher Tolkien, London: Harper Collins.

Tolkien, Chesterton, and Thomism

ALISON MILBANK

Summary

This chapter uses G. K. Chesterton's presentation of the theology of Thomas Aquinas to show how Tolkien too creates a fictional world in accord with Thomistic attitudes to the nature of being, God as Creator and the freedom and mutability of the created order (as shown by Gandalf's fireworks). In particular, Tolkien's short story 'Leaf by Niggle' is shown to be concerned with the relation of making and doing that was so central a concern of the neo-scholastic aesthetics of Jacques Maritain and Eric Gill, while the objects made by the elves embody the values of integrity, proportion and radiance that give them a religious dimension.

Outside of Tolkien's professional criticism, references to other writers are notably scant. This makes his mentions of G. K. Chesterton in his letters and elsewhere particularly significant, and it is clear that Chesterton's monograph on Dickens and his use of defamiliarising techniques was important in guiding Tolkien to his own individual conception of fantasy in his essay 'On Fairy-Stories', in which he defines and moves beyond what he calls "Chestertonian Fantasy" (OFS 58-59). In his study of Tolkien's religious vision, Stratford Caldecott makes frequent analogy with Chesterton's ideas, while not claiming any direct influence. Hobbit culture and social organisation, he also notes, has much in common with the localism and small-scale ownership of Chestertonian Distributism (Caldecott 2003:125-26). Today, however, I should like to make a bolder claim, to the effect that Chestertonian philosophy undergirds Tolkien's Middle-earth, and contributes towards its credibility and overall tone and effect.

This would not be surprising, since as a journalist and controversialist, G. K Chesterton was one of the most attractive and celebrated public characters of early twentieth-century Britain, sparring with George Bernard Shaw and H. G. Wells, delighting the public with his outrageously paradoxical essays, stories and plays, and developing the metaphysical dimension of the detective story with his creation of Father Brown. After his conversion in 1922, he was instrumental in bringing Catholicism into public debate: indeed, in making it seem thoroughly English. It would be a work by Chesterton, *The Everlasting Man*, which brought C. S. Lewis to theism before his well-known conversation with Tolkien about the truth of myth. Tolkien's poem-epistle to Lewis actually uses Chestertonian arguments to claim that myth is not a disease of language but a truthful discourse. The discussion of *Pickwick Papers* in Chesterton's study of Dickens also brings fairy-tale and myth together in the way that Tolkien would also do in his lecture 'On Fairy-Stories'. Greater than all these, however, is Chesterton's enormous emphasis on God as Creator, and on human creativity, which accords and is to some extent indebted to the revival in Thomistic theology. In what follows I shall show in what accord Chesterton's philosophy was with that of contemporary writers on Thomism, but the main focus will be on what insight this helps us to gain of Tolkien's own ideas.

It was Chesterton's prototype for Father Brown, Monsignor John O'Connor, who first translated Jacques Maritain's *Art and Scholasticism* into English in 1923, with the help of the artist and writer, Eric Gill. Along with *St. Thomas Aquinas* in 1932 and *Theonas* the next year, Maritain's writing preached the centrality of Aquinas and the scholastic tradition not only to Christian theology but to art and culture as a whole. The influence on Catholic intellectuals was immense, especially in the Ditchling community around Eric Gill and David Jones. Already, since Leo XIII's encyclical, *Aeterni Patris*, of 1879, there had been a return to Aquinas in the training given to Catholic seminarians, but it was Maritain and Etienne Gilson who drew lay Catholics like Chesterton to see his value in formulating a unified theory of civil and cultural life.

Tolkien, under the guardianship of the Birmingham Oratory priest, Father Francis Morgan, and brought up to attend mass daily, would have listened to many a homily influenced by Thomistic theology, and may very well have read Chesterton's entertaining essay on Thomas, or articles in *The Tablet*. What I am interested in showing, however, is not so much an explicit influence as the implicit Thomistic basis of the metaphysics of his fictional world, and I shall employ Chesterton's presentation of Thomas's ideas to do this. Chesterton's 'Ethics of Elfland' chapter in his intellectual autobiography, *Orthodoxy*, shows him coming to a Thomistic natural religion long before he actually read the *Summa* (if he indeed ever did so), and it may be that Tolkien too imbibed his Thomism 'naturally' with his mother's milk. It is, however my belief that Chesterton's interest in Thomas as a theological realist is central to explicating the 'realism' of Tolkien's own sub-created fictional universe.

The first and most radical of Thomas's ideas, according to Chesterton, is that "there *is* an Is" (Chesterton 2002:153). When a child looks out of the window he knows that there is something there. As Chesterton points out, it is impossible to do anything or trust the reality of the eye itself if what one sees—the grass—is "a mere green impression on the mind" (Chesterton 2002:152). From this one established point Chesterton shows how Thomas's great and complex system all proceeds. As Thomas puts it: "Our intellect, therefore, knows being [*ens*] naturally, and whatever essentially belongs to a being as such; and upon this knowledge is founded the knowledge of first principles" (Aquinas 1975, *Summa Contra Gentiles*, II, 83, 31).

There are two immediate corollaries to this central point: first, if the child sees the grass, he knows it is not true to say that he does not see it. A thing cannot be and not be, and from this, Chesterton (2002:153-54) argues, comes "the everlasting duel between Yes and No." Secondly, that which we see is not complete, because it is always in a process of change. "Ice is melted into cold water and cold water is heated into hot water; it cannot be all three at once" (Chesterton 2002:154). There is a mutability in the things we see but this does not lead to a Heraclitean flux. Rather, its incompletion, its 'becomingness' presupposes the existence of completion:

> Looking at Being as it is now, as the baby looks at the grass, we see a second thing about it; in quite popular language, it *looks* secondary and dependent. Existence exists; but it is not sufficiently self-existent; and it would never become so merely by going on existing. The same primary sense which tells us it is Being, tells us that it is not perfect Being; not merely imperfect in the popular controversial sense of containing sin or sorrow; but imperfect as Being; less actual than the actuality it implies.
> (Chesterton 2002:158)

The potentialities in the mutable phenomena that we see have their fulfilment in God, in whom they already exist. Without this potentiality there can be no concept of change at all, and Chesterton points out the inconsistency of using the language of change in evolutionary theory. The mutability of things can deceive us if we try to hold onto them as ends in themselves; but

as things tending to a greater end, they are even more real than we
think them. If they seem to have a relative unreality (so to speak) it
is because they are potential and not actual; they are unfulfilled,
like packets of seeds or boxes of fireworks. They have it in them to
be more real than they are. And there is an upper world of what the
Schoolman called Fruition or Fulfillment, in which all this relative
relativity becomes actuality; in which the trees burst into flower or
the rockets into flame. (Chesterton 2002:164-65)

There is one further element in this metaphysics that we need in order to understand Tolkien's philosophy, which is that the child does not just see one
thing but many. He sees things—grass and grain—and he sees qualities that
they hold in common, as well as ones by which they differ. It is this difference
of things that Chesterton points to as especially the worldview of Christianity;
its Creator of variety is like an artist, in contrast to an Asian philosophy of
change as a misleading veil of illusion, and individuation with it. In Thomas
this leads to a rejection of nominalism, and promotion of a moderate and participatory realism. For Tolkien the element I would stress is the otherness or
objectivity of things. Only through the reality of the world can the mind, according to Thomas, reach out to otherness, and become the object. As
Maritain (1933:9) writes, "it is in its totality reaching out towards the object,
towards the other *as* other; it needs the dominating contact of the object, but
only that it may be enriched by it [...] fertilised by being, rightly subjected to
the real."

To sum up, Aquinas, according to Chesterton, teaches "the reality of
things, the mutability of things, the diversity of things" (Chesterton
2002:168). And, as we shall see, this is a philosophy that can be found at every
level of Tolkien's fictional project, from his invention of languages, to the
workings of his fictional world and its ethics, to the meta-level of his theory of
art.

The world Tolkien invents is, of course, fictional but it is famously
realistic in its density and completeness of realisation. To invent a world at all,
as fantasy writers continue to do, is to commit to metaphysics. As Cath Filmer
(1997) has argued, it is well nigh impossible to write non-theistic fantasy because an intentionality in the act of creation of Being and beings is inherent in
the whole enterprise. It is significant that the archmodernist James Joyce, despite his rejection of Catholicism, sought the authority of Thomist aesthetics
for his Stephen Dedalus in *Portrait of the Artist as a Young Man*, and Stephen

continues his Scholastic reflections in Chapter 2 of *Ulysses*. For the fantasy writer not only mimics the Divine act of creation but he or she, by creating a self-consistent, independent world also witnesses to the existence of an Is: *Ens.*

Tolkien shows himself to be aware of this metaphysical dimension to fantasy writing in his essay 'On Fairy-Stories'. In the section discussing how fantasy can help us towards recovery, he states that "recovery (which includes return and renewal of health) is a re-gaining—regaining of a clear view. I do not say 'seeing things as they are' and involve myself with the philosophers, though I might venture to say 'seeing things as we are (or were) meant to see them'—as things apart from ourselves" (OFS 58). He goes on to move beyond what he calls 'Chestertonian fantasy', by which things are presented strangely, so that we might see them afresh, because this does not free things enough. Paradoxically it is the invention of creative fantasy which allows the gems to turn into "flowers or flames" (OFS 59), rather like the "trees burst[ing] into flower or the rockets into flame" of the upper world described in Chesterton's study of Aquinas I quoted earlier. The 'things in themselves' to which Tolkien alludes are those elements of phenomena to which Kant, an idealist, believes we have no access, and to which he gives the term, *noumena*. Despite his apologetic tone, Tolkien is actually saying something quite radical: that fiction in the form of fantastic recreation of the world can give us access to the real, by freeing the world of objects from our appropriation. Maritain states that Kant's mistake was in believing "that the act of knowing consists in *creating* the other, not in *becoming* the other, he foolishly reversed the order of dependence between the object of knowledge and the human intellect and made the human intellect the measure and law of the object" (Maritain 1933:9). In reaching out to understand the grass as grass in Thomistic fashion, rather than being trapped by the subjectivity of Kantian perception, Tolkien's story-maker becomes the lover of nature and not her slave.

This Thomistic stress on the freedom of the created order is already stressed by Chesterton in *Orthodoxy*, where he compares God to an artist: "A poet is so separate from his poem that he himself speaks of it as a little thing he has 'thrown off'" (Chesterton 1957:125-26). Similarly God, in making the world, set it free, in the manner of a dramatist, leaving its performance to human actors and stage managers. In Tolkien's own creation myth in *The Silmarillion*, Eru, 'the One' makes the great gods or spirits called the Ainur, to whom he proposes themes of music, out of which each finds his own particular melody, by which polyphony or harmony the world is conceived. It is Eru or Ilúvatar's 'secret fire' of Being, Eä, which gives existence to the world but he allows his themes to be freely developed by the Ainur, even incorporating the discord of the fallen Melkor into an even more wonderful music. This story adds a further level of freedom, so that the creation derives wholly from Ilúvatar, but has the contribution of the Ainur. However, once it has been actualised by Ilúvatar, he shows it to the Ainur as containing their own minstrelsy: he shows them themselves.

The Ainur then come to look at the creation and are amazed, especially by the children of Ilúvatar, the elves and men, who had not been part of their own thought. "Therefore when they beheld them, the more did they love them, being things other than themselves, strange and free, wherein they saw the mind of Ilúvatar reflected anew" *(Silmarillion* 18). So in each part of the creative act there is a consequent setting free of a variety of things and peoples to be themselves. Yet to have variety and diversity is not to have a dead materialism, since every work of the Ainur's hands reveals the wisdom of the Creator.

So Tolkien's myth is faithful to Thomistic philosophy in its stress on God as Creator, the freedom of creation and its diversity. Its mutability is also a strong theme throughout Tolkien's work. It is already present in his account of the creation of the two main orders of the Children of Ilúvatar: the elves are immortal except by slaughter, or at least they shall live as long as the world endures; men are mortal but have a destiny beyond the world. Human beings are therefore mutable in that their body changes and dies, but their end is a supernatural one, which accords with Thomas Aquinas's anthropology in which the natural end for man is participation in the Divine life, achievable through the Fall only by grace. The elves in contrast seem immutable in that they do not age and endure, but they witness to mutability, which they suffer, and which gives them a certain pathos. This is all the stronger in that, while not subject to death in the manner of human beings, the elves do begin to fade and lose their strength and power. To a degree greater than humanity they are wedded to the material cosmos, and yet they are always nostalgic for a return to the Blessed Realm beyond the sea, from which they are exiled. So they are in a way mutable, in that they are faded, and have lost complete actuality, but their mutability has to do with the loss of past things, whereas the mutability of men and hobbits is focused on an unachieved future.

This contrast in perspective also has something to do with the diverse vocations of humans and elves. The latter are presented primarily as artists in Tolkien's world, and the former are the ones concerned with action. This follows precisely the Thomistic distinction between *poiesis* and *praxis*, which Maritain discusses at length in *Art and Sacrament*, and David Jones in *Epoch and Artist* (Jones 1959:143-47). Action—*praxis*—in this context consists "of the *free* use [*free* being here emphatic] of our faculties or in the exercise of our free will considered not in relation to things themselves or the works of our hands, but simply in relation to the use to which we put our freedom" (Jones 1959:5). The sphere of morality and the human good is that of action, and Maritain sets up Prudence as its central virtue, by which our acts are measured against their ultimate end, which is God himself. In contrast, making (*poiesis*) is productive action, which is judged in relation to the thing produced, and its perfecting. Hence the humans in Tolkien's world are primarily men of action, involved in public projects, government and defence; it is the elves who are the makers, following the example of the Ainur such as Aulë whose "delight and pride" were "in the deed of making, and in the thing made" (*Silmarillion* 19). The ethics of this distinction are explored in the story 'Leaf by Niggle', in which Niggle the artist is wholly consumed with the desire to paint a great tree, his real picture, before he has to make what is clearly the journey of death. In the story Niggle is unable to complete his work because of constant interruptions by his neighbour Parish and his practical needs. After a spell in a purgatorial hospital in which he learns the value of practical work, Niggle is released partly because "he took a great deal of pains with leaves, just for their own sake" (Leaf 106). In Thomistic terms, he sought the perfecting of the work. At the end of a train journey he discovers the tree he had tried to paint, now an actual tree in a landscape and completely finished. "'It's a gift!' he said. He was referring to his art, and also to the result; but he was using the word quite literally" (Leaf 110). He plans more work, and with the help of Parish, who aids rather than interrupting him, Niggle completes a whole landscape, house and garden. This story is partly about the value of artistic production, but also seeks to bring together Parish's *praxis* and Niggle's *poiesis*, which find their integration and fulfillment in heaven's "mystical comradeship" as Chesterton put it in *Thomas Aquinas* (Chesterton 2002:107). It is typical of Tolkien that he should write about a piece of art coming true, since that was the triumphant theological conclusion to 'On Fairy-Stories' in which he looked to a time when all tales would come true in the eschaton. The art that is created in 'Leaf by Niggle' however, is not just a piece of fine art but also of practical use: people can come and live in it and be refreshed by it. Here Prudence has not been sacrificed to Art as Maritain (and Chesterton) claimed happened at the Renaissance, but there has been a return to an earlier medieval conception of art as serving society, which was being revived in communities like that of Eric Gill when Tolkien was writing.

The art of the elves is similarly functional in the sense that they make objects rather than paint canvases: in modern terms they make applied rather than pure art. The nearest to 'pure art' are the Silmarils made by Fëanor, either through a 'new thought' or because he dreaded the possible destruction of the Two Trees that lit the Blessed Realm, so that they "might be preserved imperishable" (*Silmarillion* 67). Although the Silmarils are wonderful as objects, Fëanor hoards them, refuses them as aid to the Valar in undoing the destruction of the Two Trees, and later they are the cause of war and all sorts of disasters. Maritain helps to make sense of the fault here. Not only should the artist aim always and solely at the good of the work itself but he makes always a new thing; he does not merely imitate an old idea. There is consequently an ambiguity in the original project, which was aimed at preservation, and this is later confirmed by Fëanor's failure to use the jewels for a good purpose. They have become evidence of an art for art's sake aesthetic, and spend much of the time locked up. Maritain does allow a look backward to artistic production, in that it restores the relation of people and things lost after the Fall: for beauty "has the savour of the terrestial paradise, because it restores, for a moment, the peace and simultaneous delight of the intellect and the senses" (Maritain 1949:19). But generally art must have a purpose that is servile because it is oriented to use or liberal in providing intellectual joy. Both purposes are located in present experience or future use.

In *The Lord of the Rings* Galadriel, Celeborn and the Lothlórien elves are presented very much as correct artists in Scholastic terms. As Maritain urges, they put themselves in all that they make: "Leaf and branch, water and stone. They have the hue and beauty of all these things under the twilight of Lórien that we love; for we put the thought of all that we love into all that we make" (*LotR* 370). Not only are all the things they make beautiful and pleasing to sight (Maritain 1949:19) but they are useful and serve the common good. Like Niggle's Parish they unite art and Prudence. Their cloaks are light and allow the wearer to blend into the landscape; their rope magically undoes itself, and their boats do not sink. Although the phial of light Galadriel gives to Frodo contains the light of Eärendil's star, it orients that ancient source of illumination to future needs. And because all these objects are given to the Fellowship, Galadriel accepts her own fading and mutability (as she does also in resisting the temptation to take the Ring when Frodo offers it to her), offering her work to an unknown world to come. Her great lament, sung as the Fellowship floats away from Lórien down the river, does mourn the loss of Eldamar, but it contains a hope that other races may indeed reach it: "maybe thou shalt find Valimar" (*LotR* 378).

Maritain also describes the qualities that the beautiful must possess for scholastic philosophy: integrity, proportion and radiance or clarity. The first refers to fullness of being, so that elvish art's enchanted quality, whereby the rope has all the qualities one might hope for—silken smoothness, toughness, easy coiling and even visiblility in the dark—to such an extent that it seems to have a life of its own, witnesses to its fullness of ropey being, or form. Elvish art clearly has proportion and unity; but most of all it has clarity or radiance, or what Aquinas terms, *splendor formae*, a splendour in its form. This means more than integrity. As Maritain (1949:20) puts it:

> *splendor formae* [...] that is to say, the principle which constitutes and achieves things in their essence and qualities, which is, finally [...] the ontological secret that they bear within them, their spiritual being, their operating mystery—the form, indeed, is above all the proper *clarity* of every thing. Besides, every form is a vestige or a ray of the creative Intelligence imprinted at the heart of created being.

Such a philosophy depends upon a neo-Platonic theory of light as intellectual energy, which is given off by a beautiful object or person from its source in God. The poet Dante constructs his whole Paradise out of such 'light intellectual full of love'. Tolkien too seems to hold to such a celestial physics in his use of objects whose radiance similarly has a heavenly origin. The Silmarils, the three rings of the elves, Narya, Nenya and Vilya, and the little phial given to Frodo, all have the radiance and clarity of divine connection, and even the rope has a silvery sheen. Their actual illumination has an intelligibility, which reveals their nature and its 'operating mystery'. For the elves all remember the realm of the gods: the ontological origins of Middle-earth itself.

Gandalf too shares the art of the elves and wears the elven ring of fire, Narya. He combines elvish understanding of the natural world with the directive energies of Prudence. In Chestertonian terms his art is even more godlike than theirs for it consists in making fireworks, which, like the Divine creation are 'thrown off' and take on a life of their own. At the beginning of my paper, I quoted Chesterton's study of Aquinas, in which he spoke of earthly things we see as being like packets of seeds or boxes of fireworks at present, to burst into flames or grow into trees and flower in the Fulfilment of the Divine life. Gandalf's fireworks not only burst into flame, as would be expected, but also take the forms of trees: "green trees with trunks of dark smoke: their leaves opened like a whole spring unfolding in a moment, and their shining branches dropped glowing flowers down upon the astonished hobbits" (*LotR* 27). Gandalf's fireworks enact the freedom that Tolkien attributed to creative fantasy, when the things of this world are set free, and the locked things fly away like cage-birds—Gandalf provides eagles and flying swans. It is, of course, Bilbo's past history that is thus re-enacted, as described in *The Hobbit*. The release of his memories into fireworks provides also a moral lesson: that he also should let things go, as he does with his living will and by leaving his home and possessions behind. Only the Ring of Power is hard to let free.

Aquinas has something also to contribute to the problem of this great Ring. Sauron, its maker, erred as an artist, in stealing knowledge to forge it from others, so that he did not put his own *habitus* within it. He erred in not seeking the good of the work but his own power. He erred also morally in separating art from Prudence completely, with no thought of the common good, or according his making to the Divine order. Despite this, the Ring appears beautiful to Frodo when he first acquires it "the gold looked very fair and pure, and Frodo thought how rich and beautiful was its colour, how perfect was its roundness. It was an admirable thing and altogether precious" (*LotR* 60). In Thomistic terms it certainly has integrity, in that it appears complete in itself. Its proportion, its inner qualities that render it round and golden, also seem unified. What it lacks is clarity or radiance because it actually hides words only visible in the fire. Moreover it lacks any vestige of its createdness: the integrity seems to subsume it, so that it becomes an isolated 'precious' object that subsumes divinity to itself. No one can free themselves from it once they own it, and therefore, as Tolkien indicated in his essay 'On Fairy-Stories', it reveals nothing of the primary world. "By the forging of Gram cold iron was revealed" (OFS 59) but the Ring's power tells us little of the virtues of gold in themselves.

Paradoxically, Sauron too becomes the slave rather than the lover of his own work, and its destruction immediately leads to his own downfall. By denying clarity and relation to origin to the Ring it became magical rather than enchanted. And in trying to be god, with his perversions of creation in his doctored orcs, Sauron is reduced to a great fiery eye, which is fixated on the object. For Tolkien shows us that to be most like God is to be creative, and to allow that creation true freedom. Tolkien as a creator, or sub-creator, has indeed given birth to a whole world of different races and landscapes, beliefs and cultures. Its success too is due to the entire devotion to *poiesis*, to the perfecting of the work itself by its author. But its satisfying depth is not just due to its complexity and detail, as if it were the Harry Potter series. It is due to its integrity, proportion but also clarity, so that it provides a philosophical clue to the primary world we know: like Middle-earth, this world means more than it seems. In a real sense *The Lord of the Rings* does not need gods or a Christian subtext to be a religious work: because there is a radiance in every detail of its world, rendering it both wholly real, and yet witnessing to a reality beyond itself: and providing, as Tolkien wrote in 'Mythopoeia' (90) "from mirrored truth the likeness of the True."

ALISON MILBANK read Theology and English Literature at Cambridge and took her PhD at Lancaster. She was John Rylands Research Fellow at Manchester and has taught at the universities of Cambridge, Middlesex and Virginia. She is Associate Professor of Literature and Theology at the University of Nottingham. Her publications include editions of Ann Radcliffe's fiction, *Daughters of the House: Modes of the Gothic in Victorian Fiction* (1992), *Dante and the Victorians* (1998), and, most recently, *Chesterton and Tolkien as Theologians: The Fantasy of the Real* (2007).

References

Abbreviations used:

Leaf: see Tolkien 2001c

LotR: see Tolkien 2004

Mythopoeia: see Tolkien 2001b

OFS: see Tolkien 2001a

Silmarillion: see Tolkien 1999

Aquinas, Thomas, 1975, *Contra Gentiles Book Two: Creation*, (translated by James P. Anderson), Notre Dame and London: Notre Dame University Press.

Caldecott, Stratford, 2003, *Secret Fire: The Spiritual Vision of J.R.R. Tolkien*, London: Darton, Longman and Todd.

Chesterton, Gilbert K., 1957, *Orthodoxy*, London: Bodley Head.

---, 2002, *Saint Thomas Aquinas and Saint Francis of Assisi*, (introductions by Ralph McInerny and Joseph Pearce), San Francisco: Ignatius Press.

Filmer-Davies, Cath, 1997, 'Presence and Absence: God in Fantasy Literature', *Christianity and Literature* 47.1:59-76.

Jones, David, 1959, 'Art and Sacrament', in *Epoch and Artist*, London: Faber, 143-79.

Maritain, Jacques, 1933, *Theonas: Conversations of a Sage*, (translated by F. J. Sheed), London: Sheed and Ward.

---, 1949, *Art and Scholasticism with Other Essays*, (translated by J. F. Scanlan), London: Sheed and Ward.

Tolkien, John Ronald Reuel, 1999, *The Silmarillion*, (first published 1977; edited by Christopher Tolkien), London: HarperCollins.

---, 2001a, 'On Fairy-Stories', in *Tree and Leaf, Including the Poem Mythopoeia*, London: HarperCollins, 3-81.

---, 2001b, 'Mythopoeia', in *Tree and Leaf, Including the Poem Mythopoeia*, London: HarperCollins, 85-90.

---, 2001c, 'Leaf by Niggle', in *Tree and Leaf, Including the Poem Mythopoeia*, London: HarperCollins, 93-118.

---, 2004, *The Lord of the Rings*, (originally published 1954-55; one-volume 50th anniversary edition), Boston: Houghton Mifflin.

The Influence of Holiness:
The Healing Power of Tolkien's Narrative

GUGLIELMO SPIRITO OFM CONV.

Summary

In the last years of his life, Tolkien received a letter from Carole Batten-Phelps, who wrote of "a sanity and sanctity" in *The Lord of the Rings*, "which is a power in itself." If sanctity inhabits an author's work, he replied, or a pervading light illumines it, then "it does not come from him but through him." What does this statement imply? It sounds very much like an authentic synthesis of the inner dynamism of Tolkien's work. But to what type of 'sanity' and 'sanctity' is he referring? Is he speaking only of a genial literary sub-creation which ultimately can be reduced to 'lies breathed through silver' (to use C.S. Lewis's famous phrase)? Or is there really an 'invisible lamp' which gives light and inner consistency to everything? And why did he think that to deny this 'lamp' would lead us "either to sadness or wrath," while by welcoming it we may become—as Frodo did—"like a glass filled with clear light for eyes to see that can."

In the life of any individual, a book that is re-read several times is one that both establishes itself as an intimate and familiar conversational partner, but which at every reading also conceals and reveals different things, opens different doors.[1] Such a book helps us to cross borders, to enter into a new and transfigured world. And that is exactly what we experience as we read Tolkien's works. He possesses to an unusual degree the gift of creative imagination. So as Chesterton (2003:81) used to say "though I could not with a crayon get the best out of the landscape, it does not follow that the landscape was not getting the best out of me."

I will try to use only two texts from Tolkien, the first being a reply to Miss Batten-Phelps written in Autumn 1971:

> You speak of 'a sanity and sanctity' in the L.R. 'which is a power in itself'. I was deeply moved. Nothing of the kind had been said to me before. But by a strange chance, just as I was beginning this letter, I had one from a man, who classified himself as 'an unbe-

---

[1] Cf. Rowan (2005:94).

liever, or at best a man of belatedly and dimly dawning religious
feeling ... but you', he said, 'create a world in which some sort of
faith seems to be everywhere without a visible source, like light
from an invisible lamp'. I can only answer: 'Of his own sanity no
man can securely judge. If sanctity inhabits his work or as a pervading light illumines it then it does not come from him but
through him. And neither of you would perceive it in these terms
unless it was with you also. Otherwise you would see and feel
nothing, or (if some other spirit was present) you would be filled
with contempt, nausea, hatred. 'Leaves out of the elf-country, gah!'
'Lembas—dust and ashes, we don't eat that.'
(Letter 328, *Letters* 413)

Tolkien is a misunderstood man precisely because he is a mythunderstood
man. He understood the nature and meaning of myth in a manner which has
not been grasped by most of his critics, though some of them, perhaps most of
them, share Lewis's conviction: "[a]s he expressed it to Tolkien, myths were
'lies and therefore worthless, even though breathed through silver.' 'No,'
Tolkien replied. 'They are not lies.'" (Pearce 2002:87).[2]

What is the applicability of this understanding to our lives today? What
is the underlying reality or truth that Tolkien would have us see?[3]

The second text from Tolkien comes from *The Two Towers* in 'The
Window on the West':

Then came the voice of Faramir close behind. 'Let them see!' he
said. The scarves were removed and their hoods drawn back, and
they blinked and gasped. They stood on a wet floor of polished
stone, the doorstep, as it were, of a rough-hewn gate of rock opening dark behind them. But in front a thin veil of water was hung,
so near that Frodo could have put an outstretched arm into it. It

---

[2]   See also OFS (50-51). "To many, Fantasy, this sub-creative art which plays
strange tricks with the world and all that is in it, combining nouns and
redistributing adjectives, has seemed suspect, if not illegitimate. To some it has
seemed at least a childish folly, a thing only for peoples or for persons in their
youth. As for its legitimacy I will say no more than to quote a brief passage from a
letter I once wrote to a man who described myth and fairy-story as 'lies'; though
to do him justice he was kind enough and confused enough to call fairy-story
making 'Breathing a lie through Silver'."

[3]   Cf. Dickerson (2003:232).

faced westward. The level shafts of the setting sun behind beat upon it, and the red light was broken into many flickering beams of ever-changing colour. It was as if they stood at the window of some elven-tower, curtained with threaded jewels of silver and gold, and ruby, sapphire and amethyst, all kindled with an unconsuming fire. 'At least by good chance we came at the right hour to reward you for your patience.' Said Faramir. 'This is the Window of the Sunset. Henneth Annun, fairest of all the falls of Ithilien, land of many fountains. Few strangers have ever seen it. But there is no kingly hall behind to match it. Enter now and see!' Even as he spoke the sun sank, and the fire faded in the flowing water. (*LotR* 700)

To reject the reality of this spirit "leads to sadness or to wrath" said Tolkien (OFS 65). This passage and those surrounding it are the key texts for interpreting the heart of Tolkien's work. He was an artist who created a secondary world that has "the inner consistency of reality" for most, though not all of his readers. But he was also a Christian, and his Christianity gave him the joy and vision that find expression in his work.[4]

Sadness immobilizes us internally, because in the place of light it puts the deepest darkness. In the time of sadness we take no account of anything, neither of God, nor of our neighbour, nor even of ourselves—we experience a kind of annihilation. Darkness renders everything indistinguishable, whereas light enables us to distinguish and discriminate, and within its truth the human person makes real progress.[5] Sadness turns darkness inward and wrath outward.

The Desert Fathers, who are experts in the workings of the human soul, know that anger awakens within us the most uncompassionate feelings, that it destroys any disposition to become more refined and provokes the drunkenness of darkness, which extinguishes reason and renders every feeling blind. Anger is expressed as if from a position of strength, but it is born in weakness. We become angry because something hinders us and surpasses us, threatens to surround us with insecurity. The soul's serenity and tranquility, by contrast,

---

[4]   Cf. Purtill (2003:188-89): "Not all of those who dislike and reject Tolkien's work do so in an Orcish spirit. No doubt some of Tolkien's critics hate God, and others merely hate Elves."

[5]   Cf. Ramfos (2000:159). On the symbolism of darkness, cf. Devaux (2003).

witness to a firm faith and inner security, a spiritual state independent of human feelings of power or weakness.[6]

> The consolation of fairy-stories, the joy of the happy ending: or more correctly, of the good catastrophe, the sudden joyous 'turn' (for there is no true end to any fairy-tale): this joy which is one of the things which fairy-stories can produce supremely well, is not essentially 'escapist' or 'fugitive'. In its fairy-tale—or otherworld—setting, it is a sudden and miraculous grace, never to be counted on to recur. It does not deny the existence of *dyscatastrophe*, of sorrow and failure: the possibility of these is necessary to the joy of deliverance: it denies (in the face of much evidence, if you will), universal final defeat, and in so far is *evangelium*, giving a fleeting glimpse of Joy, Joy beyond the walls of the world, poignant as grief. (OFS 62)

Tolkien chooses the term 'eucatastrophe' to emphasize that the sudden 'turning' or unexpected deliverance at the end of a true tale of Faërie must be experienced not as an achievement of triumphant revenge, but rather as a divine gift. The joy produced by such a happy ending requires a surprise, a deliverance that no human effort could have made possible. In a letter to his son Christopher, Tolkien uses the example of a boy dying of tubercular peritonitis who was taken to the Grotto at Lourdes, but not cured. However, on the train ride home, as he passed within sight of the Grotto again, he was healed. Tolkien writes that this story, "with its apparent sad ending and then its sudden unhoped-for happy ending" gave him that peculiar emotion which comes from eucatastrophe, because it is a "sudden glimpse of the Truth [...] a ray of light through the very chinks of the universe about us" (*Letters* 100f.). One of the principal mythological forms to represent holiness and sanctity is *light*, taken not as a symbol but as an embodiment of holiness.[7]

'Presence' has a depth that lives behind the form or below the surface. There is a well of presence within everything, but it is usually hidden from the human eye. This comes to the surface in different ripples. No human can ever see anything fully. All we see are aspects of things. Being human is like being

---

[6]   Cf. Ramfos (2000:160).

[7]   Irigaray (1999:210). Cf. also *LotR* (514-16) where light emanates from the resurrected Gandalf.

in a room of almost total darkness. The walls are thick and impenetrable, but there are crevices which let in the outside light. Each time you look out, all you see is a single angle or aspect of something. From within this continual darkness, you are unable to control or direct the things outside this room. You are utterly dependent on them to offer you different views of themselves. All you ever see are dimensions. This is why it is so difficult to be certain of anything. As St Paul says, "Now we see in a glass darkly, then we shall see face to face."[8]

In English the phrase that a person 'has presence' is hard to define. There are people whose being here and now is felt, even though they do not put themselves centre-stage by action or speech. There are other people who may be here all the time, and no one will be aware of them. We say of a person whose outer appearance communicates something of his indwelling power or greatness, whose soul is radiant and conveys itself without words, that he has presence. Similarly, the outer appearance of the world communicates something of the indwelling greatness of God, which is radiant and conveys itself without words. *The whole earth is full of His glory.* "There is no speech, there are no words, neither is their voice heard," and yet, "their radiance goes out through all the earth and their words to the end of the world" (Psalm 19:4-5).

This glory is neither an esthetic nor a physical category. It is sensed in grandeur, but it is more than grandeur. It is, as we said, a living presence or the effulgence of a living presence. Standing face to face with the world, we often sense a spirit which surpasses our ability to comprehend. The world is too much for us. It is crammed with marvel, and the glory is not an exception but an aura that is cast about all being, a spiritual setting of reality. The perception of the glory is a rare occurrence in our lives. We usually fail to wonder, we fail to respond to the presence. This is the tragedy of every man; 'to dim all wonder by indifference'. Life is routine and routine is resistance to wonder.

Heschel (1991:82-83, 85) writes:[9]

'Replete is the world with a spiritual radiance, replete with sublime and marvellous secrets. But a small hand held against the eye hides it all,' said the Baal Shem. 'Just as a small coin held over the face

---

[8] Cf. O'Donohue (2002:54, 204).

[9] Cf. also Fernandez (2005:67).

can block out the sight of a mountain, so can the vanities of living block out the sight of the infinite light.' [...] 'Of what avail is an open eye, if the heart is blind?'

Awe is the awareness of *transcendent meaning*, of a spiritual suggestiveness of reality, an allusiveness to transcendent meaning. The world in its grandeur is full of a spiritual radiance, for which we have neither name nor concept.

Awe, then is more than a feeling. It is an answer of the heart and mind to the presence of mystery in all things, *an intuition for a meaning that is beyond the mystery*, an awareness of the *transcendent worth of the universe*.

The imperative of awe is its certificate of evidence, a universal certificate which we all seal with tremor and fascination; not because we desire to, but because we are stunned and cannot brave it. There is so much more meaning in reality than the soul can take in. To our sense of mystery and wonder the world is too incredible, too meaningful for us, and its existence the most unlikely, the most unbelievable fact, contrary to all reasonable expectations. Even our ability to wonder fills us with amazement. This, then is an insight we gain in acts of wonder; not to measure meaning in terms of our own mind, but to sense a meaning infinitely greater than ourselves.[10]

Chesterton (2003:131) used to say that "Fairyland is nothing but the sunny country of common sense. It is not Earth that judges Heaven, but Heaven that judges Earth."

'The best lack all conviction'. George Steiner wrote a book called *Real Presences: Is There Anything in What We Say?* And the title says it all. Steiner maintains that the profound crisis in which we are living has its roots in the last century, and the collapse of shared belief that our words have anything to do with how things are. They disclose nothing. The covenant between word and world is broken. It is this break of the covenant between word and world which constitutes one of the few genuine revolutions of spirit in western history and which defines modernity itself.[11]

---

[10]   Cf. Heschel (1991:106f.). See also Williams (2003:4, 5, 8, 9, 10, 58) and Chryssavgis (2004:110f.).

[11]   Cf. Radcliffe (1999:234f.).

So, if the sun didn't shine, they would have not seen anything. The glittering drops are not the source of their own light!

'The Window on the West' "invites us to surrender the safe security of the disengaged reader, to lose our mastery, to give up being 'little mortal absolutes', to entrust ourselves to the flow and thrust of a story beyond our control, like the one who, we believe, gave himself into other people's hands so that we might live" (Radcliffe 2001:212).

Up to now, we have been speaking of light, and of beauty. Light is the life-blood of the world, of all things the most desirable, for it is the 'luminous form of the beautiful'. It carries within itself the music of meaning. But the source of both light and beauty, according to Tolkien, is fire.[12]

Carl Kerenyi (1951:2-4, 8, quoted in Curry 1997:131) defined the stuff of mythology as:

> an immemorial and traditional body of material contained in tales about gods and god-like beings, heroic battles and journeys to the Underworld—*mythologem* is the best Greek word for them—tales already well-known but not unamenable to further reshaping. Myth is the *movement* of this material. ... In a true mythologem this meaning is not something that could be expressed just as well and just as fully in a non-mythological way. [...]
>
> Myth gives a ground, lays a foundation. It does not answer the question 'why?' but 'whence?'

A fantasy like *The Lord of the Rings* can help us not only to imagine wonder, but realise it by returning to our world and seeing it afresh. It offers renewal not through escapism, but reconnection.

There is no tale ever told, Tolkien (OFS 65) says of the Gospel, "that men would rather find was true, and none which so many sceptical men have accepted as true on its own merits. [...] To reject it leads either to sadness or to wrath." The phrasing is curiously cautious; 'would rather' is in the subjunctive, not the indicative or declarative mood. It is a story that has been 'accepted as true', which suggests what men *want* rather than what men *know*. This is not

---

[12] See Hans Urs von Balthasar (1982:441) and also Caldecott (2005:103-7).

to suggest that Tolkien did not believe the story was true. Nothing in his life is clearer than his commitment to his faith.

Perhaps the key lies in the underlying, light-associated nature of directional movement. It can be seen most clearly at those points of intersection where westward-moving, light-seeking men cross the path of eastward-moving, light-declining Elves. But Gandalf said to himself about Frodo:

> He is not half through yet, and to what he will come in the end not
> even Elrond can foretell. Not to evil, I think. He may become like
> a glass filled with a clear light for eyes to see that can.
> (*LotR* 239)

Gandalf's auxiliary verb is significant. He does not say Frodo *will* become, or *must* become, but that he *may* become. This is speculation, not prediction. *May*, Anglo-Saxon *magan*, 'to be able', describes capacity, not actuality. What Gandalf sees in Frodo is potential; it may or may not be realized.[13]

But that potential of Frodo's is our own: "Things that are covered up from men in this world will become transparent as globes of crystal" (Heschel 2003:34).[14]

The fact that *The Lord of the Rings* is indirectly responsible for (or at least involved in) nearly everything of value in my present life, becomes insignificant next to that best of magic—the ability to make reality itself more real.[15]

The doctrine of Creation teaches us to see the world as created, which is to say as given. Our eyes are opened to the pure gratuitousness of being. Nothing need exist. Everything is a gift. To ask God for what I desire and to thank God when I receive it is living in the real world. It is opening our eyes to the pure gratuity of being. The word 'thank' derives from 'think'.[16]

---

[13]   Flieger (2002:30, 124, 156, 157). See also John Paul II (1995:32). This process of becoming ever more moderate and sparing, more transparent to himself, can cause him to fall into pride and intransigence if he comes to believe that these are the fruits of his own ascetic efforts.

[14]   See Ramfos (2000:248) and also Wood (2003:142-43).

[15]   Cf. Duane (2001:129).

[16]   Ayto (1990:526) quoted in Radcliffe (2006:127).

Thanking is thinking truly, and prayer helps us to think well. So if I am to describe a human being truthfully, Timothy Radcliffe said, it is not enough for me to just describe what is before my eyes. I am reaching out for what cannot be fully told now, what can only be glimpsed at the edge of language. Seamus Heaney describes a poem by Dylan Thomas as giving "the sensation of language on the move towards a destination in knowledge." He (quoted in Radcliffe 2006:127f.) writes,

> We go to poetry, we go to literature in general, to be forwarded within ourselves. The best it can do is to give us an experience that is like foreknowledge of certain things which we already seem to be remembering.

As O'Donohue (2002:2) explains,[17]

> To be human is to belong. Belonging is a circle that embraces everything; if we reject it, we damage our nature. The word 'belonging' holds together the two fundamental aspects of life: Being and Longing, the longings of our Being and the being of our Longing.

We know no more where the Window on the West lies, but the sun still glitters and shines, the sun *is*, there is a source of light, the one that was shining through Frodo. So there *is* a light which has, through us, a sanity and sanctity which refreshes us. However, it doesn't come from us but through us![18]

In the words of Pope John Paul II (1995:11, 54f.):

> The light of the East has illumined the universal Church, from the moment when 'a rising sun' appeared above us (Lk 1:78): Jesus Christ, our Lord, whom all Christians invoke as the Redeemer of man and the hope of the world.
>
> On the threshold of the third millennium we all hear the cry of those oppressed by the burden of grave threats, but who, perhaps even without realizing it, long to know what God in his love intended. These people feel that a ray of light, if it is welcomed, is capable of dispelling the shadows which cover the horizon of the Father's tenderness.
>
> Mary, 'Mother of the star that never sets', 'dawn of the mystical

---

[17] See also O'Donohue (2002:229-30).

[18] See Fernandez (2005:62, 66) and also Ramfos (2000:253-54).

day', 'rising of the sun of glory', shows us the *Orientale Lumen*. Every day in the East the sun of hope rises again, the light that restores life to the human race. It is from the East, according to a lovely image, that our Savior will come again (cf. Mt 24:27).

There is a story from the Fathers of the Egyptian Desert:

> Abba Isaiah called one of the brethren, washed his feet, put a handful of lentils into the pot and brought them to him as soon as they had boiled. The brother said to him, 'They are not cooked, Abba.' The old man replied, '*Is it not enough simply to have seen the fire? That alone is a great consolation.*' (Ward 1984:70)

Also for us! Having glimpsed the splintering light which comes from the radiance of the Living Sun, who is and ever shall be, that could be enough for us ... for a while at least! Until we meet the Shining Sun face to face in the Everlasting West.

GUGLIELMO SPIRITO, OFM Conv., is a Franciscan friar, Vice-Dean of the Theological Institute of Assisi (ITA) and Professor of Spirituality and Christian and Non-Christian Mystics. Father Guglielmo has taught in Russia, Romania, and Croatia, as well as in the Theological Faculty of Saint Bonaventure in Rome. He is the author of two books and numerous articles on Tolkien, and in 2005 organized a conference on the fiftieth anniversary of Tolkien's visit to Assisi.

References

Abbreviations used:

Biography: see Carpenter 1977

Letters: see Carpenter 2000

LotR: see Tolkien 1992a

OFS: see Tolkien 1992b

Ayto, John, 1990, *Bloomsbury Dictionary of Word Origins*, London: Bloomsbury.

Balthasar, Hans Urs von, 1982, *The Glory of the Lord*, San Francisco: Ignatius Press.

Caldecott, Stratford, 2005, *The Power of the Ring. The Spiritual Vision Behind the Lord of the Rings*, New York: Crossroad.

Carpenter, Humphrey, 1977, *Tolkien: A Biography,* Boston: Houghton Mifflin.

---, (with the assistance of Christopher Tolkien) (ed.), 2000, *The Letters of J.R.R. Tolkien*, (first published 1981), Boston: Houghton Mifflin.

Chesterton, Gilbert K., 2003, *Essential Writings*, Maryknoll, NY: Orbis Books.

Chryssavgis, John, 2004, *Light Through Darkness. The Orthodox Tradition*, London: Darton Longman Todd.

Curry, Patrick, 1997, *Defending Middle-earth. Tolkien: Myth and Modernity*, Edinburgh: Floris Books.

Devaux, Michaël, 2003, 'Les anges de l'Ombre chez Tolkien: chair, corps et corruption', in Michaël Devaux, 2003, *Tolkien, les racines du légendaire*, Geneva: Ad Solem, 191-245.

Dickerson, Matthew T., 2003, *Following Gandalf. Epic Battles and Moral Victory in The Lord of the Rings*, Michigan: Brazos Press.

Duane, Diane, 2001, *Meditations on Middle-earth*, New York: St. Martin's Press.

Fernandez, Irène, 2005, *C.S. Lewis – Mythe, raison ardente*, Geneva: Ad Solem.

Flieger, Verlyn, 2002, *Splintered Light. Logos and Language in Tolkien's World*, Kent, OH: The Kent State University Press.

Heschel, Abraham Joshua, 1991, *God in Search of Man. A Philosophy of Judaism*, New York: The Noonday Press.

---, 2003, *The Sabbath. Its Meaning for Modern Man*, Boston: Shambhala.

Irigaray, Ricardo, 1999, *Elfos, Hobbits y Dragones. Una investigacion sobre la simbologia de Tolkien*, Buenos Aires: Tierra Media.

John Paul II, 1995, *The Light of the East (Orientale lumen)*, (apostolic letter), Boston: Paoline Book & Media.

Kerenyi, Carl, 1951, 'Prolegomena', in Carl Gustav Jung and Carl Kerenyi, 1951, *Introduction to a Science of Mythology: The Myth of the Divine Child and the Mysteries of Eleusis*, London: Routledge & Kegan Paul.

O'Donohue, John, 2002, *Eternal Echoes. Celtic Reflections on Our Yearning to Belong*, New York: HarperCollins.

Pearce, Joseph, 1999, *Tolkien: Man and Myth*, London: Harper Collins.

---, 2002, 'True Myth. The Catholicism of *The Lord of the Rings*', in John G. West Jr. (ed.), 1999, *Celebrating Middle-earth. The Lord of the Rings as a Defense of Western Civilization*, Seattle: Inklings Books, 83-94.

Purtill, Richard L., 2003, *J.R.R. Tolkien: Myth, Morality, and Religion*, San Francisco: Ignatius Press.

Radcliffe, Timothy OP, 1999, *Sing a New Song. The Christian Vocation*, Dublin: Dominican Publications.

---, 2001, *I Call You Friends*, London and New York: Continuum.

---, 2006, *What is the Point of Being a Christian?* London and New York: Burns & Oates.

Ramfos, Stelios, 2000, *Like a Pelican in the Wilderness. Reflections on the Sayings of the Desert Fathers*, Brookline, Massachussetts: Holy Cross Orthodox Press.

Rowan, Williams, 2005, *Why Study the Past? The Quest for Historical Church*, London: Darton Longman Todd.

Tolkien, John Ronald Reuel, 1992a, *The Lord of the Rings*, (first published 1954-55; one volume edition), London: Grafton.

---, 1992b, 'On Fairy-Stories', in *Tree and Leaf*, (edited by Christopher Tolkien), London: Grafton, 9-73.

Ward, Benedicta, 1984, *The Sayings of the Desert Fathers*, Kalamazoo, Mich.: Cistercian Publication.

West, John G. Jr. (ed.), 1999, *Celebrating Middle-earth. The Lord of the Rings as a Defense of Western Civilization*, Seattle: Inklings Books.

Williams, Rowan, 2003, *The Dwelling of the Light. Praying with Icons of Christ*, Norwich: The Canterbury Press.

Wood, Ralph C., 2003, *The Gospel According to Tolkien. Visions of the Kingdom in Middle-earth*, Louisville and Westminster: John Knox Press.

Tolkien's Project[1]

STRATFORD CALDECOTT

Summary

The purpose of this paper is to draw together some of the threads of the volume, and to encourage the further opening up of Tolkien Studies. I will be trying to say a little bit for what it is that Tolkien's work tells us about England, the country he almost died trying to defend in the First World War. And I will touch on the controversial question of Christianity and Paganism.

In Search of England

So, what is England? The question is especially current at the moment, for several reasons. Firstly, because our relationship to the mainland has been radically changing ever since we began the process of European integration. The vision—or nightmare—of the European Union is the Oliphaunt in the bedroom of political discourse. Power is draining away from Westminster to Brussels, and connected with this is a movement towards devolution: that is, the creation of separate governing assemblies for Wales, Scotland, and Northern Ireland. While many members of Her Majesty's present government are in fact of Scottish origin, it appears that the binding force holding the parts of the United Kingdom together is currently weaker than at any time since the death of Queen Victoria.

Secondly, we have been through an accelerating process of cultural change since the end of the Second World War, and just at the moment many people feel that what used to define us as a culture is in danger of disappearing forever. That is to say, our accent, our language, our shared values, our sense of fairness, our national health system, our innate courtesy, not to mention our pre-eminence on the football pitch, are all in question. Our farms are being converted into state-subsidized parkland, the Church of England is in virtual schism with itself, Big Brother rules the airwaves and the tabloids.

---

[1] Some paragraphs of this essay are borrowed from Caldecott (2005).

Back in 1943, Tolkien had already expressed some anxieties about the effects of globalization:

> The bigger things get the smaller and duller or flatter the globe gets. It is getting to be all one blasted little provincial suburb. When they have introduced American sanitation, morale-prep, feminism, and mass production throughout the Near East, Middle East, Far East, USSR, the Pampas, el Gran Chaco, the Danubian Basin, Equatorial Africa, Hither Further and Inner Mumbo-land, Gondhwanaland, Lhasa, and the villages of darkest Berkshire, how happy we shall be. At any rate it ought to cut down travel. There will be nowhere to go. So people will (I opine) go all the faster. Col. Knox says 1/8 of the world's population speaks 'English', and that is the biggest language group. If true, damn shame—say I. May the curse of Babel strike all their tongues till they can only say 'baa baa'. It would mean much the same. I think I shall have to refuse to speak anything but Old Mercian.
> (Letter 53, *Letters* 65)

Thirdly, as in most of Europe, our native population is ageing and dying. A flood of immigrants may compensate for the lack of young people to keep the economy going, but it will change the national culture almost beyond recognition. At any rate, the whole prospect has stirred a debate on the nature of 'British' or 'English' values and how to pass them on through the education system (if indeed such values do exist and we can agree on what they are).

The point I want to make is that 'England' cannot be perceived—we will miss it entirely—if we do not view it as an imaginative construction, in other words as a *story*. We talk, dream, and imagine something called 'England' into existence, and if we cease to believe in it, it will cease to be. A National Census or a Gallup Poll cannot reveal England. Adding a module on Citizenship to our national curriculum will not preserve it. It can only be known in the myths and folklore that tell us what it feels like to belong to this landscape and this tradition. It can only be perpetuated by storytellers and mythmakers.

In an essay called 'The Spirit of England', Tolkien's soul-mate G.K. Chesterton (1923:284-87) wrote:

> What is wanted for the cause of England today is an Englishman with enough imagination to love his country from the outside as well as the inside. That is, we need somebody who will do for the

English what has never been done for them, but what is done for any outlandish peasantry or even any savage tribe. We want people who can make England attractive; quite apart from whether England is strong or weak [...]. To express this mysterious people, to explain or suggest why they like tall hedges and heavy breakfasts and crooked roads and small gardens with large fences, and why they alone among Christians have kept quite consistently the great Christian glory of the open fireplace, here would be a strange and stimulating opportunity for any of the artists in words, who study the souls of strange peoples.

He goes on to say that this would be the true way to create a friendship between peoples and nations, for "Nations can love each other as men and women love each other, not because they are alike but because they are different" (and if they are really alike, they are not really nations). And he closes by saying this:

The particular kind of beauty there is in an English village, the particular kind of humour there is in an English public-house, are things that cannot be found in lands where the village is far more simply and equally governed, or where the vine is far more honourably served and praised. Yet we shall not save them by merely sinking into them with the conservative sort of contentment, even if the commercial rapacity of our plutocratic reforms would allow us to do so. We must in a sense get far away from England in order to behold her; we must rise above patriotism in order to be practically patriotic; we must have some sense of more varied and remote things before these vanishing virtues can be seen suddenly for what they are; almost as one might fancy that a man would have to rise to the dizziest heights of the divine understanding before he saw, as from a peak far above a whirlpool, how precious is his perishing soul. (Chesterton 1923:294)

These passages seem to express the semi-conscious intention behind *The Hobbit* and *The Lord of the Rings*. Here we have the work of "an Englishman with enough imagination to love his country from the outside as well as the inside." Tolkien presents England in the guise of the Shire, the cultivated landscape of an obscure tribe or race of Hobbits on the edge of Wilderland. And he writes of how the 'particular beauty' of this little country might be saved, not by the 'conservative contentment' evidenced by the majority of the placid Hobbits, but by a journey 'there and back again' from the illusory security of the Shire into the world of 'more varied and remote things', where one acquires the strength of character to defend the values of home.

The Fellowship of English Romantics

Tolkien wrote a story that seemed to C.S. Lewis like 'lightning from a clear sky', yet they both knew it was part of a tradition. The Inklings were Englishmen of a particular stripe. I have described them as Romantics, and many of them were of course, roughly speaking, *Christian* Romantics, or Christian Platonists. One of Tolkien's great forebears was Samuel Taylor Coleridge, whose poems (such as 'The Ancient Mariner') often possess a Tolkienian 'flavour'. Another was William Blake, who decried in modernity the same things as Tolkien, and sought to resurrect the spirit of England through his mythological saga of Albion. As Kathleen Raine (1986:97-101) once wrote, mythological thought is "the highest and most complete form of symbolic imagination; as it is also the rarest," for in myth the various symbolic figures and elements are integrated as parts within a living, dynamic whole. Blake, she says, "created an imaginative universe comparable with those of ancient pantheons," but he did so as a poet suffering from the lack of a traditional form: "He was a man crying out for a mythology, and trying to make one because he could not find one to his hand. Had he been a Catholic of Dante's time he would have been well content with Mary and the angels." But in fact as Michaël Devaux (2003) has explored in his book, Tolkien, a Catholic who possessed the same rare gift, found that the myth-making faculty is stimulated rather than destroyed by the Gospel and Church teaching. He did something comparable to Blake, but arguably with a more orthodox theological intention.[2]

Tolkien did not, as far as I know, acknowledge any debt to Blake in particular. Mostly he looked back further to medieval and ancient sources, to *Beowulf* and the Norse sagas. But there were some modern writers who cer-

---

[2]   Verlyn Flieger and Patrick Curry would, of course, see more of a separation between the mythological and religious elements in his thought than this. My view, as I will explain later, is that his earlier work should be set in the context and read within the intention manifest in his later work, where the Christianity is more evident, but it is clearly legitimate also to read the earlier work as primary.

tainly played a role in awakening his imagination, and who could be called predecessors if not influences—though Tolkien sought to discourage the search for them. One may easily detect echoes here and there of stories by H. Rider Haggard and E.R. Eddison, for example. Eddison drew heavily on Icelandic legend and folklore to create a series of saga-like novels in the 1920s, the best-known of which is *The Worm Ouroboros* (1922), which contains many of the same quest-elements as *The Lord of the Rings*. Even J.M. Barrie should not be neglected. We know that Tolkien saw and enjoyed the play *Peter Pan*, and there is something, some note of Elvish poignancy, about Peter's doomed relationship with Wendy that reminds one of the 'Athrabeth'.

William Morris (an earlier graduate of Exeter College, whose family Tolkien later came to know) has been mentioned as a particularly important point of reference, linking him to the arts and crafts movement. Tolkien's attitude to modern technology is close to that evidenced in the machineless rural England of Morris's *News From Nowhere* (1891). Morris is important, too, for the prose romances he wrote in the 1880s, set between the fourth and the fourteenth centuries and based on Old English and Old Icelandic forms— stories such as *The Roots of the Mountains* (1889).

Another predecessor is George MacDonald, that remarkable Scottish clergyman who linked the German Romantics to the Pre-Raphaelites and was an even more important influence on Tolkien's friend C.S. Lewis. MacDonald's profoundly Celtic Christian spirituality radiates a kindliness and love of animals and nature that Tolkien must have found attractive, and his ancient, magical feminine figures reminiscent of the Virgin Mary, rather out of place in Calvinism but found in most of his fairy tales, recall Galadriel in *The Lord of the Rings*.

Tolkien's mind was therefore already richly furnished when he arrived at Exeter College, struggling with Victorian and Edwardian notions of myth and magic, modernity and medievalism.[3] Talking specifically about the English Romantics and their search for 'a dimension beyond the mundane', John Garth has told us that Tolkien gave a talk on the Catholic Poet Francis Thompson to the Essay Club at Exeter College in March 1914, in which he

---

[3]   Chris Hopkins (1995) points to the close similarity in feeling between Tolkien's early writing and Tennyson's 'The Lady of Shallot'.

claimed Thompson as an example of the type of writer who could bridge Rationalism and Romanticism, highlighting "the images drawn from astronomy and geology, and especially those that could be described as Catholic ritual writ large across the universe." "One must begin with the elfin and delicate and progress to the profound: listen first to the violin and flute, and then learn to hearken to the organ of being's harmony" (Garth 2003:36). It is a fair description of the progress of Tolkien's own writing.

Missionary to the English

It was John Garth's book *Tolkien and the Great War* that made me realize how 'driven' Tolkien was at this point by a sense of mission to accomplish the poetic 'rescue' of the English. Garth highlights the role of Tolkien's earliest literary fellowship in all this. Dating back to his schooldays in Birmingham and inextricably tangled up with Oxbridge and the War, Tolkien felt that the four members of the Tea Club and Barrovian Society, with their refined sense of honour and poetry and beauty, "had been granted some spark of fire [...] that was destined to kindle a new light, or, what is the same thing, rekindle an old light in the world" (Letter 5, *Letters* 10). Through them he found in 1914 his sense of vocation. He believed that the TCBS "was destined to testify to God and Truth in a more direct way even than by laying down its several lives in this war"—in a work that may be done "by three or two or one survivor" (Letter 5, *Letters* 10), always inspired in part by the others. It was Tolkien who, in the end, carried the torch for the TCBS, by constructing a literary vehicle in which to transmit its vision to the wider world. As Tolkien's character Ramer (*Sauron Defeated* 228) much later remarks: "I don't think you realise, I don't think any of us realise, the force, the daimonic force that the great myths and legends have. From the profundity of the emotions and perceptions that begot them, and from the multiplication of them in many minds—and each mind, mark you, an engine of obscure but unmeasured energy." [4]

Tolkien wanted to harness this 'obscure but unmeasured energy'. His *legendarium* was intended to capture something of the essence, the inner

---

[4]   The TCBS set a pattern in Tolkien's life that was echoed in other literary clubs he joined or formed, notably the Viking Club at Leeds (1924), the Coalbiters at Oxford (1926) and, of course, the Inklings during the 1930s.

meaning or 'form', of this nation—a form which is the archetypal root or cause of what we are now, and which may serve to perpetuate and even regenerate it through the multiplication of its effect in many minds and hearts. He used his knowledge of languages and folklore and how they evolve over time in the real or 'primary' world to explore what lies within language and behind the place names and fragmentary traditions, the national character and geography of these islands. What lies 'behind' in this sense is not merely another, earlier period of the same nature as our own, even though he feigns a kind of historical continuity as a way of connecting the events of the stories with our present reality. In 1951 (Letter 131, *Letters* 145) he writes that he always had "the sense of recording what was already 'there', somewhere: not of 'inventing'."

The land of Faërie is not merely a dream-landscape into which we can escape from the real world, but a land of *vision*. It reveals or 'makes luminous' the things of which the primary world is made. That is why it is such a serious matter to deprive a nation of its fairy-tales, its native mythology, leaving only historical narratives and political ideologies for people to nourish their souls upon. Tolkien believed that the Norman invasion of 1066 had effectively suppressed the imaginative life and oral traditions of the Anglo-Saxons; and it was this that Tolkien set himself single-handedly to rebuild, in the way Elias Lönnrot had done for Finland, the brothers Grimm for Germany, and Snorri Sturluson, much earlier, for Iceland.

The English and the Celts

It is important to make a distinction between England and Britain. Britain, like 'Breton', derives from the old Latin word for the Celtic peoples, who in the north and western parts of Europe—especially in Ireland, Scotland, and Wales—were never fully assimilated by Roman civilization. The 'Celtic' British have always possessed a wealth of stories, including many that survived the Norman conquest and were used by Geoffrey of Monmouth in his *History of the Kings of Britain* (around 1135) to build the legend of Arthur and his knights. In Geoffrey's Arthur, the Normans and their successors found a hero capable of defending the national identity against the inheritors of the Roman Imperium, the Franks and Germans. Rather than looking to Charlemagne and Alexander, they wanted the nation to remember Arthur and Troy. For they looked for the earliest founding of Britain and the origin of its name to the mythical Brutus, an exiled prince of Troy, great-grandson of Aeneas and (some even supposed) ancestor of Uther Pendragon.

Understandably the Normans did not turn for heroes to the Saxons whom they had recently conquered, and whose kings, Alfred the Great (d. 899, warrior, theologian, translator, and educator), or Alfred's grandson Athelstan, the first King of all England (d. 939), were in many ways as heroic as the mythical Arthur of medieval fantasy. These 'English', or Angles and Saxons, displaced the Celts in the central and southern parts of these islands,[5] coming from northern Germany and the area around Denmark, but we know much less about their legends than we do about those of the Welsh or Irish or Scots. It was this lost Anglo-Saxon culture that most fascinated Tolkien, as he caught its far-off gleam in the poetry of Cynewulf and the saga of Beowulf. Rohan, Gondor and Hobbiton are all attempts to capture one or other aspect of the lost civilization—as lost (thanks to the Normans) as the drowned island of Atlantis/Númenor, though through no fault of its own. His kings of Gondor are descended from Elendil and Isildur, who escaped from the great Deluge that buried their ancient home.

But the Celtic world was not excluded from Tolkien's vision. How could it be, when Welsh was one of his favourite languages, and George MacDonald one of his favourite writers? In fact I believe that Elvendom and Elvishness were Tolkien's attempt to capture the best in the Celtic spirit. (Like the Celts, the Elves in his stories are drifting or being forced westward, their magical influence gradually fading from the lands of Middle-earth.)[6] But it was

---

[5] Recent genetic research, according to Prof. Stephen Oppenheimer, indicates that the invasion of the Anglo-Saxons cannot have been quite as violent as it has often been painted, beginning with the tract 'On the Ruin of Britain' by the 6th-century monk Gildas. Anglo-Saxon male gene types account for only 5% of the present population, which shows a less invasive impact than that of the Vikings. Three-quarters of the modern British gene-pool (two thirds in England) derives from a much earlier group, perhaps earlier than the 'Celts', namely peaceful settlers from the Basque country who arrived as the ice-caps were retreating and before the creation of the English Channel, between 7,500 and 15,000 years ago. See Professor Oppenheimer's book *The Origins of the British: A Genetic Detective Story*.

[6] "They planted Britain, and gave to the seas and mountains names which are poems, and imitate the pure voices of nature." Thus wrote the American Romantic poet Ralph Waldo Emerson of the race of Celts (chapter IV) in his *English Traits* of 1856.

more than that. It was Tolkien's attempt to heal the deepest wound in our culture—the breach between the Celts and the English, the Celts and the Anglo-Saxons.

In the light of all this I make no apology for quoting again Tolkien's revealing letter of 1951 (Letter 131, *Letters* 144-45) to an editor at Collins.

> Do not laugh! But once upon a time (my crest has long since fallen) I had a mind to make a body of more or less connected legend, ranging from the large and cosmogonic, to the level of romantic fairy-story—the larger founded on the lesser in contact with the earth, the lesser drawing splendour from the vast backcloths—which I could dedicate simply to: to England; to my country. It should possess the tone and quality that I desired, somewhat cool and clear, be redolent of our 'air' (the clime and soil of the North West, meaning Britain and the hither parts of Europe: not Italy and the Aegean, still less the East), and, while possessing (if I could achieve it) the fair elusive beauty that some call Celtic (though it is rarely found in genuine ancient Celtic things), it should be 'high', purged of the gross, and fit for the more adult mind of a land now steeped in poetry.[7]

What he calls here the 'gross' is set in contrast with the 'high', the 'fair elusive beauty' that he attempted to portray in the Elves. But observe that in this passage he speaks both of England and of Britain. Though I have just tried to distinguish them, I believe Tolkien was trying to reconcile the two, to bring about through *poesis* a healing of the wound inflicted by the Normans, to find a mythological solution that would weave together the Celtic with the Anglo-Saxon threads in our culture. This is reflected in the *legendarium* by the way the race of Men is intermingled with that of the Elves through a series of marriages, notably that of Beren and Lúthien, Aragorn and Arwen. The 'fair elusive beauty' that Tolkien sought from his earliest days as a linguist was found in Anglo-Saxon as well as Celtic things, and in fact represented the highest aspect of both cultures, that element or spirit in which the two were united. United, we might say, against the 'gross' crudity of the Norman conquerors who turned the two cultures against each other, stealing the Arthurian stories

---

[7] I find it interesting that for Tolkien an 'adult' mind is one that is 'steeped in poetry'.

from the Celts to forge a national *mythos* in which Anglo-Saxon would be submerged.

Let us probe a little further. It is notable, for example, that the 'English' (that is, Anglo-Saxon) royal families represented themselves as "descended from a boy who came ashore in a boat, clad in armour in one version, with a sheaf of corn in another, on an island off the coast of Denmark" (Every 1993:408), a shipwrecked child called Skyld or Sceaf, whom some say had been born in the Ark or descended from one who was, bringing with him skills not known in the North. Tolkien's version of this legend of 'King Sheave', the 'Corn God' of the Danes who is eventually sent back to his mysterious home in the far West over the great sea, can be found in *The Lost Road and Other Writings* (85-97). There he refers to "older and more mysterious traditions" in which Skyld was known as Ing (I suppose a possible root for the word 'English').

The association of Ing with Tolkien's Ingwë/Inwë or his son Ingil is explored by Christopher Tolkien in *The Book of Lost Tales Part II* (301-12). In Tolkien's later writings, of course, Ingwë the High King of the Vanyar had departed from Middle-earth long before the coming of Men, and never returned. But earlier in the development of the *legendarium*, when he appears as Ing, he is the King of Albion or Luthany (from which term for the British Isles Tolkien once considered deriving the name Lúthien); that is, the 'Land of Friendship' between Elves and Men. This Ing is human, though he drinks the Elvish draught of immortality. He (or perhaps his son) is the builder of the great tower in Kortirion. He assists Eärendel on his mission to the Elves, is caught up in the great war, and shipwrecked. It is in this way that he comes among the East Danes as their teacher and king, eventually departing for Tol Eressëa, which in this version of the Tales lies over the sea to the west of Luthany. Aelfwine ('Elf-friend'), called Eriol in the earlier versions, is one of his Anglo-Saxon descendants. Meanwhile the English Channel has been carved out by the Elves to separate Luthany from mainland Europe. Despite this protection, Luthany is invaded seven times by Men, ending with the Romans (from whom the Elves fled) and finally the returning Anglo-Saxons, the Elf-friends.

All of this is admittedly extremely complicated (I have glossed over as much as I can),[8] and one senses Christopher's frustration in trying to make sense of it, but it all testifies to Tolkien's intention: his vision of an island kingdom where Celts and Anglo-Saxons could live together in peace and friendship.[9]

In Search of Atlantis

Implicit in the early *legendarium*, but gradually more explicit in the later versions, is the idea drawn both from Celtic and from Anglo-Saxon sources (not to mention Plato) of a land in the West that has been drowned in the sea. In the Bible, of course, we find the story of the Flood, and Tolkien was aware that nearly all ancient peoples have similar legends. The oldest is recorded in the epic of Gilgamesh, and it is this account that seems to lie behind the Biblical one. Tolkien, who no doubt knew the speculations of his colleagues in the field of ancient history, believed that Man first 'awoke' (as he put it) in Mesopotamia, and I believe he tried to work this into the wider framework for his English mythology. (As far as I can tell, not much has been done on this particular aspect of Tolkien's inspiration, so my speculation is intended to encourage others to look into it.)

As Tolkien was aware, city-based civilization can be traced to the fourth millennium BC within the 'fertile crescent' between the Tigris and Euphrates. Indeed painted ceramics have been found in the north as early as 6000 BC. By the year 3000 there were highly developed cities in Mespotamia and Egypt, a thousand years earlier than those of India and China. The domestication of the waters and marshlands of southern or lower Mesopotamia by the Sumerians is

---

[8] See Honegger (2007) for a more detailed discussion of this topic.

[9] King Arthur is supposed to have been a Roman chieftain who held back for a time the Saxon invasion. Tolkien may have intended to re-write the legend of Arthur by tracing his ancestry back to Aragorn and Lúthien. In this way the Norman-Plantagenet hijacking of Celtic Arthurian mythology in order to bolster their suppression of the English spirit could have been subverted. Clearly there are resemblances between the pair Aragorn and Gandalf on the one hand, and Arthur and Merlin on the other, and there is a prophecy in the Appendices of *The Lord of the Rings* to the effect that Aragorn's line will never be extinguished.

perhaps enough to explain an early legend that the secrets of civilization had been taught to Men by Enki, the fish-god, or by the 'fish-people' associated with him.[10] For Tolkien, however, we must remember that the early history of Man is preceded by that of the Elves, and before the events known to historians are those concerning Númenor, which have left their traces in our earliest epics. Men were raised to almost superhuman heights by their friendship with the Elves in the Second Age. Could it not be that elements of human civilization in Mesopotamia were fostered through benign contact with the Elves, or with the seafaring men of Númenor? That, too, may have lain behind the ancient reference to 'fish-people'.

And more intriguing still, what was the mysterious disaster that befell European and Middle-eastern civilization around 1200 BC, plunging it into a long dark age, and known to historians as the invasion of the 'Peoples of the Sea'? The origin and destination of the Peoples of the Sea remain totally unknown. The Mycenaean palaces were burnt around 1230 BC, the Hittite Empire collapsed in 1200. The Egyptians describe these enemies as "of great stature, with tall white bodies, fair hair and blue eyes," and as coming from "the Great Green Sea"—which to me sounds more like the Atlantic than the Aegean—adding as to their origin that "the islands shook, and vomited forth their nations all at once" (Braudel 2001:178, 180).

Was the collapse of Bronze Age civilization, then, something to do with the corruption and decline of Númenor in its later phase, culminating in the destruction of the island by an act of God? Tolkien does inform us that the Númenoreans of the later period ventured into Middle-earth mainly to conquer and pillage. Perhaps it was the evil Men of Númenor themselves, under the influence of Sauron, and later, fleeing the destruction; perhaps it was peoples of Middle-earth who had fallen under the sway of the island empire who

---

[10]   See Temple (1991:xxii). In the Sumerian pantheon, Enlil corresponds to Tolkien's Eru, Anu to Manwë, and Inanna perhaps to Yavanna, though with aspects of Elbereth. Enki corresponds to Ulmo, the Lord of the Waters, who has always taken more of an interest in human history than others of the Valar. Tolkien's interest in this region and its legends is suggested also by the use he made of the name Uruk (as in Uruk-Hai; see Ryan 1988), which was the largest city of the Sumerians around 3400 BC, holding a population of 20,000. The name Gilgalad is also reminiscent of Gilgamesh, the great king of Uruk.

now, upon the destruction of their overlords, decided to do some rampaging on their own account. Meanwhile the *good* Númenoreans landed further north and established more enlightened kingdoms, the echo of which has come down to us in the legend of King Sheave and the stories of the Ark.[11]

In her book *Interrupted Music*, Verlyn Flieger has explored the way, with growing confidence in his powers as a writer, and driven to make greater sense of the Atlantis dream that haunted him (the dream of a great wave towering over green fields), Tolkien began to search for an even more intimate way of binding the matter of his *legendarium* into the fabric of modern England. The new method involved a kind of time-travel through inherited memory (not, I think, as Flieger suggests, a form of reincarnation, but rather a tuning-in to the memories and experiences of direct ancestors). In the early *Book of Lost Tales*, the narrator Eriol had journeyed to Tol Eressëa from Scandinavia, and simply recorded what he learnt there from the Elves. (Tol Eressëa is at that time conceived as being the island of Britain, and the town in its centre, Kortirion, is later the city of Warwick where Tolkien is to be married.) The more science-fictional idea of time-travel back to Atlantis entered the picture in a second phase, starting with Tolkien's famous 'bargain' with C.S. Lewis around 1936.

In *The Lost Road*, it is a contemporary historian, Oswin Errol, vacationing in Cornwall with his son Alboin, who finds and travels the 'straight road' into the far West, the road that persists (for Elves and Elf-friends) after the world was 'bent' into a sphere by the drowning of Atlantis and the removal of the gods from our plane of existence. This gives way ten years later, in 1946, to a much more successful story, *The Notion Club Papers*. It starts with the discovery in the early 21st century of the papers of the Notion Club, itself a version of the Inklings projected into Tolkien's future. Gradually the members of the Club have discovered through dreams and intuitions the key to the ancient languages and the memories of Númenor bound up with their personal genetic identity.

The Notion Club Papers would have been an extraordinary work, if completed. It would have underlined the continuity between the mythical

---

[11]   One may trace Tolkien's development of these ideas in the various versions of 'The Drowning of Anadûnê' in *Sauron Defeated*.

world of the *legendarium* and modern England. Unfinished as it is, it gives us many insights into the conversations of the Inklings, and how Tolkien worked with his own dreams.

The Scouring of the Shire

I have indicated some loose ends and false starts, but Tolkien's major task, I believe, was nevertheless achieved, despite his niggling dissatisfaction with the result. It was achieved in his major published work, *The Lord of the Rings*. That task was to encode within a story the true spirit of the English civilization that had almost been extinguished, for those to rekindle who might. He had led millions of readers to a place in their imagination where they could glimpse the light that shines beyond the world's end, and above every horizon. It was more than Englishness, but Englishness was included within it. Tolkien uncovered this light for others by going deep within himself. The true centre of *The Lord of the Rings* is not in Gondor, after all, it is in the Shire.

That is why Peter Jackson's film missed the heart of the book when he omitted 'The Scouring of the Shire'. The whole point of the journey 'there and back again' is not just to return, but to return 'initiated' and transformed. In the case of *The Lord of the Rings*, Tolkien's portrayal of England in the Shire at the beginning of the novel is full of unresolved tensions. The Hobbits are peaceful and contented, it is true, but they are also (mostly) small-minded, self-satisfied, and suspicious of strangers. One thinks especially of Ted Sandyman and the Sackville-Bagginses. Their small vices contain the seeds of a greater evil, the possibility of a corruption later brought to them by Saruman and his minions. The Shire under martial law therefore comes close to being a prophetic statement on Tolkien's part about the state of modern Britain. It is to become capable of dealing with this spiritual threat to the Shire that the Hobbits, according to Gandalf, have been sent on their long adventure.

I only recently noticed the striking similarities—right down to the vocabulary and precise turns of phrase—between Tolkien's description of the scouring of the Shire and Charles Kingsley's description of the return of Hereward the Wake to an England just taken over by the Normans—the French 'ruffians'.[12] Hereward is an Anglo-Danish princeling exiled on the eve of the

---

[12]   See Kingsley (1954), chapter 19.

invasion, who through a series of adventures abroad learns both maturity and chivalry enough to return as a hero of the resistance. Like the returning Hobbits, he is short in stature compared to the invaders. The fenland which he defends could be said to represent the drowned world of English civilization. By planting echoes of this earlier work within his own, Tolkien was underlining the connection between the Normans and the forces of modernity overrunning the Shire, in the context of his wider project of healing the wounds inflicted by the invasion on the English psyche.

But there is another thread in the tapestry that ought to be mentioned at this point, and that is Tolkien's Catholicism. As we know from the *Letters* and biographies, Tolkien was a daily Mass-goer, who believed his mother's early death from illness brought on by poverty was the direct result of her conversion to Catholicism. He identified with the Catholic minority in England, who at times had been a persecuted minority. His ideal of England is therefore a Christian, even a Catholic one.

I believe a strong case can be made that a Catholic vision of human nature and indeed of reality informed the whole of Tolkien's project—taming, purifying, and even inspiring the use he made of non-Christian legends—though I am not going to make it in detail here.[13] Instead I will contrast my view with that of Nicholas Boyle in his book, *Sacred and Secular Scripture: A Catholic Approach to Literature*. Boyle also argues for a Catholic reading of the novel. For him, part of its claim to greatness lies in the way Tolkien has created "a piece of popular literature that, in the spirit of G.K. Chesterton, reclaims the myth of England for Catholicism and uses that myth both to represent a more general twentieth-century experience of historical uprooting and to give new sense to the old tradition of the ascetic life lived in imitation of Christ and in the communion of saints" (Boyle 2004:266).

But, Boyle argues, Tolkien has done this precisely by making the Hobbits 'irreligious' in a peculiarly modern way. They do not even have a ritual moment of recollection before meals, as Faramir does. "This setting in a world that does not yet know the Christian, or even the Jewish, revelation has the

---

[13]   Cf. Caldecott (2003) *Secret Fire: The Spiritual Vision of J.R.R. Tolkien*. See also Ian Boyd and Stratford Caldecott (2003), *The Hidden Presence: Catholicism in The Lord of the Rings*.

singular advantage that it also, as it were, prefigures a world so secularized that
it has largely forgotten them: the archaic, or archaizing, features of the book
are the metaphors for its ultra-modernity. The hobbits find themselves wan-
dering through a landscape, both natural and human, that, metaphorically at
least, is post-Christian" (Boyle 2004:259). Religion is represented by the old
myths and stories, which to the Hobbits gradually, through their adventures,
begin to seem more real than the sheltered enclave of the Shire.

In the end, for Boyle, "the planting of the fairy tree, which puts the
Shire under the special protection of an Elf Queen, is something like the return of England, Mary's Dowry, to the Roman faith. The ultimate answer to
our question, what are the hobbits? must then be that they are, at least by the
end of the book, the representatives of a Catholic England which has resisted
the temptation to secular modernity, in particular to Britishness, and has accepted its place within Christendom" (Boyle 2004:263). The Elves, then, represent both the magic of nature and the magic of Catholicism.

I agree with Boyle that for Tolkien, Elvishness and Catholicism were
closely related. I think you can detect a 'hidden code' that refers to Catholic
themes and ideas, such as the Eucharist and the Blessed Virgin Mary, in *The
Lord of the Rings*.[14] The description of *lembas* is very suggestive, for example,
and when Gandalf gives the date of the Ring's destruction as 25 March
Catholics recall that this is the Marian feast of the Annunciation. The carrying
of the Ring to its destruction on Mount Doom, with Frodo's several falls under the growing weight, echoes the Stations of the Cross in popular Catholic
devotion. (In fact, in Catholic theology it is paradoxically Christ's carrying of

---

[14] While I was writing a paper recently on C.S. Lewis, I happened to pick up Lewis's
personal copy of Coventry Patmore's *Poetical Works*, one of the books he had been
reading in 1930 around the time of his conversion. A deeply Catholic work, with
a high mystical doctrine of 'sacred *eros*' in marriage that Lewis felt somewhat dis-
turbing, the book had later belonged to Lewis's former pupil and now fellow-Ink-
ling George Sayer. Out of the book fell an unpublished letter addressed to Dame
Felicitas Corrigan of Stanbrook Abbey, from whom I had received it. In this letter
Sayer wrote that Lewis "never recovered from his N.I. Prot attitude to Our Lady.
His grandfather Hamilton, the local Belfast vicar, was violently anti-R.C." By
contrast, he adds, his friend Tolkien was deeply devoted to the Virgin Mary.
"Tolkien in a letter to me (still unpublished) wrote: 'I attribute whatever there is
of beauty and goodness in my work to the influence of the Holy Mother of God.'"

the Cross and his death upon it that makes possible the Annunciation....) But in the end I think Boyle turns Tolkien's novel into too much of an allegory. I do not believe the scouring of the Shire was code for a Catholic restoration. It is a more complex and sophisticated symbol than that. As Catherine Madsen (2004:37) points out, Tolkien "was not a simple person, and how his Christianity worked on his storytelling is not a simple matter."

Madsen goes on to say that for years she tried to find in Christianity what she had found in Tolkien, but to little avail. Commentators, she says, have 'mined' the book for Christian content, but only succeeded in taking the enchantment out of it. My own feeling is that there are good reasons why *The Lord of the Rings* has a huge appeal to modern self-styled 'Pagans'. What such readers find evoked and celebrated in the book is worth celebrating: the enchantment of a natural world full of living presences, of stars associated with a benign femininity, of beauty and kindness allied with heroism, a freshness of vision giving rise to ineffable gratitude, a sense of wickedness integrated into some greater harmony. I would say simply that none of this is incompatible with Christianity, though historically many Christians have denied these very things. In that sense Tolkien is pointing us towards a richer and more beautiful conception of Christianity, and of Christian England, than any we might find in a Catholic polemic, even a coded one.

Elves and Men

Tolkien's final lesson about England and Englishness is located in his portrait of the Hobbit soul, its weaknesses and its potentiality for greatness. The greatness is demonstrated by the interior strength of Merry, Pippin and Sam as they face down the evil and uproot it. Frodo has a greatness of a different sort. He is weakened, not strengthened, by his experience of bearing the Ring and having it torn from him unwillingly. Thus he is living the tragedy of evil in his own person, bearing the wound of it so that others can live more freely and happily.

Tolkien teaches us that strength of character is just as important in apparently small things as in the great—perhaps more so. One of the unresolved tensions at the outset of the book is between Sam Gamgee and the hobbit-maiden Rosie. It is in the resolution of this tension that we must look for the final integration of Elvishness into human nature, according to the pattern of the romance as a whole. For Sam's growth to maturity and the healing of the Shire go hand in hand. The story identifies this double process with Sam's winning of the hand of the girl he loves, and the book ends not with Aragorn's coronation or glorious marriage, or with Frodo's departure into the West, but with Sam's return home to a loving wife and family.

> And he went on, and there was yellow light, and fire within; and
> the evening meal was ready, and he was expected. And Rose drew
> him in, and set him in his chair, and put little Elanor upon his lap.
> He drew a deep breath. 'Well, I'm back,' he said. (*LotR* 1031)

The long-postponed marriage of Samwise to Rosie represents the 'earthing' in ordinary domestic life of the more distant epic marriages of Men and Elves. Of course, Rosie Cotton is not an Elven princess, any more than Tolkien's wife Edith was.[15] Nonetheless, it is a fact that when Sam names his first child (who, he says, takes after Rosie), he chooses to identify her with a flower, *elanor*, 'sun-star', that blooms only in Lothlórien. Christopher Tolkien tells us that his father's projected Epilogue to *The Lord of the Rings* makes a point of referring to Elanor, "who by a strange gift has the looks and beauty of an elven-maid; in her all [Sam's] love and longing for Elves is resolved and satisfied" (*Sauron Defeated* 132).

The Elves, I have suggested above, may represent the purified Celtic strand in our civilization, just as the human kingdoms of Middle-earth represent the Anglo-Saxon. But in trying to heal and weave together these two strands of our culture in his narrative Tolkien found himself exploring a deeper tragedy than the loss of a folk tradition or even a language. The Elves also represent the *feminine* aspect of our civilization, just as the Normans for him represented the cruder masculine aspect, because the deeper tragedy of our times is a severance and distortion in the relationship of masculine to feminine—reflected also, at another level in the story, by the separation of the Ents and the Entwives. Into the Elves Tolkien placed qualities that he associated very largely with women, and with his wife Edith at the moment he fell in love

---

[15]   Nor is Sam a Beren. However, a subtle identification of the two is effected by Sam's remark to Frodo after the destruction of the Ring and the loss of his finger: "I would have spared him a whole hand of mine rather" (*LotR* 947).

with her: qualities such as delicacy, creativity, musicality, beauty, unfailing memory, profound wisdom, lasting fidelity.[16]

The first encounter of Beren and Lúthien is based upon Tolkien's living vision of Edith dancing among the hemlocks in a Yorkshire glade in 1917. Tolkien is only just recovering from his experience of the War.

> Beren came stumbling into Doriath grey and bowed as with many years of woe, so great had been the torment of the road. But wandering in the summer in the woods of Neldoreth he came upon Lúthien, daughter of Thingol and Melian, at a time of evening under moonrise, as she danced upon the unfading grass in the glades beside Esgalduin. Then all memory of his pain departed from him, and he fell into an enchantment; for Lúthien was the most beautiful of all the Children of Ilúvatar. Blue was her raiment as the unclouded heaven, but her eyes were as grey as the starlit evening; her mantle was sewn with golden flowers, but her hair was as dark as the shadows of twilight. As the light upon the leaves of trees, as the voice of clear waters, as the stars above the mists of the world, such was her glory and her loveliness; and in her face was a shining light. (*Silmarillion* 165)

We have seen how in one of its earliest manifestations the mythology was associated with Ronald and Edith's marriage in Warwick, the ancient Elvish capital. It could be argued that all through Tolkien's life the stories were a running commentary on that marriage and its interior meaning for him. That is why it is so appropriate that the names Beren and Lúthien were written over the grave of Tolkien and his wife in Wolvercote.[17] Tolkien knew or sensed that the

---

[16] That is why, despite the presence of strong masculine characters among the Elves, Elvishness seems most perfectly and completely represented in the feminine of the species; for example, in Galadriel rather than Celeborn, Legolas or Glorfindel. Certainly it is through the marriage of a series of female Elves to a series of human males, rather than the other way around, that Elvishness is "wound like a thread" into the tapestry of human history (Letter 156, *Letters* 204, fn). Beren and Lúthien make the first such marriage, Idril and Tuor the second. The Halfelven line descends from these two marriages in the persons of Eärendil and Elwing, who become the parents of Elrond and Elros, the latter being first mortal king of Númenor. Finally in Aragorn's marriage to Arwen—the descendant of Elros to the daughter of Elrond—the lines are reunited and a new dynasty founded.

[17] Another and sadder aspect of that marriage is perhaps explored in a fragmentary way in the unfinished tale of Aldarion and Erendis.

deeper problem with industrial modernity—in England, which was the starting point for the Industrial Revolution, after all, but also elsewhere throughout
the modern world—is the imbalance of the metaphysical masculine and feminine principles, reflected in the relation of the sexes. The final resolution or
healing of *this* tension can come about only through a union of the human and
Elvish elements in our nature. More than that, the resolution will not be at the
level of the couple only, but of a fruitful couple; that is to say, a couple that is
the source of new life. It is not simply with his marriage to Rosie that Sam's
eros—his love and longing for Elves, the motivation for his journey—is fulfilled and blessed, but with the birth and growth within his home of Elanor
and the other children.

Thus in the end Tolkien's mythology for England, or let us say his
rediscovery of the true meaning of England, is the revelation of moral depths
and cosmic significance within the domestic world itself. There is something
small, something domestic, about England. Englishness is not about having an
empire, or even being a part of one, but about the civilization of the hearth,
the fireside, the kitchen table, the conversation down the pub, supported and
sustained not by the State but in medieval times by the guilds and the Church,
not by the imposition of belief but by the nourishing and passing on of a living
tradition, a sensibility expressed in folklore, common sense, and popular devotion. Ordinary family life, the life of the Shire, is threatened by forces so immense they can only be described in epic terms, and it must be defended by
developing 'ordinary virtues' such as loyalty, courage, integrity and humility.
These are ultimately stronger than any darkness, because they spring from the
very source of creation, where goodness is one with truth in beauty. The true
England has almost gone, but her seeds remain in the barren ground, as
though waiting for the first touch of spring. *The Lord of the Rings* is one of
those seeds.

STRATFORD CALDECOTT was the Chairman of the Oxford
Tolkien Conference at Exeter College in 2006. He is the author of
Secret Fire: The Spiritual Vision of J.R.R. Tolkien (US title: *The
Power of the Ring*), and *The Seven Sacraments: Entering the Mysteries
of God* (Crossroad/Alban Books). He is also the editor of the jour-
nal *Second Spring* and directs the Thomas More College Center for
Faith & Culture in Oxford, England.
See *www.secondspring.co.uk* .

References

Abbreviations used:

Letters: see Carpenter 1995

Lost Road: see Tolkien 1987

Lost Tales II: see Tolkien 1983

LotR: see Tolkien 2004

Sauron Defeated: see Tolkien 1993

Silmarillion: see Tolkien 1977

Boyd, Ian and Stratford Caldecott (eds.), 2003, *The Hidden Presence: Catholicism in The Lord of the Rings*, South Orange, NJ and Oxford, UK: Chesterton Institute Press.

Boyle, Nicholas, 2004, *Sacred and Secular Scripture: A Catholic Approach to Literature*, London: Darton, Longman & Todd.

Braudel, Fernand, 2001, *The Mediterranean in the Ancient World*, London and New York: Allen Lane.

Caldecott, Stratford, 2003, *Secret Fire: The Spiritual Vision of J.R.R. Tolkien*, London: Darton, Longman & Todd.

---, 2005, 'Tolkien's Elvish England', *The Chesterton Review*, Fall/Winter 2005. See http://academic.shu.edu/chesterton.

Carpenter, Humphrey (with the assistance of Christopher Tolkien) (eds.), 1995, *The Letters of J.R.R. Tolkien*, (first published 1981), London: HarperCollins.

Chesterton, Gilbert K., 1923, *What I Saw in America*, London: Hodder & Stoughton.

Devaux, Michaël (ed.), 2003, *Tolkien, les racines du légendaire: cahier d'études tolkieniennes reunies sous la direction de Michaël Devaux*, Geneva: Ad Solem.

Emerson, Ralph Waldo, 1856, *English Traits*, accessed 17 January 2008, http://www.infomotions.com/alex2/authors/emerson-ralph/emerson-english-749.

Every, George, 1993, 'What Englishness Is', *New Blackfriars* (September 1993), 408-9.

Flieger, Verlyn, 2005, *Interrupted Music*, Kent, Ohio: The Kent State University Press.

Garth, John, 2003, *Tolkien and the Great War*, London: HarperCollins.

Honegger, Thomas, 2007, 'A Mythology for England? Looking a Gift Horse in the Mouth', in Eduardo Segura and Thomas Honegger (eds.), 2007, *Myth and Magic. Art According to the Inklings*, (Cormarë Series 14), Zurich and Berne: Walking Tree Publishers, 109-30.

Hopkins, Chris, 1995, 'Tolkien and Englishness', in Patricia Reynolds and Glen. H. GoodKnight (eds.), 1995, *Proceedings of the J.R.R. Centenary Conference. Keble College, Oxford, 1992*, (*Mythlore 80/Mallorn* 30), Milton Keynes and Altadena: The Tolkien Society and The Mythopoetic Press, 278-80.

Kingsley, Charles, 1954, *Hereward the Wake*, (first published 1866), London: Collins.

Madsen, Catherine, 2004, 'Light from an Invisible Lamp. Natural Religion in *The Lord of the Rings*', in Jane Chance (ed.), 2004, *Tolkien and the Invention of Myth. A Reader*, Lexington, Kentucky: The University Press of Kentucky, 35-47.

Oppenheimer, Stephen, 2006, *The Origins of the British: A Genetic Detective Story*, London: Constable.

Raine, Kathleen, 1986, *Yeats the Initiate*, London: Allen & Unwin.

Ryan, John, 1988, 'Indo-European Race-Memories and Race-Fears from the Ancient City of Uruk', *Angerthas* 22:27-46.

Temple, Robert, 1991, *He Who Saw Everything: A Verse Translation of the Epic of Gilgamesh*, London: Rider.

Tolkien, John Ronald Reuel, 1977, *The Silmarillion*, (edited by Christopher Tolkien), New York: Houston Mifflin.

---, 1983, *The Book of Lost Tales: Part 2*, (volume two of *The History of Middle-earth*, edited by Christopher Tolkien), London: George Allen & Unwin.

---, 1987, *The Lost Road and Other Writings*, (volume five of *The History of Middle-earth*, edited by Christopher Tolkien), London: George Allen & Unwin.

---, 1993, *Sauron Defeated*, (volume nine of *The History of Middle-earth*, edited by Christopher Tolkien), London: Harper Collins.

---, 2004, *The Lord of the Rings*, (originally published 1954-55; one-volume 50th anniversary edition), Boston: Houghton Mifflin.

A Look into Galadriel's Mirror

CONCLUSION BY
THOMAS HONEGGER

We all know that it is a perilous undertaking to try and make predictions out-side the clearly defined and restricted framework of natural laws—and yet, men and women have always been fascinated by the (as yet) Unknown and tempted to peep behind the curtain of the Now into the hidden Future. Yet without either a palantir or a magic mirror at our disposal, we must rely on traditionally acquired bits and pieces of information in order to formulate an educated guess as to what the future holds for Tolkien studies.

Taking stock, we can summarise the situation as follows:[1] Tolkien stud-ies have established themselves as a regular part of academia. The successful launching of *Tolkien Studies* in 2004 has given us a yearbook that lives up to the criteria of a peer-reviewed journal and it offers, for the first time, an inter-nationally recognised scholarly platform for studies dealing (almost) exclusively with Tolkien's work. It unites contributions by established scholars next to papers by young and up-coming talents.[2]

Another player in the field that has acquired greater importance over the last few years is Walking Tree Publishers (sorry for blowing our own trumpet a bit). It is a non-commercial organisation dedicated (since 1997) to publishing academic and scholarly studies on Tolkien. The number of publications has increased to about four to five books per year and submissions are now evalu-ated by an independent board of advisors comprising leading scholars and 'general' readers.

---

[1] The following highly subjective overview is limited to publications in English—important work is also done in French and other languages, but that would take us too far.

[2] At the same time, *Hither Shore*, the yearbook of the German Tolkien Society, came into being. Each volume has a thematic focus and the majority of contribu-tions are based on papers given at the annual German Tolkien Society Seminar. *Hither Shore* has been designed as a bilingual German and English publication, but it is only during the last two years that we have seen a significant increase of items in English.

Next to these 'specialised' platforms, there are, of course, numerous other publishing houses that include individual volumes on Tolkien in their programmes.

The recent past has also seen the coming of age of a new generation of academics—scholars who no longer consider it anathema to discuss Tolkien's work and who do not hesitate to include books such as *The Hobbit, The Lord of the Rings* or even *The Silmarillion* in their examination reading lists. Thus, many large-scale academic conferences (such as the MLA, the IMC Leeds, Kalamazoo, ESSE etc.) feature not merely individual papers on Tolkien, but devote entire sections to his work. Also, with more and more open-minded scholars in permanent positions of academic influence, it has become possible for interested and gifted students to write their thesises in this field and quite a number of the more recent monographs as well as articles have their origin in their authors' work towards a university degree. The range of approaches to Tolkien, which have as yet been (compared to the wider field of post-/modernist literature) rather limited, is thus likely to broaden considerably in the not-too distant future (see also the papers in the recent volumes of *Tolkien Studies*).

A volume such as Robert Eaglestone's *Reading The Lord of the Rings. New Writings on Tolkien's Classic* (2005), which comprises papers by literary critics who are (in the majority of cases) not primarily Tolkien scholars, can be seen as the typical product of this new 'pragmatic' approach. Some of the essays may show minor mistakes due to the fact that not every author has mastered the deep ramifications of the professor's work, but I accept these slight drawbacks rather than having the discussion of Tolkien's writings limited to specialists only. Publications such as Eaglestone's book show that Tolkien studies are no longer the domain of an in-group but have become part of normal academic discourse.

This development is, to some extent, also due to the fact that *The Lord of the Rings* is seen more and more in the context of 'modernist' and other 20th-century literature (see Simonson 2008 and Hiley 2009). There is, however, as Shippey has pointed out most recently, still a lot of work to be done on "the influences on him of writers of the nineteenth and twentieth centuries, so often now deeply unfashionable, forgotten and out of print" (Shippey 2008:3).

Another and very different approach is taken by explicitly Catholic scholars. Due to the popular success of Peter Jackson's movies, many an evangelical Christian author (predominantly in the US) with the urge to spread his Christian message has hijacked *The Lord of the Rings* for his purposes (see Schneidewind and Weinreich 2005). Although Tolkien's work, and especially *The Lord of the Rings*, is based upon a (common-ground) Christian understanding of the world, it is his (medieval) Catholic background that determines and shapes many of the ethically and philosophically vital points in his writings. If, for Tolkien, the Norman Conquest represents the linguistic fall from grace in the history of England, then the dissolution of the English monasteries and the creation of the Anglican Church is the analogous event in the religious sphere. So the mere focus on individual Christian elements does not do justice to the intricate theological underpinnings of his work—and it has been a number of Catholic scholars (see, for example, Pearce 1998, Boyd and Caldecott 2003, or Caldecott 2003) who took on the task of saving Tolkien from the 'terrible simplificateurs' by making explicit the specifically Catholic elements and their role in Tolkien's work.

Biographical studies have also received an unexpected booster by the fact that the documents stored in the WW I archives are now publicly accessible. John Garth's fine study *Tolkien and the Great War* (2003) has proved that Carpenter's standard biography on Tolkien, published more than thirty years ago, may profit from a revision, updating and supplementing (see also his essay in this volume). Apart from large-scale investigations into Tolkien's life, we also need more (complementary) work that focuses on specialised aspects of his career. Gilliver, Marshall and Weiner's (2006) research into Tolkien's time working for the *Oxford English Dictionary* is a case in point.

John Rateliff's two volumes on the history of *The Hobbit* (2007) have, at long last, filled the gap that had become more and more noticeable ever since much of the material that constitutes the legendarium and the drafts of *The Lord of the Rings* have been edited and published by Christopher Tolkien in *The History of Middle-earth*. These resources, together with Hammond and Scull's *Companion* (Hammond and Scull 2005) and *Chronology* (Scull and Hammond 2006), provide Tolkien scholars with unique and powerful critical tools for research. Furthermore, over the last years we witnessed the publication of critical editions of shorter literary works—such as *Smith of Wootton Major* (Flieger 2005)—that are of importance for the interpretation of

Tolkien's longer writings, as well as the critical incorporation of scholarly works such as 'Beowulf: The Monsters and the Critics' (cf. Drout 2002) and 'On Fairy-Stories' (Anderson and Flieger 2008 forthcoming). The Bodleian Library, whom the Tolkien Estate has entrusted with Tolkien's academic writings, holds many a smaller treasure[3] worth editing along the lines of Drout's meticulous work.

So it seems quite safe to say that the future of Tolkien studies will be one of new challenges and new horizons. The building on the strong foundations already laid is going to be continued while at the same time new areas of study will be opened up. The diversification and specialisation of the individual approaches is bound to go on, and it is thus all the more important that the proponents of the different traditions remain in close contact and keep up a mutually inspiring dialogue—for which the Exeter College conference has set an excellent example and there are plans for a follow-up conference in the not-too distant future in Granada (Spain).

---

[3] See, for example, Honegger (2007) for a preliminary study of the numerous drafts of *The Homecoming of Beorhtnoth*.

References

Anderson, Douglas and Verlyn Flieger (eds.), 2008 forthcoming, *J.R.R. Tolkien: On Fairy-Stories*, London: HarperCollins.

Boyd, Ian and Stratford Caldecott (eds.), 2003, *The Hidden Presence: Catholicism in The Lord of the Rings*, South Orange, NJ and Oxford, UK: Chesterton Institute Press.

Caldecott, Stratford, 2003, *Secret Fire: The Spiritual Vision of J.R.R. Tolkien*, London: Darton, Longman and Todd.

Drout, Michael D.C., 2002, *Beowulf and the Critics by J.R.R. Tolkien*, (Medieval and Renaissance Texts and Studies 248), Tempe, Arizona: The Arizona Center for Medieval and Renaissance Studies.

Eaglestone, Robert, 2005, *Reading The Lord of the Rings. New Writings on Tolkien's Classic*, London and New York: Continuum.

Flieger, Verlyn (ed.), 2005, *J.R.R. Tolkien: Smith of Wootton Major*, (extended edition), London: HarperCollins.

Garth, John, 2003, *Tolkien and the Great War*, London: HarperCollins.

Gilliver, Peter, Jeremy Marshall, and Edmund Weiner, 2006, *The Ring of Words. Tolkien and the Oxford English Dictionary*, Oxford: Oxford University Press.

Hammond, Wayne G. and Christina Scull, 2005, *The Lord of the Rings. A Reader's Companion*, London: HarperCollins.

Hiley, Margaret, 2009 forthcoming, *Aspects of Modernism in the Works of C.S. Lewis, J.R.R. Tolkien and Charles Williams*, Zurich and Jena: Walking Tree Publishers.

Honegger, Thomas, 2007, '*The Homecoming of Beorhtnoth*: Philology and the Literary Muse', *Tolkien Studies* 4:189-99.

Pearce, Joseph, 1998, *Tolkien: Man and Myth. A Literary Life*, London: HarperCollins.

Schneidewind, Friedhelm and Frank Weinreich, 2005, 'Beispiele der Instrumentalisierung von Mittelerde' in Thomas Honegger, Andrew J. Johnston, Friedhelm Schneidewind and Frank Weinreich, 2005, *Eine Grammatik der Ethik*, Saarbrücken: Edition Stein und Baum, 27-38.

Rateliff, John D., 2007a, *The History of The Hobbit. Part One: Mr. Baggins*, London: HarperCollins.

Rateliff, John D., 2007b, *The History of The Hobbit. Part Two: Return to Bag-End*, London: HarperCollins.

Scull, Christina and Wayne G. Hammond, 2006, *The J.R.R. Tolkien Companion and Guide. Chronology*, London: HarperCollins.

Shippey, Tom A., 2008, 'Guest Editorial: An Encyclopedia of Ignorance', *Mallorn* 45:3-5.

Simonson, Martin, 2008, *The Lord of the Rings and the Western Narrative Tradition*, Zurich and Jena: Walking Tree Publishers.

Walking Tree Publishers

Walking Tree Publishers was founded in 1997 as a forum for publication of material (books, videos, CDs, etc.) related to Tolkien and Middle-earth studies. Manuscripts and project proposals can be submitted to the board of editors (please include an SAE):

Walking Tree Publishers
CH-3052 Zollikofen
Switzerland
e-mail: info@walking-tree.org
http://www.walking-tree.org

Cormarë Series

The *Cormarë Series* has been the first series of studies dedicated exclusively to the exploration of Tolkien's work. Its focus is on papers and studies from a wide range of scholarly approaches. The series comprises monographs, thematic collections of essays, conference volumes, and reprints of important yet no longer (easily) accessible papers by leading scholars in the field. Manuscripts and project proposals are evaluated by members of an independent board of advisors who support the series editors in their endeavour to provide the readers with qualitatively superior yet accessible studies on Tolkien and his work.

News from the Shire and Beyond. Studies on Tolkien
Peter Buchs and Thomas Honegger (eds.), Zurich and Berne 2004, Reprint, First edition 1997 (Cormarë Series 1), ISBN 3-9521424-5-X

Root and Branch. Approaches Towards Understanding Tolkien
Thomas Honegger (ed.), Zurich and Berne 2005, Reprint, First edition 1999 (Cormarë Series 2), ISBN 3-905703-01-7

Richard Sturch, *Four Christian Fantasists. A Study of the Fantastic Writings of George MacDonald, Charles Williams, C. S. Lewis and J.R.R. Tolkien*
Zurich and Berne 2007, Reprint, First edition 2001 (Cormarë Series 3), ISBN 978-3-905703-04-7

Tolkien in Translation
Thomas Honegger (ed.), Zurich and Berne 2003 (Cormarë Series 4), ISBN 3-9521424-6-8

Mark T. Hooker, *Tolkien Through Russian Eyes*
Zurich and Berne 2003 (Cormarë Series 5), ISBN 3-9521424-7-6

Translating Tolkien: Text and Film
Thomas Honegger (ed.), Zurich and Berne 2004 (Cormarë Series 6), ISBN 3-9521424-9-2

Christopher Garbowski, *Recovery and Transcendence for the Contemporary Mythmaker. The Spiritual Dimension in the Works of J.R.R. Tolkien*
Zurich and Berne 2004, Reprint, First Edition by Marie Curie Sklodowska, University Press, Lublin 2000, (Cormarë Series 7), ISBN 3-9521424-8-4

Reconsidering Tolkien
Thomas Honegger (ed.), Zurich and Berne 2005 (Cormarë Series 8),
ISBN 3-905703-00-9

Tolkien and Modernity 1
Frank Weinreich and Thomas Honegger (eds.), Zurich and Berne 2006 (Cormarë
Series 9), ISBN 978-3-905703-02-3

Tolkien and Modernity 2
Thomas Honegger and Frank Weinreich (eds.), Zurich and Berne 2006 (Cormarë
Series 10), ISBN 978-3-905703-03-0

Tom Shippey, *Roots and Branches. Selected Papers on Tolkien by Tom Shippey*
Zurich and Berne 2007 (Cormarë Series 11), ISBN 978-3-905703-05-4

Ross Smith, *Inside Language. Linguistic and Aesthetic Theory in Tolkien*
Zurich and Berne 2007 (Cormarë Series 12), ISBN 978-3-905703-06-1

How We Became Middle-earth. A Collection of Essays on The Lord of the Rings
Adam Lam and Nataliya Oryshchuk (eds.), Zurich and Berne 2007 (Cormarë
Series 13), ISBN 978-3-905703-07-8

Myth and Magic. Art According to the Inklings
Eduardo Segura and Thomas Honegger (eds.), Zurich and Berne 2007 (Cormarë
Series 14), ISBN 978-3-905703-08-5

The Silmarillion - Thirty Years On
Allan Turner (ed.), Zurich and Berne 2007 (Cormarë Series 15)
ISBN 978-3-905703-10-8

Martin Simonson, *The Lord of the Rings and the Western Narrative Tradition*
Zurich and Jena 2008 (Cormarë Series 16), ISBN 978-3-905703-09-2

*Beyond Middle-earth: Tolkien's Shorter Works. Proceedings of the 4th Seminar of the
Deutsche Tolkien Gesellschaft & Walking Tree Publishers Decennial Conference*
Margaret Hiley and Frank Weinreich (eds.), Zurich and Jena 2008 (Cormarë Series 17)
ISBN 978-3-905703-11-5

Tolkien's The Lord of the Rings: Sources and Inspirations
Stratford Caldecott and Thomas Honegger (eds.), Zurich and Jena 2008

Constructions of Authorship in and around the Works of J.R.R. Tolkien
Judith Klinger (ed.), Zurich and Jena, forthcoming

Rainer Nagel, *Hobbit Place-names. A Linguistic Excursion through the Shire*
Zurich and Jena, forthcoming

Tales of Yore Series

The *Tales of Yore Series* grew out of the desire to share Kay Woollard's whimsical stories and drawings with a wider audience. The series aims at providing a platform for qualitatively superior fiction with a clear link to Tolkien's world.

Kay Woollard, *The Terror of Tatty Walk. A Frightener*
CD and Booklet, Zurich and Berne 2000 (Tales of Yore Series 1)
ISBN 3-9521424-2-5

Kay Woollard, *Wilmot's Very Strange Stone or What came of building "snobbits"*
CD and booklet, Zurich and Berne 2001 (Tales of Yore Series 2)
ISBN 3-9521424-4-1

Ossie felt the back of his neck go prickly....

Lightning Source UK Ltd.
Milton Keynes UK
UKOW041903170713

213982UK00006B/431/P

9 783905 703122